The Amazing Life of Jesus Christ
Part Two

BIG DREAM MINISTRIES

His Rejection, Death, and Resurrection

ISBN 10: 1-932199-53-5
ISBN 13: 978-1932-199-53-6

Cover design by Melissa Swanson
Cover image from iStock Photos
Creative Team: Terry Behimer, Pat Reinheimer, and Leslie Strader

Printed in the United States

2 3 4 5 6 7 8 9 10 / 23 22 21 20 19 18

TABLE OF CONTENTS

Introduction: Jesus Is Amazing . . . 4

About This Study . . . 5

Acknowledgements . . . 7

Map of Jesus' Journeys to Galilee and Judea . . . 8
Week 13: Jesus, Light of the World . . . 9

Map of Jesus' Journeys to Galilee and Judea . . . 26
Week 14: Jesus, the Provider . . . 27

Map of Jesus in Judea and Jerusalem . . . 46
Week 15: Jesus, the Good Shepherd . . . 47

Map of Ministry Beyond Galilee . . . 66
Week 16: Jesus, the Narrow Door . . . 67

Map of Jesus in Judea and Jerusalem . . . 88
Week 17: Jesus, the Resurrection and the Life . . . 89

Map of Passion Week . . . 108
Week 18: Jesus, Son of David . . . 109

Map of Passion Week . . . 124
Week 19: Jesus, the Judge . . . 125

Map of Passion Week . . . 142
Week 20: Jesus, the Way, the Truth, and the Life . . . 143

Map of Passion Week . . . 162
Week 21: Jesus, Son of Man . . . 163

Map of Passion Week . . . 180
Week 22: Jesus, the Suffering Servant . . . 181

Week 23: Jesus, Redeemer and Savior . . . 195

Week 24: Jesus, King of Kings . . . 213

Endnotes . . . 227

Timeline for the Life of Jesus . . . 229

INTRODUCTION

JESUS IS AMAZING

In history and religion, there is no more controversial or captivating figure, no one who has made a greater impact on individuals or institutions, than Jesus of Nazareth. Jesus is amazing! Every word on every page of Scripture proclaims this truth. The Gospel writers were given the inspired privilege of breathing literary life into the Word made flesh. And we get to bask in the glory.

So much of the life of Jesus is familiar, whether you grew up in church or not. Who hasn't heard of the One who turned water into wine, walked on top of the waves, and fed thousands with a few fish and bits of bread? Or how He cast out demons and healed the incurable diseases of the day—even the incurable conditions of *our* day? Blindness, paralysis, and leprosy didn't stand a chance at the hand of the Great Physician. He cured with compassion. He restored life and hope.

And when He taught, Jesus' words were more than moving, beyond simply radical thinking. Every time He opened His mouth, Jesus spoke life-changing truth, and it fell on ears and hearts like rain on parched land. Stray sheep heard the voice of the Good Shepherd at last. Following Him, however, was another story.

It is all of these things and more that we will examine together in *The Amazing Life of Jesus Christ*. Rather than rushing through the "Sunday school stories" some know by heart, we will slow our pace. These words are treasures and so we will hold them tightly, turn them over in our hands, and watch them sparkle in the light.

The permanence of Scripture offers us an extraordinary opportunity: we can carefully (and joyfully!) explore the life of the One who left the beauty, perfection, and glory of heaven to *"be made like his brethren in all things, so that he might become a merciful and faithful high priest in things pertaining to God, to make propitiation for the sins of the people."* (Hebrews 2:17)

Pray for eyes to see Him as He was on earth—a Man fully human and perfectly divine, and as He is today—seated at His Father's right hand, His work completed, waiting to return.

Thanks be to God for His indescribable gift! (2 Corinthians 9:15)

With joy,

Leslie Strader

ABOUT THIS STUDY

Theme:

Instead of focusing on one book in the Gospels, *The Amazing Life of Jesus Christ* weaves together Scripture primarily from Matthew, Mark, Luke, and John in chronological order, journeying from the preexistence of Jesus to His future return. At the same time, this study will focus on a particular aspect of Jesus' character each week. From Son of Man to King of Kings, we will slow down the Gospel story and examine the teaching, miracles, words, and heart of the One who came to save.

Teaching:

The weekly teacher presentations will offer additional information that will enhance the understanding of Christ's life on earth. Each section of Scripture is unfolded in a way that will draw your heart into the story and encourage you to sense the great impact Jesus had on those around Him and the power of the battle that began even as He was an infant.

Introduction:

To help calibrate the timeline and set your mind, take time to read through the introduction at the beginning of each week. This will give you an overview of what you will be studying and orient you to where we are in the life of Christ.

Maps:

Where relevant to the content of the passage, maps are included to give an additional visual connection to where Jesus is, how far He might have traveled, and where He's going.

Memory Verses:

Each week begins with a verse from the passage of Scripture you'll be studying. Cut out the cards in the back and read over them as you move through your day. Ask the Holy Spirit to help you commit these short verses to memory, and you will be encouraged by the truths written on your heart for the rest of your life!

Scripture:

We have included the portions of Scripture that you'll be studying in the workbook itself. Having the passage right in front of you will help with continuity and focus. Of course context matters, so please open your Bible at any point along the way to get a bigger picture of the scene.

Questions:

Rather than days, *The Amazing Life of Jesus Christ* is divided into studies. Depending on the content, some weeks will be longer than others, so you may need to adjust your time accordingly. There are five studies each week, and each contains an introduction, questions about the passage, and questions for personal application.

- Before you begin each study, pray and ask the Holy Spirit to open your eyes to see Jesus as never before. Pray for insights into His life and ministry. Pray for understanding and a teachable spirit. Pray that you would love Jesus more each day as you grow in your knowledge and understanding of Him and His mission on earth.

- Read completely through the blocked passage of Scripture before answering the questions.
- The first grouping of questions are about the passage itself and will encourage you to prayerfully think and observe truths from God's Word.
- Each section will have an **Application** question that will help you apply the truths of the passage to your own life.
- Sometimes, you'll discover a section titled **A Deeper Look**. This portion is optional, but will lead you into a deeper investigation of a specific truth seen in God's Word.

Wrapping Up:

This section is a simple summary of the theme, ideas, and truths from the week. As you read through these and digest what you've learned, stop and thank God for the ways He's revealed more of Himself and His Son to you each day, through His Word and by His Spirit.

ACKNOWLEDGEMENTS

The Amazing Life of Jesus Christ is based on the outstanding scholarly works of those who, through the centuries, have endeavored to put the life of Jesus Christ in chronological order. Using excerpts from the four Gospels, the events are placed during the time they most likely occurred. Although it is difficult to be absolutely certain of the following order of events, what *is* certain is that each event took place.

We are indebted to those who have done the hard work of placing the events in order, such as John MacArthur, Robert L. Thomas, Stanley N. Gundry, Johnston M. Cheney and others. Dr. Dwight Pentecost's and Dr. Oswald Sanders' works on Jesus were tremendously helpful as well.

A very special note of appreciation to the Lockman Foundation for giving us permission to use Scripture from the New American Standard Version and to B&H Publishing Group for the use of the maps taken from The Holman Bible Atlas.

I first met Leslie Strader several years ago at a leadership conference given by Dallas Theological Seminary. I was immediately impressed with her knowledge of Scripture and her joy for life. Years later, I invited her to come to a planning retreat with the board of Big Dream Ministries. This time I was impressed with her creativity and insights. When I found out she was a writer for a ministry magazine, I knew right away I wanted her to author the workbook for *The Amazing Life of Jesus Christ.* I will be forever grateful for that providential meeting in Dallas, and so appreciate her willingness to work with us on this study. Leslie is the wife of Ross, senior pastor of Bethel Bible Church, a thriving church in Tyler, Texas, and the mother of three children.

Pat Harley
President
Big Dream Ministries

~ Map of Jesus' Journeys to Galilee and Judea ~

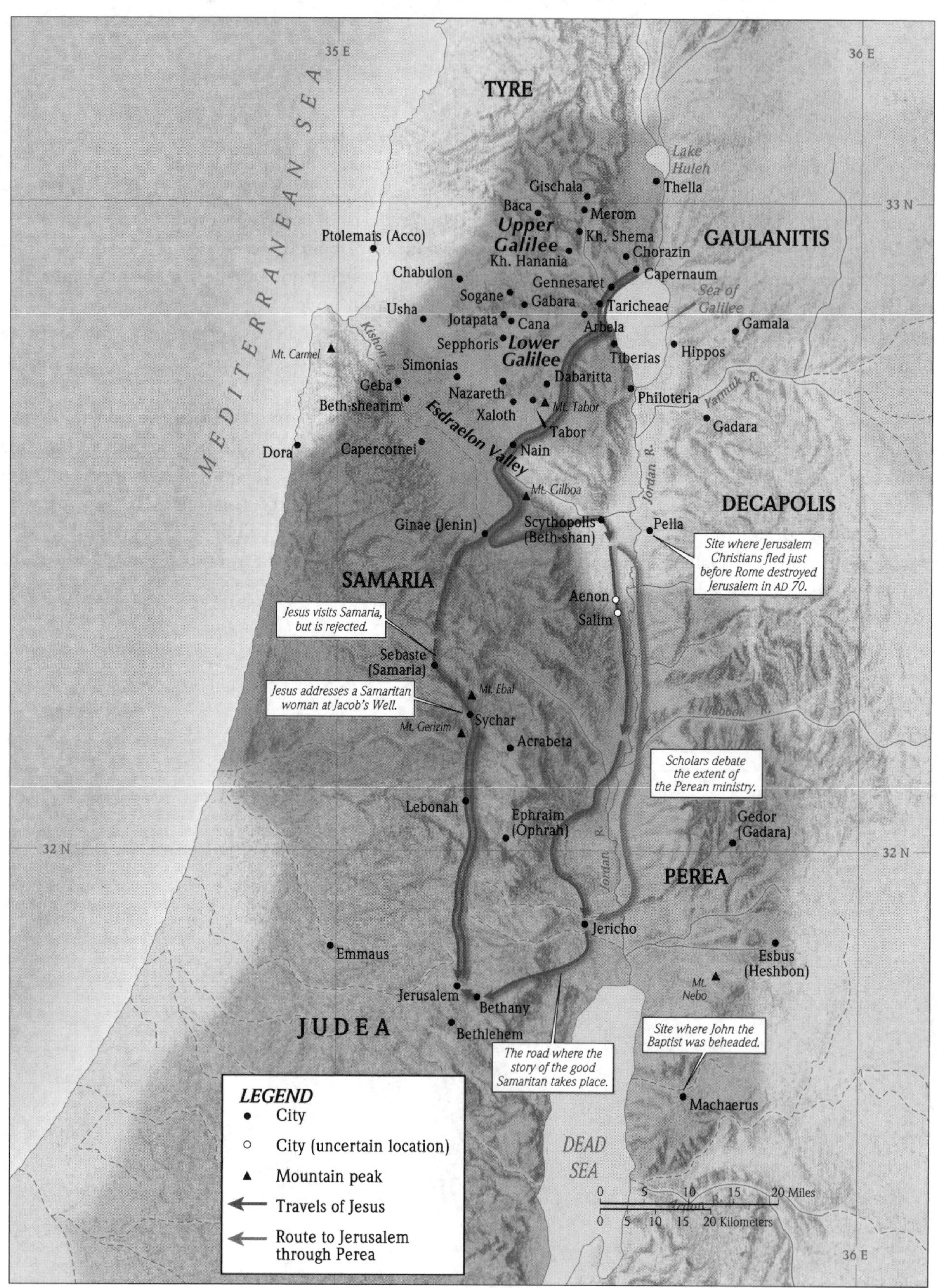

JESUS, LIGHT OF THE WORLD

"Then Jesus again spoke to them, saying, 'I am the Light of the world; he who follows me will not walk in the darkness, but will have the light of life.'"
JOHN 8:12

From the glowing embers of prehistoric fires to Edison's first light bulb, human beings have long searched for ways to burn away the darkness. We cannot live without the gift of light. Not only does it supply heat, enable sight, and generate growth, it provides revelation of things unseen. We would live in cold, gloomy fear without it.

The fact that Jesus spoke of Himself as Light ignites images of warmth and comfort. The Light of Jesus also gives names to the shadows hidden in the corners of our hearts. Through His Word, Jesus shines Truth on monsters like pride, envy, bitterness, and greed—natural enemies to which our flesh tries desperately to cling. They imprison us; Jesus desires to set us free.

When His Spirit graciously exposes these beasts within, we must agree their presence in our lives does not correspond to the person we are in Christ. While His death extinguished sin's authority over us, we are still in a daily battle against the powers of this dark world. And Light is our greatest weapon.

In the beginning, darkness hovered over the deep; God spoke light into it and morning dawned. Through Jesus, God spoke His Word into the darkness once again. A single ray pierced the night, and covered the whole world with brilliant hope. And now we can walk as children of the day.

STUDY ONE
Jesus at the Feast of Booths

By this time, Jesus has revealed His purpose on earth to His disciples, who responded with either despair or disbelief. The setting here was a feast, a time of celebration, commemoration, and community. But it must have been a lonely time for Jesus, who knew His course was set for rejection, betrayal, and death. He had no fear of the opposition He faced; in fact, He used it as a teachable moment, training His disciples to turn the other cheek. *Following me is not about recognition and honor*, He told them. *Faithfulness and focus make you fit for My kingdom.*

John 7:2–10
"2 Now the feast of the Jews, the Feast of Booths, was near. 3 Therefore His brothers said to Him, 'Leave here and go into Judea, so that Your disciples also may
see Your works which You are doing. 4 For no one does anything in secret when
he himself seeks to be known publicly. If You do these things, show Yourself to
the world.' 5 For not even His brothers were believing in Him. 6 So Jesus said to
them, 'My time is not yet here, but your time is always opportune. 7 The world
cannot hate you, but it hates Me because I testify of it, that its deeds are evil. 8 Go
up to the feast yourselves; I do not go up to this feast because My time has not
yet fully come.' 9 Having said these things to them, He stayed in Galilee. 10 But
when His brothers had gone up to the feast, then He Himself also went up, not
publicly, but as if, in secret."

Luke 9:51–62
"51 When the days were approaching for His ascension, He was determined to
go to Jerusalem; 52 and He sent messengers on ahead of Him, and they went
and entered a village of the Samaritans to make arrangements for Him. 53 But
they did not receive Him, because He was traveling toward Jerusalem. 54 When
His disciples James and John saw this, they said, 'Lord, do You want us to command fire to come down from heaven and consume them?' 55 But He turned and
rebuked them, [and said, 'You do not know what kind of spirit you're of; 56 for
the Son of Man did not come to destroy men's lives, but to save them.'] And they
went on to another village.

57 As they were going along the road, someone said to Him, 'I will follow You
wherever You go.' 58 And Jesus said to him, 'The foxes have holes and the birds of
the air have nests, but the Son of Man has nowhere to lay His head.' 59 And He
said to another, 'Follow Me.' But he said, 'Lord, permit me first to go and bury
my father.' 60 But He said to him, 'Allow the dead to bury their own dead; but as
for you, go and proclaim everywhere the kingdom of God.' 61 Another also said,
'I will follow You, Lord; but first permit me to say good-bye to those at home.'
62 But Jesus said to him, 'No one, after putting his hand to the plow and looking
back, is fit for the kingdom of God.'"

1. What is the Feast of Booths? (See Leviticus 23:33–44 and Nehemiah 8:13–18)

2. What did Jesus' brothers advise Him to do and why? (vv. 3–4) In contrast, what was the constant focus and purpose of Jesus' mission? (review Matthew 16:21)

3. What does verse 5 disclose about the brothers' attitude toward Jesus? What fundamental principle about faith does this story illustrate?

4. How did Jesus demonstrate He was living by God's time and not man's time? (vv. 6–10)

5. As Jesus moved toward the cross, what opposition does He face in Luke 9:52–53?

6. Why did the Samaritans reject Jesus in verse 53? (for the history of this relationship, see 2 Kings 17:24–41)

7. Who did the disciples ask to rebuke in verse 54? Who did Jesus rebuke in verse 55? How does this contrast display the tolerance of Jesus toward those who rejected Him?

8. How did the disciple's response in verse 54 echo that of an Old Testament story from 2 Kings 1:1–12?

9. How did James and John exhibit zeal without knowledge in this passage?

10. Typically, leaders try to attract followers. Jesus' responses sound as though He's trying to drive them away. But how is His honesty helpful? What can we learn about the cost of being a follower of Christ from His words?

Application

How tolerant are you of others who believe differently from you? What is the difference between tolerating the beliefs of another and accepting the beliefs of another?

STUDY TWO
Division

The city was crowded with Jews who had come to celebrate God's faithfulness for a fruitful harvest, but it appears their attention was elsewhere. Grumbling distracts us from giving thanks, so when Jesus began to teach in the temple, His words fell on fallow ground. The Jews trusted in their enlightened human minds, but Jesus' teaching came from His heavenly Father. And rather than by debate or discussion, Jesus said the only way they could completely grasp His words was if they were willing to do what He said. Faith brings understanding, not the other way around. While the Jews were breathing threats they could not carry out, Jesus was promising grace: a little more time to believe in Him and the future gift of the Holy Spirit.

John 7:11–39

"11 So the Jews were seeking Him at the feast and were saying, 'Where is He?'
12 There was much grumbling among the crowds concerning Him; some were
saying, 'He is a good man'; others were saying, 'No, on the contrary, He leads
the people astray.' 13 Yet no one was speaking openly of Him for fear of the Jews.
14 But when it was now the midst of the feast Jesus went up into the temple,
and began to teach. 15 The Jews then were astonished, saying, 'How has this man
become learned, having never been educated?' 16 So Jesus answered them and
said, 'My teaching is not Mine, but His who sent Me. 17 If anyone is willing to
do His will, he will know of the teaching, whether it is of God or whether I speak
from Myself. 18 He who speaks from himself seeks his own glory; but He who is
seeking the glory of the One who sent Him, He is true, and there is no unrighteousness in Him.
19 'Did not Moses give you the Law, and yet none of you carries out the
Law? Why do you seek to kill Me?' 20 The crowd answered, 'You have a demon!
Who seeks to kill You?' 21 Jesus answered them, 'I did one deed, and you all
marvel. 22 For this reason Moses has given you circumcision (not because it is
from Moses, but from the fathers), and on the Sabbath you circumcise a man.
23 If a man receives circumcision on the Sabbath so that the Law of Moses will
not be broken, are you angry with Me because I made an entire man well on the
Sabbath? 24 Do not judge according to appearance, but judge with righteous
judgment.'
25 So some of the people of Jerusalem were saying, 'Is this not the man whom
they are seeking to kill? 26 Look, He is speaking publicly, and they are saying
nothing to Him. The rulers do not really know that this is the Christ, do they?
27 However, we know where this man is from; but whenever the Christ may
come, no one knows where He is from.' 28 Then Jesus cried out in the temple,
teaching and saying, 'You both know Me and know where I am from; and I have
not come of Myself, but He who sent Me is true, whom you do not know. 29 I
know Him, because I am from Him, and He sent Me.' 30 So they were seeking
to seize Him; and no man laid his hand on Him, because His hour had not yet
come. 31 But many of the crowd believed in Him; and they were saying, 'When
the Christ comes, He will not perform more signs than those which this man has,
will He?'
32 The Pharisees heard the crowd muttering these things about Him, and the
chief priests and the Pharisees sent officers to seize Him. 33 Therefore Jesus said,

‘For a little while longer I am with you, then I go to Him who sent Me. 34 You
will seek Me, and will not find Me; and where I am, you cannot come.’ 35 The
Jews then said to one another, ‘Where does this man intend to go that we will not
find Him? He is not intending to go to the Dispersion among the Greeks, and
teach the Greeks, is He? 36 What is this statement that He said, ‘You will seek Me,
and will not find Me; and where I am, you cannot come’?’
37 Now on the last day, the great day of the feast, Jesus stood and cried out,
saying, ‘If anyone is thirsty, let him come to Me and drink. 38 He who believes
in Me, as the Scripture said, ‘From his innermost being will flow rivers of living
water.’ 39 But this He spoke of the Spirit, whom those who believed in Him were
to receive; for the Spirit was not yet given, because Jesus was not yet glorified.”

1. What is the atmosphere in Jerusalem when Jesus arrives? (vv. 11–13) What were the two opinions expressed by the Jews in verse 12 about Jesus?

2. Read verses 14–15 and make the following observations from the description of events:

    - Who was there?
    - Where did it take place?
    - When did it take place?
    - What happened?
    - How did the Jews respond?

3. What did Jesus explain about His teaching, His relationship with God, and His character in verses 16–18?

4. What does verse 15 reveal the religious leaders believed was necessary for understanding God’s teaching? What does Jesus say was necessary in verse 17?

5. What is the "one deed" Jesus is referring to in verse 21? (see John 5:10–18)

6. How does Jesus point out the hypocrisy of the Jews in verses 22–24?

7. What does Jesus say is missing from the way the Jews judge the acceptability of others in verse 24?

8. There is confusion among the people of Jerusalem as to the true identity of Jesus. Summarize their confusion in your own words from verses 25–27.

9. How does the Light of the world boldly speak into the darkness of their doubt in verses 28–29?

10. How does verse 30 illustrate God's sovereignty over Jesus' betrayal and death?

11. How did the Pharisees and chief priests respond in this situation? (v. 32)

12. To what event is Jesus cryptically referring in verses 33–34? How do verses 35–36 confirm there is still darkness blinding the Jews?

13. Verse 37 says Jesus "cried out." Considering the time stamp in this verse, what was the urgency behind Jesus' cry? What need was He addressing?

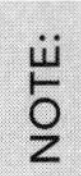

Notice in each passage the celebration and joy of people who return to the Lord.

14. Who is the invitation to and what is the condition? (v. 37) What is the promise? (v. 38) How is the promise delivered? (v. 39)

Application

What do grumbling and fear expose about our hearts? What kind of behavior often comes from a critical, fearful spirit? (see Numbers 12 for an example)

A DEEPER LOOK

How does God's Word say we experience the Living Water from within us?

Psalms 51:10

Ezekiel 36:27

Romans 6:11–14

Galatians 2:20–21

Galatians 5:16–26

Hebrews 13:20–21

STUDY THREE
The Adulterous Woman

The officers of the temple returned empty-handed. Their mission had been to seize Jesus, but His words had captured their hearts instead. A familiar character—Nicodemus—presented a defense for those judged by the Pharisees but, in a foreshadowing of future events, he was ridiculed and ignored. In the light of day, the religious leaders offered another accusation in the sins of an adulterous woman. Stones in hand, they brought her shame before Jesus to test His loyalty to the Law. In a counter move, Jesus cast His own indictment that landed squarely on their hearts. The Jews walked away with wounded pride. The woman was released as well—sin exposed and grace given.

John 7:40–8:11

"**40** Some of the people therefore, when they heard these words, were saying, 'This certainly is the Prophet.' **41** Others were saying, 'This is the Christ.' Still others were saying, 'Surely the Christ is not going to come from Galilee, is He? **42** Has not the Scripture said that the Christ comes from the descendants of David, and from Bethlehem, the village where David was?' **43** So a division occurred in the crowd because of Him. **44** Some of them wanted to seize Him, but no one laid hands on Him.

45 The officers then came to the chief priests and Pharisees, and they said to them, 'Why did you not bring Him?' **46** The officers answered, 'Never has a man spoken the way this man speaks.' **47** The Pharisees then answered them, 'You have not also been led astray, have you? **48** No one of the rulers or Pharisees has believed in Him, has he? **49** But this crowd which does not know the Law is accursed.' **50** Nicodemus (he who came to Him before, being one of them) said to them, **51** 'Our Law does not judge a man unless it first hears from him and knows what he is doing, does it?' **52** They answered him, 'You are not also from Galilee, are you? Search, and see that no prophet arises out of Galilee.' **53** Everyone went to his home.

1 But Jesus went to the Mount of Olives. **2** Early in the morning He came again into the temple, and all the people were coming to Him; and He sat down and began to teach them. **3** The scribes and the Pharisees brought a woman caught in adultery, and having set her in the center of the court, **4** they said to Him, 'Teacher, this woman has been caught in adultery, in the very act. **5** Now in the Law Moses commanded us to stone such women; what then do You say?' **6** They were saying this, testing Him, so that they might have grounds for accusing Him. But Jesus stooped down and with His finger wrote on the ground. **7** But when they persisted in asking Him, He straightened up, and said to them, 'He who is without sin among you, let him be the first to throw a stone at her.' **8** Again He stooped down and wrote on the ground. **9** When they heard it, they began to go out one by one, beginning with the older ones, and He was left alone, and the woman, where she was, in the center of the court. **10** Straightening up, Jesus said to her, 'Woman, where are they? Did no one condemn you?' **11** She said, 'No one, Lord.' And Jesus said, 'I do not condemn you, either. Go. From now on sin no more.'"

1. What was the division among the people in verses 40–44? What was right and wrong about their opinions?

2. Why did the officers say they did not arrest Jesus? (v. 46)

3. Who came to the defense of the officers (and, ultimately, Jesus) in verses 50–51? What does the Mosaic Law teach about judgment? (see Deuteronomy 1:16–17) Based on all this, what is the irony of verse 49?

4. Read Ezekiel 34:1–10. How is this prophecy seen in this passage?

5. Who are the characters in this scene in John 8:1–11? Where and when does it take place? What was Jesus doing?

6. What was the charge against the woman by the scribes and Pharisees? (vv. 3–4) Why did the Pharisees condemn this woman to death? (See Deuteronomy 22:22–24)

7. Based on verses 6–7, who were the religious leaders really seeking to accuse?

8. In verse 7, Jesus summarized His previous teaching from Matthew 7:1–5. Review that passage now. Based on His instruction, what would have been the appropriate, biblical heart response of the Pharisees in that moment?

9. Read Romans 3:20. Where is the law at work in this scene? Where is grace visible in this scene?

10. What promise and exhortation did Jesus give the woman?

11. Notice the order of Jesus' words to the woman in verse 11. How does that exhibit grace? (Romans 6:1–2, 12–14)

Application

In his book *Knowing God*, J.I. Packer talks about God's love for us being "utterly realistic, based at every point on prior knowledge of the worst about (us), so that no discovery can disillusion him… ." Reflecting on this truth—and on Romans 8:1—record your thoughts of thanksgiving to God for His boundless mercy and love.

A DEEPER LOOK

This passage is full of disunity, among the people and among the leaders. What does the Bible say about the importance of unity in the body of Christ?

Psalms 133:1

Galatians 3:26–28

Malachi 2:10

Ephesians 4:16

Romans 12:4–5

Hebrews 10:24–25

1 Corinthians 12:27

1 Peter 2:9–10

STUDY FOUR
The Light of the World

Light played a particular role in the Feast of Tabernacles each year. One of the most joyous seasons in the Jewish calendar, this feast incorporated light into the heart of the celebration. Torches reflected in brass bowls lit up the temple at night, adding a special brightness to the festivities. It is in the midst of these blazing fires that Jesus proclaimed Himself not the Light of the temple or even the Light of Israel, but the Light of the world. The darkness of the Pharisees' spiritual sight was all the more pronounced in this illuminated setting. Jesus referenced a revelation to come through His death on the cross—an event that will shine like a spotlight in history, evidence that Jesus was the true Light of life.

John 8:12–30

"**12** Then Jesus again spoke to them, saying, 'I am the Light of the world; he who follows Me will not walk in the darkness, but will have the Light of life.' **13** So the Pharisees said to Him, 'You are testifying about Yourself; Your testimony is not true.' **14** Jesus answered and said to them, 'Even if I testify about Myself, My testimony is true, for I know where I came from and where I am going; but you do not know where I come from or where I am going. **15** You judge according to the flesh; I am not judging anyone. **16** But even if I do judge, My judgment is true; for I am not alone in it, but I and the Father who sent Me. **17** Even in your law it has been written that the testimony of two men is true. **18** I am He who testifies about Myself, and the Father who sent Me testifies about Me.' **19** So they were saying to Him, 'Where is Your Father?' Jesus answered, 'You know neither Me nor My Father; if you knew Me, you would know My Father also.' **20** These words He spoke in the treasury, as He taught in the temple; and no one seized Him, because His hour had not yet come.

21 Then He said again to them, 'I go away, and you will seek Me, and will die in your sin; where I am going, you cannot come.' **22** So the Jews were saying, 'Surely He will not kill Himself, will He, since He says, 'Where I am going, you cannot come?' **23** And He was saying to them, 'You are from below, I am from above; you are of this world, I am not of this world. **24** Therefore I said to you that you will die in your sins; for unless you believe that I am He, you will die in your sins.' **25** So they were saying to Him, 'Who are You?' Jesus said to them, 'What have I been saying to you from the beginning? **26** I have many things to speak and to judge concerning you, but He who sent Me is true; and the things which I heard from Him, these I speak to the world.' **27** They did not realize that He had been speaking to them about the Father. **28** So Jesus said, 'When you lift up the Son of Man, then you will know that I am He, and I do nothing on My own initiative, but I speak these things as the Father taught Me. **29** And He who sent Me is with Me; He has not left Me alone, for I always do the things that are pleasing to Him.' **30** As He spoke these things, many came to believe in Him."

1. How does Jesus identify Himself in verse 12? What does Jesus promise to those who follow the Light?

2. In verse 14, how did Jesus say the Pharisees missed the point in verse 13?

3. What does Jesus say is "true?" How are these things true? (vv. 14–18)

4. What is the judgment Jesus pronounces on the Pharisees in verse 19?

5. Why did no one oppose Jesus in verse 20?

6. What does Jesus say saves us from dying in our sin? (v. 24)

7. How does Jesus, the Son, say we are able to know God, the Father? (v. 28)

8. How do the Pharisees and Jews demonstrate they are "in the dark" in this passage? What does Jesus say will eventually "enlighten" them? (vv. 27–28)

9. How does Jesus explain and describe His relationship with His Father in this passage?

10. What illumination took place in verse 30 as a result of Jesus' teaching?

Application

Read 1 John 1:5–7 and Matthew 5:14–16 and connect them to Jesus' words in John 8. What are the promises for us as followers of the Light? How do we bring the Light of the gospel to the world? What can we do to draw others to the Light?

A DEEPER LOOK

What does the Bible say about light in relationship to God?

Psalms 27:1

Isaiah 60:19–20

Isaiah 9:2

1 Timothy 6:16

Isaiah 49:6

Revelation 21:23–24

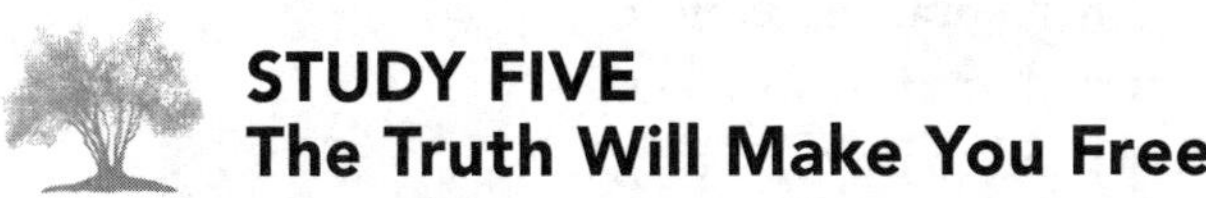

STUDY FIVE
The Truth Will Make You Free

Many Jews said they believed in Jesus as He proclaimed Himself the Light, but the conversation that followed revealed it was a shallow faith. Jesus gave them a command that would ensure their continued growth in Him: abide in the truth of My teaching, not just that day, but every day. Jesus encouraged them to persevere in their desire to know the Lord and walk in His way. That will bring freedom. Jesus also confronted these new converts with their enslavement to sin and offered them deliverance. The Jews' faith begins to falter here as they misunderstand Jesus' motives and mission. So they traded in their belief for accusations of blasphemy, and dropped their fragile faith among the temple stones.

John 8:31–59

"31 So Jesus was saying to those Jews who had believed Him, 'If you continue in
My word, then you are truly disciples of Mine; 32 and you will know the truth,
and the truth will make you free.' 33 They answered Him, 'We are Abraham's
descendants and have never yet been enslaved to anyone; how is it that You say,
'You will become free'?

34 Jesus answered them, 'Truly, truly, I say to you, everyone who commits sin
is the slave of sin. 35 The slave does not remain in the house forever; the son does
remain forever. 36 So if the Son makes you free, you will be free indeed. 37 I know
that you are Abraham's descendants; yet you seek to kill Me, because My word has
no place in you. 38 I speak the things which I have seen with My Father; therefore
you also do the things which you heard from your father.'

39 They answered and said to Him, 'Abraham is our father.' Jesus said to
them, 'If you are Abraham's children, do the deeds of Abraham. 40 But as it is,
you are seeking to kill Me, a man who has told you the truth, which I heard from
God; this Abraham did not do. 41 You are doing the deeds of your father.' They
said to Him, 'We were not born of fornication; we have one Father: God.' 42 Jesus
said to them, 'If God were your Father, you would love Me, for I proceeded forth
and have come from God, for I have not even come on My own initiative, but
He sent Me. 43 Why do you not understand what I am saying? It is because you
cannot hear My word. 44 You are of your father the devil, and you want to do the
desires of your father. He was a murderer from the beginning, and does not stand
in the truth because there is no truth in him. Whenever he speaks a lie, he speaks
from his own nature, for he is a liar and the father of lies. 45 But because I speak
the truth, you do not believe Me. 46 Which one of you convicts Me of sin? If I
speak truth, why do you not believe Me? 47 He who is of God hears the words of
God; for this reason you do not hear them, because you are not of God.'

48 The Jews answered and said to Him, 'Do we not say rightly that You are a
Samaritan and have a demon?' 49 Jesus answered, 'I do not have a demon; but I
honor My Father, and you dishonor Me. 50 But I do not seek My glory; there is
One who seeks and judges. 51 Truly, truly, I say to you, if anyone keeps My word
he will never see death.' 52 The Jews said to Him, 'Now we know that You have a
demon. Abraham died, and the prophets also; and You say, 'If anyone keeps My
word, he will never taste of death.' 53 Surely You are not greater than our father
Abraham, who died? The prophets died too; whom do You make Yourself out to
be?' 54 Jesus answered, 'If I glorify Myself, My glory is nothing; it is My Father
who glorifies Me, of whom you say, 'He is our God'; 55 and you have not come to
know Him, but I know Him; and if I say that I do not know Him, I will be a liar
like you, but I do know Him and keep His word. 56 Your father Abraham rejoiced
to see My day, and he saw it and was glad.' 57 So the Jews said to Him, 'You are
not yet fifty years old, and have You seen Abraham?' 58 Jesus said to them, 'Truly,
truly, I say to you, before Abraham was born, I am.' 59 Therefore they picked up
stones to throw at Him, but Jesus hid Himself and went out of the temple."

1. Who is Jesus talking to in verse 31?

2. What does Jesus say makes a true disciple in verses 31–32? What does it mean to "continue in My word?"

3. What did the Jews declare about themselves and their identity? (see vv. 33, 39, 53)

4. What does Jesus say the people were enslaved by (vv. 34–36) and what makes them free?

5. Who does Jesus say is the "father" of these Jews? How does He prove His point? (vv. 43–44)

6. What does Jesus say in verses 42–47 that kept the "unbelieving believers" from accepting the truth about Him?

7. What "scandal" were these Jews referring to in verse 41? (see Luke 1:26–38)

8. How does Jesus describe His relationship with His Father in this passage?

9. What declaration does Jesus make about Himself and those who believe in Him in verses 51–59? What promise does Jesus make in verse 51?

10. Based on Leviticus 24:16, why did these Jews believe they had the right to stone Jesus?

11. John 5:24 is a commentary on Jesus' words in verse 51. How does Jesus' earlier teaching help interpret His teaching here?

12. Read Exodus 3:14. In light of this verse, what is Jesus saying in verse 58? Why would the truth have been offensive to these Jews?

13. What evidence from this passage demonstrates that these "believing Jews" did not have a "saving faith" in Jesus?

Application

Jesus was shining a light on the true heart condition of the Jews and they responded defensively and rejected the truth. Give an example of when the Holy Spirit illuminated truth in your life. What did He reveal to you?

A DEEPER LOOK

Read the verses below and record the difference between a false faith that doesn't truly believe and a true faith that eternally saves.

Isaiah 29:13

Romans 10:9

Ephesians 2:8–9

Titus 1:16

James 2:19

1 John 2:9

WRAPPING UP

In one of his later letters, John revisits the theme of Light:

"This is the message we have heard from Him and announce to you, that God is Light, and in Him there is no darkness at all. If we say that we have fellowship with Him and yet walk in the darkness, we lie and do not practice the truth; but if we walk in the Light as He Himself is in the Light, we have fellowship with one another, and the blood of Jesus His Son cleanses us from all sin." (1 John 1:5–7)

These verses show us the dual purpose of light: it is a gift we need, but it is also a gift we can provide for others. Walking with Jesus is the key to fellowship with God. And in our union with God, we become "light" for those around us.

To our brothers and sisters in Christ, our light can be a reminder to one another of the glorious hope we have in Jesus. And to the lost around us, we shine Christ's love and point them to the Son.

Whether it's into a foggy mist or the deepest darkness, pray for compassion and courage to let your light shine—through your Spirit-empowered works and God-honoring words—so that all the world will see the Light of life.

~ Map of Jesus' Journeys to Galilee and Judea ~

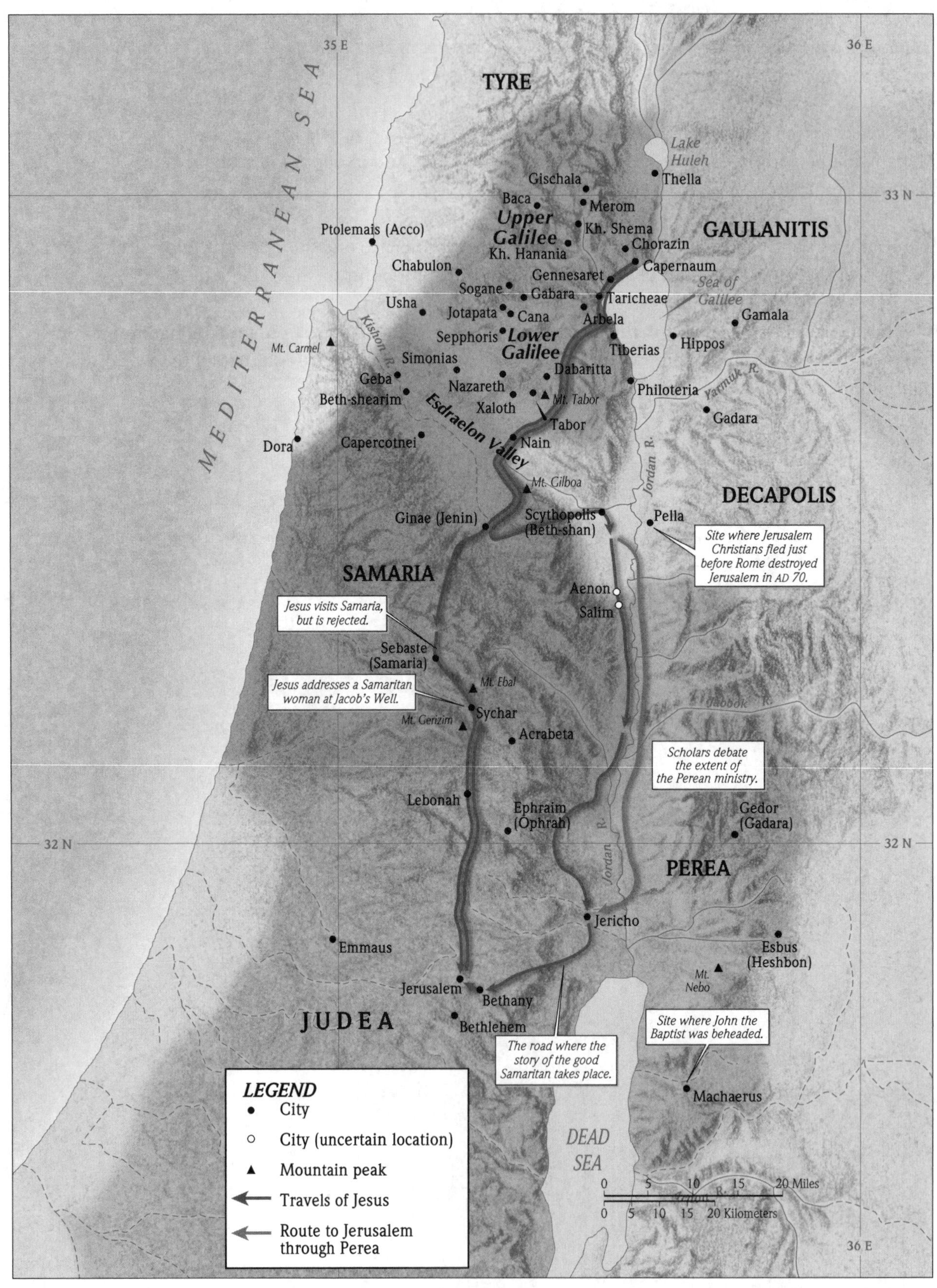

WEEK 14

JESUS, THE PROVIDER

"And do not seek what you will eat and what you will drink, and do not keep worrying. For all these things the nations of the world eagerly seek; but your Father knows that you need these things. But seek His kingdom, and these things will be added to you."
Luke 12:29–31

One of the most difficult things for us to admit is that we are in need. No one wants to be "needy." The word itself has almost become a curse in our self-sufficient culture, used as a warning to signal others to stay away or be bled dry.

With our self-reliant standards so high, it is interesting to see that Jesus is not only drawn to those "red flags" of neediness, He watches for them to wave. In 2 Corinthians 12:9–10, Paul tells us our weakness is the ideal condition for the power of Christ to work flawlessly in our lives. That is when His perfect power rests and works best in us.

We consider need a weakness, a critical condition that requires an immediate remedy. Jesus teaches that we were created to live in a constant state of dependence on Him. He is not repelled by our frailty; He came to seek the lost, feed the hungry, and strengthen the weary. Need opens a door in our hearts, giving Jesus full access to lavish His riches on all the places we are poor.

Jesus doesn't want us to wait until we are lying battered and beaten on the side of the road before we cry out to Him. Jesus is generous and finds joy in giving to His children. But His provision comes with a caveat: we must acknowledge we are needy, and that it's not a passing phase. Every day and in every way, we are desperate for all our Provider supplies.

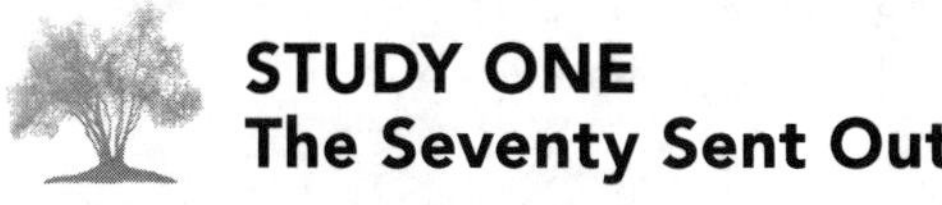

STUDY ONE
The Seventy Sent Out

The provision of Jesus is tied to trust in Him as He sends seventy men out to sow seeds of faith. Jesus promised to sustain His disciples through the obedience and generosity of others, an abiding principle we experience today. Jesus provided faith and basic needs for these laborers, as well as the power and authority to heal, bless, and curse. The men were encouraged after a fruitful mission, buoyant over the wonders they saw and performed. Jesus righted their perspective by reminding them of their true reason for rejoicing: they were blessed for having seen God work but, even more, because they belonged to Jesus.

Luke 10:1–29

"Now after this the Lord appointed seventy others, and sent them in pairs ahead of Him to every city and place where He Himself was going to come. **2** And He was saying to them, 'The harvest is plentiful, but the laborers are few; therefore beseech the Lord of the harvest to send out laborers into His harvest. **3** Go; behold, I send you out as lambs in the midst of wolves. **4** Carry no money belt, no bag, no shoes; and greet no one on the way. **5** Whatever house you enter, first say, 'Peace be to this house.' **6** If a man of peace is there, your peace will rest on him; but if not, it will return to you. **7** Stay in that house, eating and drinking what they give you; for the laborer is worthy of his wages. Do not keep moving from house to house. **8** Whatever city you enter and they receive you, eat what is set before you; **9** and heal those in it who are sick, and say to them, 'The kingdom of God has come near to you.' **10** But whatever city you enter and they do not receive you, go out into its streets and say, **11** 'Even the dust of your city which clings to our feet we wipe off in protest against you; yet be sure of this, that the kingdom of God has come near.' **12** I say to you, it will be more tolerable in that day for Sodom than for that city.

13 'Woe to you, Chorazin! Woe to you, Bethsaida! For if the miracles had been performed in Tyre and Sidon which occurred in you, they would have repented long ago, sitting in sackcloth and ashes. **14** But it will be more tolerable for Tyre and Sidon in the judgment than for you. **15** And you, Capernaum, will not be exalted to heaven, will you? You will be brought down to Hades!

16 'The one who listens to you listens to Me, and the one who rejects you rejects Me; and he who rejects Me rejects the One who sent Me.'

17 The seventy returned with joy, saying, 'Lord, even the demons are subject to us in Your name.' **18** And He said to them, 'I was watching Satan fall from heaven like lightning. **19** Behold, I have given you authority to tread on serpents and scorpions, and over all the power of the enemy, and nothing will injure you. **20** Nevertheless do not rejoice in this, that the spirits are subject to you, but rejoice that your names are recorded in heaven.'

21 At that very time He rejoiced greatly in the Holy Spirit, and said, 'I praise You, O Father, Lord of heaven and earth, that You have hidden these things from the wise and intelligent and have revealed them to infants. Yes, Father, for this way was well-pleasing in Your sight. **22** All things have been handed over to Me by My Father, and no one knows who the Son is except the Father, and who the Father is except the Son, and anyone to whom the Son wills to reveal Him.'

23 Turning to the disciples, He said privately, 'Blessed are the eyes which see the things you see, **24** for I say to you, that many prophets and kings wished to see the things which you see, and did not see them, and to hear the things which you hear, and did not hear them.'

25 And a lawyer stood up and put Him to the test, saying, 'Teacher, what shall I do to inherit eternal life?' **26** And He said to him, 'What is written in the Law? How does it read to you?' **27** And he answered, "You shall love the Lord your God with all your heart, and with all your soul, and with all your strength, and with all your mind; and your neighbor as yourself.' **28** And He said to him, 'You have answered correctly; do this and you will live.' **29** But wishing to justify himself, he said to Jesus, 'And who is my neighbor?'"

1. Who is "the Lord" in verse 1? What is He doing? Where were they to go?

2. What was the first instruction Jesus gave the disciples in verse 2 (review various translations for clarity)?

3. How did Jesus describe those He was sending out in verse 3? How does Jesus characterize the people to whom He is sending them? What does that say will be necessary in the tone and posture of their heart and ministry?

4. What instruction does Jesus give in verses 4–7?

NOTE: Moses' words to Aaron in Numbers 6:24–26 are an example of a typical blessing of peace of the day.

5. What were the disciples to do and say in cities that received them? (vv. 8–9)

6. When were the disciples to wipe the dust off their feet and what does that act symbolize? (vv. 10–11)

7. How does Jesus affirm the authority of the seventy in verse 16?

8. How did the disciples return and what report did they give of their ministry in verse 17?

9. What confirmation did Jesus give in verses 18–19? How did He help adjust their perspective in verse 20?

10. What does verse 21 say Jesus did in response to the disciples' ministry experience? What did Jesus praise His Father for? Who might Jesus have been referring to when He said "the wise and intelligent?" Who were the "infants?"

11. Who does Jesus say knows who He is in verse 22? Why are the disciples blessed? (vv. 23–24)

12. What did the lawyer stand up and ask in verse 25? What was the intent of his heart in asking the question? How did Jesus respond?

13. How did the lawyer use the Law to answer Jesus? (see Deuteronomy 6:5)

14. After Jesus affirms the lawyer's answer, the lawyer takes things a step further. What does he ask and what is the meaning behind his question in verse 29?

Application

What are the benefits of participating in ministry with others vs. "Lone Ranger" style? What do you consider your "ministry" in life? What about it gives you joy?

A DEEPER LOOK

What is a "man of peace?" (see v. 6) Where does peace come from?

Psalms 29:11

1 Corinthians 14:33

Isaiah 26:3

Philippians 4:6–7

Romans 5:1

2 Thessalonians 3:16

Romans 15:13

STUDY TWO
The Samaritan and the Sisters

The character of man and communion with Jesus are connected in story and life as Jesus teaches about the condition of our hearts. Provision came from an unexpected place in a parable about loving your neighbor. Jesus wanted His disciples and dissenters to know that obedience to God's commandments meant loving Him by loving others, even those you would rather leave on the side of the road. Two sisters provided an illustration about priorities in relationships. While one sat at the feet of her Friend, the other was distressed about dishes and dusting and having to do it alone. Jesus doesn't shame this servant; He gently reminds her of what matters most. Jesus continued to make disciples as He made His way through Israel, exemplifying and exhorting an attitude of dependence on the Father in prayer.

Luke 10:30–11:13

"**30** Jesus replied and said, 'A man was going down from Jerusalem to Jericho, and
fell among robbers, and they stripped him and beat him, and went away leaving
him half dead. **31** And by chance a priest was going down on that road, and when
he saw him, he passed by on the other side. **32** Likewise a Levite also, when he
came to the place and saw him, passed by on the other side. **33** But a Samaritan,
who was on a journey, came upon him; and when he saw him, he felt compassion,
34 and came to him and bandaged up his wounds, pouring oil and wine on them;
and he put him on his own beast, and brought him to an inn and took care of
him. **35** On the next day he took out two denarii and gave them to the innkeeper

and said, 'Take care of him; and whatever more you spend, when I return I will
repay you.' 36 Which of these three do you think proved to be a neighbor to the
man who fell into the robbers' hands?" 37 And he said, 'The one who showed
mercy toward him.' Then Jesus said to him, 'Go and do the same.'

38 Now as they were traveling along, He entered a village; and a woman named
Martha welcomed Him into her home. 39 She had a sister called Mary, who was
seated at the Lord's feet, listening to His word. 40 But Martha was distracted with
all her preparations; and she came up to Him and said, 'Lord, do You not care
that my sister has left me to do all the serving alone? Then tell her to help me.'
41 But the Lord answered and said to her, 'Martha, Martha, you are worried and
bothered about so many things; 42 but only one thing is necessary, for Mary has
chosen the good part, which shall not be taken away from her.'

1 It happened that while Jesus was praying in a certain place, after He had finished, one of His disciples said to Him, 'Lord, teach us to pray just as John also
taught his disciples.' 2 And He said to them, 'When you pray, say:

'Father, hallowed be Your name.
Your kingdom come.
3 'Give us each day our daily bread.
4 'And forgive us our sins,
For we ourselves also forgive everyone who is indebted to us.
And lead us not into temptation.'

5 Then He said to them, 'Suppose one of you has a friend, and goes to him
at midnight and says to him, 'Friend, lend me three loaves; 6 for a friend of mine
has come to me from a journey, and I have nothing to set before him'; 7 and
from inside he answers and says, 'Do not bother me; the door has already been
shut and my children and I are in bed; I cannot get up and give you anything.'
8 I tell you, even though he will not get up and give him anything because he is
his friend, yet because of his persistence he will get up and give him as much as
he needs.

9 'So I say to you, ask, and it will be given to you; seek, and you will find;
knock, and it will be opened to you. 10 For everyone who asks, receives; and he
who seeks, finds; and to him who knocks, it will be opened. 11 Now suppose one
of you fathers is asked by his son for a fish; he will not give him a snake instead
of a fish, will he? 12 Or if he is asked for an egg, he will not give him a scorpion,
will he? 13 If you then, being evil, know how to give good gifts to your children,
how much more will your heavenly Father give the Holy Spirit to those who ask
Him?'"

1. What happened to the man in verse 30?

NOTE: Jesus does not say this, but it is implied the man was Jewish because he was leaving Jerusalem.

2. Who enters the story in verses 31–32 and how did they respond to the man? Jesus does not say, but why do you think the two men responded like they did?

3. What do we know about Samaritans? Use the Quick Reference Dictionary at www.biblestudytools.com to refresh your memory.

4. As the storyteller, Jesus could have inserted any kind of person He wanted into this story. What do you think Jesus was saying by making a Samaritan the "provider" of kindness and help?

5. Why does Jesus say he stopped to help in verse 33? Read verses 34–35 and describe that feeling in action. How does he go "above and beyond?"

6. How did the lawyer describe the Samaritan in verse 37? What is Jesus' exhortation to us in verse 37?

7. Consider this: what if Jesus was "the Good Samaritan?" Then what might be the message of this parable?

8. Whose home did Jesus enter in verse 38? Describe this scene in verses 39–40 in your own words. From what we see in Scripture, describe Mary and Martha.

9. How does Jesus describe Martha in verse 41? Based on the truth from Romans 8:1, what do we know Jesus was NOT saying to her?

10. How does this story instruct us about priorities (Matthew 6:33)?

11. What is the promise for Mary and us in this passage when we "choose the good?" (v. 42)

12. What did the disciples ask Jesus to do in Luke 11:1? What had Jesus been doing before they asked?

NOTE: This is the only time recorded in Scripture the disciples ask Jesus to teach them anything.

13. Observe and write down the elements of Jesus' teaching on prayer. How does His teaching help inform your prayer life?

14. Jesus then gives a parable about prayer. What is Jesus teaching about Himself and His Father as Provider in this parable?

15. What is our responsibility in prayer outlined in verse 9?

16. Why should we not give up asking, seeking, and knocking according to verse 10?

17. How does Hebrews 4:16 help us interpret this story?

18. What do we know about God and how He responds to our needs and requests? (Isaiah 55:8–9, Ephesians 3:20–21, 1 John 5:14–15)

19. What does Jesus say is an even greater gift than material blessings? (v. 13) How do we receive that gift? (Romans 8:9, 1 John 3:23–24, and 4:13)

Application

Are you more task-oriented or people-oriented? If task, does focusing on getting the job done or the list checked off ever hinder your relationship with Jesus or with others? If people, does connecting with others ever distract you from doing the things you know you need to do, or that others are counting on you to do?

Is there anything you need to do to inject more balance in your life?

A DEEPER LOOK

What is the "one thing" that is necessary for all of us?

Numbers 18:20

Psalms 84:10

Psalms 16:5

Psalms 142:5

Psalms 73:26

Lamentations 3:24

STUDY THREE
Pharisees' Blasphemy

Jesus cast a mute demon out of a man, amazing some Jews and angering others. Jesus does not waste time addressing their words; He goes straight to their thoughts. Using logic and truth, Jesus challenged their belief that His power came from the very demons He cast out. They were accusing Jesus of blasphemy while speaking it themselves. The divided house Jesus used in the metaphor was true in reality in Israel. Jesus came to light the lamp of truth, providing the only sign anyone needed that He was their promised Redeemer. But the Jews who should have known could not see.

Luke 11:14–36

"14 And He was casting out a demon, and it was mute; when the demon had gone
out, the mute man spoke; and the crowds were amazed. 15 But some of them
said, 'He casts out demons by Beelzebul, the ruler of the demons.' 16 Others,
to test Him, were demanding of Him a sign from heaven. 17 But He knew their
thoughts and said to them, 'Any kingdom divided against itself is laid waste; and
a house divided against itself falls. 18 If Satan also is divided against himself, how
will his kingdom stand? For you say that I cast out demons by Beelzebul. 19 And
if I by Beelzebul cast out demons, by whom do your sons cast them out? So they
will be your judges. 20 But if I cast out demons by the finger of God, then the
kingdom of God has come upon you. 21 When a strong man, fully armed, guards
his own house, his possessions are undisturbed. 22 But when someone stronger
than he attacks him and overpowers him, he takes away from him all his armor
on which he had relied and distributes his plunder. 23 He who is not with Me is
against Me; and he who does not gather with Me, scatters.

24 'When the unclean spirit goes out of a man, it passes through waterless
places seeking rest, and not finding any, it says, 'I will return to my house from
which I came.' 25 And when it comes, it finds it swept and put in order. 26 Then
it goes and takes along seven other spirits more evil than itself, and they go in and
live there; and the last state of that man becomes worse than the first.'

27 While Jesus was saying these things, one of the women in the crowd raised
her voice and said to Him, 'Blessed is the womb that bore You and the breasts at
which You nursed.' 28 But He said, 'On the contrary, blessed are those who hear
the word of God and observe it.'

29 As the crowds were increasing, He began to say, 'This generation is a wicked
generation; it seeks for a sign, and yet no sign will be given to it but the sign of
Jonah. 30 For just as Jonah became a sign to the Ninevites, so will the Son of Man
be to this generation. 31 The Queen of the South will rise up with the men of this
generation at the judgment and condemn them, because she came from the ends
of the earth to hear the wisdom of Solomon; and behold, something greater than
Solomon is here. 32 The men of Nineveh will stand up with this generation at the
judgment and condemn it, because they repented at the preaching of Jonah; and
behold, something greater than Jonah is here.

33 'No one, after lighting a lamp, puts it away in a cellar nor under a basket,
but on the lampstand, so that those who enter may see the light. 34 The eye is the
lamp of your body; when your eye is clear, your whole body also is full of light;
but when it is bad, your body also is full of darkness. 35 Then watch out that the

light in you is not darkness. 36 If therefore your whole body is full of light, with no dark part in it, it will be wholly illumined, as when the lamp illumines you with its rays.'"

1. What did Jesus do in verse 14?

2. What was the response to Jesus' miracle in verse 14? How did the people try to explain His ability to do this in verses 15–16?

3. Based on their accusations that He colluded with Satan, what is Jesus arguing in verses 17–19?

4. How does Jesus say He casts out demons? What is He saying that means with regard to this time in history? (v. 20)

5. Who are the two characters in battle in verses 21–22? Who is always "someone stronger?" Who are the "possessions?"

6. What are the options with regard to following Jesus in verse 23? What does this say about those who say they are "ambivalent" or "neutral" about Jesus?

7. How do verses 24–25 describe the current condition of the man from verse 14?

NOTE: As John MacArthur explains in *One Perfect Life*, "Christ was characterizing the work of the phony exorcists. What appears to be a true exorcism is really a temporary respite, after which the demon returns with seven others."

8. What is the danger of leaving your "inner house" empty? (v. 26) What needs to fill it?

9. How does Jesus deflect the woman's praise of His mother in verses 27–28?

10. How was Jonah a sign to the Ninevites (Jonah 3)? How is Jesus a similar sign to the people?

11. What does it mean that the eye is a lamp for the body? (v. 34) Consider:

    - What is a lamp?
    - How does a lamp work?
    - What does a lamp need?

12. What does light represent? (Psalms 27:1, Psalms 119:105, 130)

Application

How can your "lamp" (eye) be clear to illumine darkness?

STUDY FOUR
Woes upon the Pharisees

It is usually considered bad manners to insult your dinner host—unless you're Jesus and the invitation to the meal was more like the summons from the spider to the fly. No doubt Jesus quickly lost His appetite as the criticism from the Pharisees came before anyone could say "Amen." Jesus compared the hypocrisy of these religious men to eating off a dirty plate. You can call it clean, but the evidence is clear. Like a well-manicured graveyard, their spiritual lives appeared holy, but their hearts were as lifeless as a tomb. The lawyers were supposed to tell "the whole truth and nothing but the truth" about the Law. Jesus charged them with imprisoning the people with unnecessary burdens while they got off scot-free.

Luke 11:37–54

"37 Now when He had spoken, a Pharisee asked Him to have lunch with him; and He went in, and reclined at the table. 38 When the Pharisee saw it, he was surprised that He had not first ceremonially washed before the meal. 39 But the Lord said to him, 'Now you Pharisees clean the outside of the cup and of the platter; but inside of you, you are full of robbery and wickedness. 40 You foolish ones, did not He who made the outside make the inside also? 41 But give that which is within as charity, and then all things are clean for you.

42 'But woe to you Pharisees! For you pay tithe of mint and rue and every kind of garden herb, and yet disregard justice and the love of God; but these are the things you should have done without neglecting the others. 43 Woe to you Pharisees! For you love the chief seats in the synagogues and the respectful greetings in the market places. 44 Woe to you! For you are like concealed tombs, and the people who walk over them are unaware of it.'

45 One of the lawyers said to Him in reply, 'Teacher, when You say this, You insult us too.' 46 But He said, 'Woe to you lawyers as well! For you weigh men down with burdens hard to bear, while you yourselves will not even touch the burdens with one of your fingers. 47 Woe to you! For you build the tombs of the prophets, and it was your fathers who killed them. 48 So you are witnesses and approve the deeds of your fathers; because it was they who killed them, and you build their tombs. 49 For this reason also the wisdom of God said, 'I will send to them prophets and apostles, and some of them they will kill and some they will persecute, 50 so that the blood of all the prophets, shed since the foundation of the world, may be charged against this generation, 51 from the blood of Abel to the blood of Zechariah, who was killed between the altar and the house of God; yes, I tell you, it shall be charged against this generation.' 52 Woe to you lawyers! For you have taken away the key of knowledge; you yourselves did not enter, and you hindered those who were entering.'

53 When He left there, the scribes and the Pharisees began to be very hostile and to question Him closely on many subjects, 54 plotting against Him to catch Him in something He might say."

1. Who was Jesus with in verse 37 and why? What surprised the Pharisee in verse 38?

2. Where did the practice of ceremonially washing before meals come from: the Law of Moses or the tradition of man? (see Matthew 15:2 and Mark 7:1–4)

3. What hypocrisy did Jesus point out to His host? (vv. 39–40)

4. What is "that which is within" us? What act did Jesus say would demonstrate the Pharisees were fully devoted to God? (v. 41)

5. What are the three woes Jesus pronounced on the Pharisees? (vv. 42–44)

6. What heart attitudes do these three woes/indictments reveal?

NOTE: The lawyers, or scribes, interpreted the Law of Moses. The Pharisees promoted and enforced it.

7. What are the three woes pronounced against the lawyers? (vv. 46–48, 52) What heart attitudes do they reveal?

8. What was this generation guilty of according to verses 49–51?

9. As interpreters of the Law, how have the lawyers taken away the "key of knowledge" and what has been the result? (v. 52)

10. What was the response of the scribes and Pharisees after the pointed rebuke of Jesus? (vv. 53–54)

Application

How had religious leaders confused their zeal for observing the Law for true righteousness and submission to God? How do we do the same thing?

STUDY FIVE
Beware Of Hypocrisy

With thousands clamoring for His time and attention, Jesus hit the height of popularity. But Jesus did not adjust His message to make it more palatable for the masses. He continued to teach about the real meaning of discipleship. *The Pharisees' example is not one to follow,* He said, *nor are they to be feared. Fear the One who can see your heart and follow Him whatever the cost. The closer your walk with Me, the greater your clarity and perspective will become. But when you wonder, the birds, the lilies, and the grass can testify that My care is constant and complete.* So do not worry, be on your guard, and seek His kingdom. All that you lose for the sake of the Son will be recovered as untold treasure in heaven.

Luke 12:1–34

"Under these circumstances, after so many thousands of people had gathered
together that they were stepping on one another, He began saying to His disciples first of all, 'Beware of the leaven of the Pharisees, which is hypocrisy. 2 But
there is nothing covered up that will not be revealed, and hidden that will not
be known. 3 Accordingly, whatever you have said in the dark will be heard in the
light, and what you have whispered in the inner rooms will be proclaimed upon
the housetops.

4 'I say to you, My friends, do not be afraid of those who kill the body and
after that have no more that they can do. 5 But I will warn you whom to fear:
fear the One who, after He has killed, has authority to cast into hell; yes, I tell
you, fear Him! 6 Are not five sparrows sold for two cents? Yet not one of them is
forgotten before God. 7 Indeed, the very hairs of your head are all numbered. Do
not fear; you are more valuable than many sparrows.

8 'And I say to you, everyone who confesses Me before men, the Son of Man
will confess him also before the angels of God; 9 but he who denies Me before
men will be denied before the angels of God. 10 And everyone who speaks a word
against the Son of Man, it will be forgiven him; but he who blasphemes against
the Holy Spirit, it will not be forgiven him. 11 When they bring you before the
synagogues and the rulers and the authorities, do not worry about how or what
you are to speak in your defense, or what you are to say; 12 for the Holy Spirit will
teach you in that very hour what you ought to say.'

13 Someone in the crowd said to Him, 'Teacher, tell my brother to divide the
family inheritance with me.' 14 But He said to him, 'Man, who appointed Me a
judge or arbitrator over you?' 15 Then He said to them, 'Beware, and be on your
guard against every form of greed; for not even when one has an abundance does
his life consist of his possessions.' 16 And He told them a parable, saying, 'The
land of a rich man was very productive. 17 And he began reasoning to himself,
saying, 'What shall I do, since I have no place to store my crops?' 18 Then he said,
'This is what I will do: I will tear down my barns and build larger ones, and there
I will store all my grain and my goods. 19 And I will say to my soul, 'Soul, you
have many goods laid up for many years to come; take your ease, eat, drink and
be merry.' 20 But God said to him, 'You fool! This very night your soul is required
of you; and now who will own what you have prepared?' 21 So is the man who
stores up treasure for himself, and is not rich toward God.'

22 And He said to His disciples, 'For this reason I say to you, do not worry

about your life, as to what you will eat; nor for your body, as to what you will put
on. 23 For life is more than food, and the body more than clothing. 24 Consider
the ravens, for they neither sow nor reap; they have no storeroom nor barn, and
yet God feeds them; how much more valuable you are than the birds! 25 And
which of you by worrying can add a single hour to his life's span? 26 If then
you cannot do even a very little thing, why do you worry about other matters?
27 Consider the lilies, how they grow: they neither toil nor spin; but I tell you,
not even Solomon in all his glory clothed himself like one of these. 28 But if God
so clothes the grass in the field, which is alive today and tomorrow is thrown into
the furnace, how much more will He clothe you? You men of little faith! 29 And
do not seek what you will eat and what you will drink, and do not keep worrying. 30 For all these things the nations of the world eagerly seek; but your Father
knows that you need these things. 31 But seek His kingdom, and these things
will be added to you. 32 Do not be afraid, little flock, for your Father has chosen
gladly to give you the kingdom.

33 'Sell your possessions and give to charity; make yourselves money belts
which do not wear out, an unfailing treasure in heaven, where no thief comes
near nor moth destroys. 34 For where your treasure is, there your heart will be
also."

1. Who is Jesus speaking to in verse 1? Based on the scene, does the scribes' and Pharisees' hostility toward Jesus have an affect on His popularity?

2. What is leaven or yeast? How does it work?

3. What is the "leaven" of the Pharisees? What earlier encounter with a Pharisee in chapter 11 might have been on Jesus' mind?

4. What warning is Jesus giving in verses 2–3? (see Numbers 32:23)

5. Who does Jesus say is to be feared and why in verses 4–5? What promises do believers have in 2 Timothy 2:11–13?

6. How do verses 6–7 encourage or instruct you about God's awareness of and love for us as our Provider? How can a better understanding of who God is help us to "fear not?"

7. What is the contrast in verses 8–10? Which posture is driven by a fear of man? Which by a fear of God?

8. What are the disciples told to expect and what is promised? (vv. 11–12)

9. What did the man want Jesus to do in verse 13? What was Jesus' indictment in verse 15?

10. Circle the words "I" and "my" in this story in verses 17–19. What does the repetition of this word tell you?

11. How is verse 19 the spiritual turning point for this man? What did God say to him in verse 20? (see Psalms 14:1)

12. Write down the things from this passage (vv. 22–34) that Jesus says God as His Father does. What does that tell you about Him?

13. What does Jesus say to those who choose to worry rather than trust Him? (v. 28) What does verse 31 say we are to do instead of worrying? What does that look like for you?

14. Jesus had acknowledged the risks of being His disciple in verses 11–12. How do His words in verses 22–34 bring comfort in the face of persecution?

15. How does Jesus teach us in this passage to approach our needs, material and otherwise?

Application

Can someone who is poor be greedy? How is greed idolatry?

A DEEPER LOOK

What does the Bible say about being a fool?

Proverbs 13:20

Proverbs 14:1, 7–9, 16

Proverbs 17:28

Proverbs 18:2

Proverbs 23:9

Proverbs 28:26

Proverbs 29:11

Ecclesiastes 7:9

WRAPPING UP

Jesus is not a magic genie we summon to make our wishes come true. Neither is He a lonely grandfather who hands out ten dollar bills whenever we make the time to visit. Jesus desires to bless and provide for His children, but always on His timetable and with purposes far beyond simply meeting a need or making us happy.

We see in Scripture that the provision of Jesus seems often to be linked with trust in Him. While He is able to meet our needs apart from our belief that He can, the sins of worry or self-sufficiency prevent us from praising Him in the midst of need or recognizing the way our trials conform us to His image.

Philippians 4:19 promises that "…my God will supply all your needs according to His riches in glory in Christ Jesus." He has been doing this since creation and will continue until He returns, when every need we have will be forever satisfied.

~ Map of Jesus in Judea and Jerusalem ~

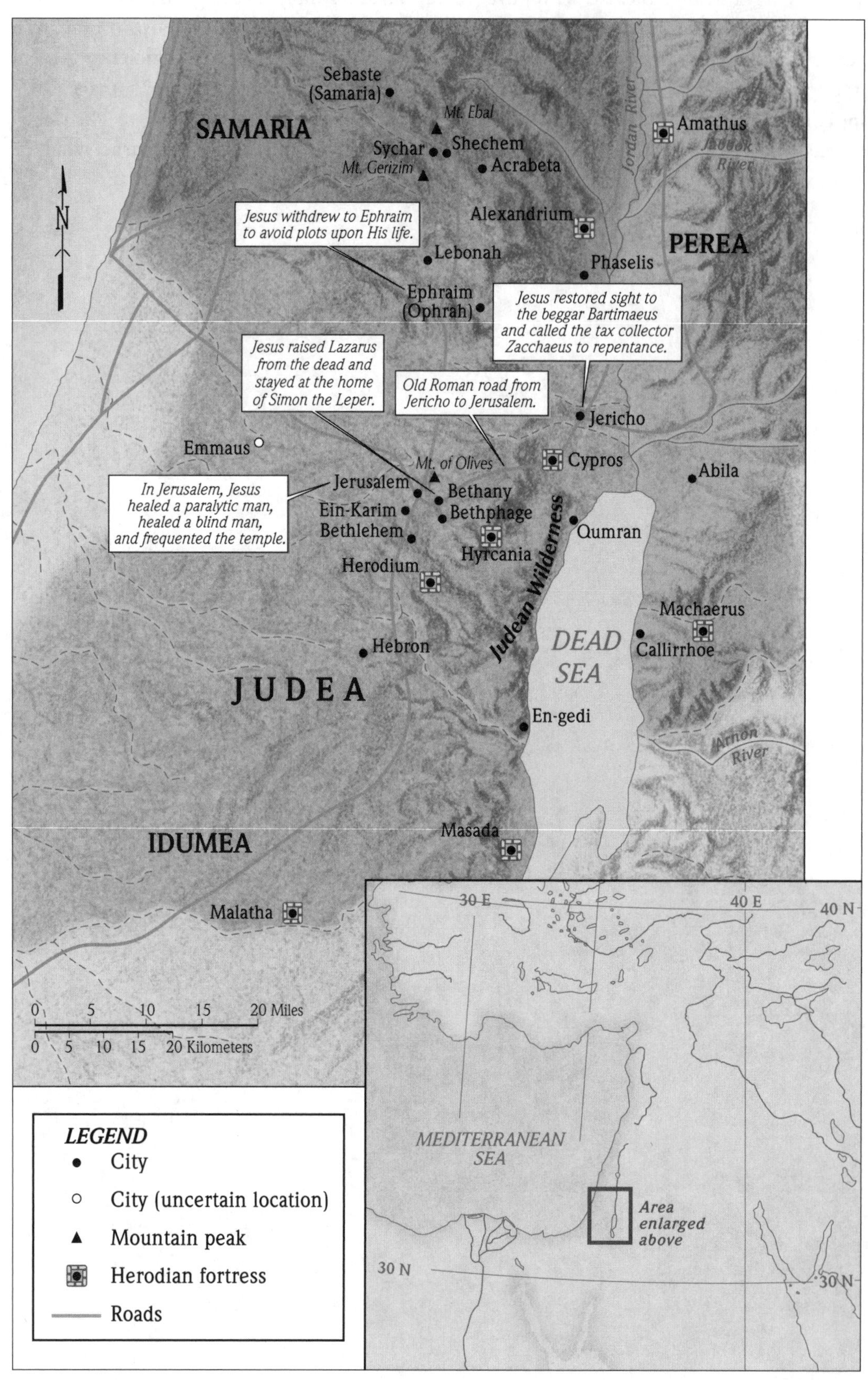

WEEK 15

JESUS, THE GOOD SHEPHERD

"I am the good shepherd, and I know My own and My own know Me, even as the Father knows Me and I know the Father; and I lay down My life for the sheep."
JOHN 10:14–15

Every third grade Sunday school class has one hanging on the wall. It's a peaceful, pastoral scene: a cloudless, bright blue sky, rolling hills blanketed in soft, green grass. And Jesus—sometimes sitting, sometimes standing—in the center of the print, holding a fluffy white lamb in His arms.

The colors are muted; the figures sometimes a little blurry around the edges, for effect. But Jesus is always portrayed gently gazing at His flock, a reminder that we are the helpless sheep, and He keeps us safe from harm.

When Jesus called Himself the "Good Shepherd" for the first time in Scripture, the setting was a little less peaceful. There was implied contention and contrast in His proclamation. God had appointed shepherds over Israel in the form of the priests and Levites (Numbers 8). But, unlike Jesus, they did not care for their sheep. Their only concerns were for perfect adherence to the Law and holding on to their position of power. They behaved like hired hands, working for a wage rather than laboring out of love.

In the face of this division, Jesus painted a clear picture of what the Good Shepherd does for His sheep: He cares for their needs, He knows them specifically and intimately, and He is willing to give up His life to save them. And as the sheep of His fold, we thrive when we acknowledge His authority, listen to His voice, and receive His offer of abundant life.

STUDY ONE
Be Ready

Jesus speaks here of the future, a time when the master returns, families divide, and accounts are settled. The words of Jesus sound harsh, but they are harsh like a parent keeping his child's hand from the flame. His message was urgent for those with no thought for the future because ambivalence leads to judgment and death. His message was crucial for His flock because they must live in expectation, ready and longing for signs of Christ's return. Why? A blessing awaits His faithful servants, those who have stewarded their time, gifts, and relationships with an eye toward eternity. But for those who chose to ignore the signs, a storm was brewing.

Luke 12:35–59

"35 'Be dressed in readiness, and keep your lamps lit. 36 Be like men who are waiting for their master when he returns from the wedding feast, so that they may
immediately open the door to him when he comes and knocks. 37 Blessed are
those slaves whom the master will find on the alert when he comes; truly I say to
you, that he will gird himself to serve, and have them recline at the table, and will
come up and wait on them. 38 Whether he comes in the second watch, or even in
the third, and finds them so, blessed are those slaves.

39 'But be sure of this, that if the head of the house had known at what hour
the thief was coming, he would not have allowed his house to be broken into.
40 You too, be ready; for the Son of Man is coming at an hour that you do not
expect.'

41 Peter said, 'Lord, are You addressing this parable to us, or to everyone else
as well?' 42 And the Lord said, 'Who then is the faithful and sensible steward,
whom his master will put in charge of his servants, to give them their rations at
the proper time? 43 Blessed is that slave whom his master finds so doing when he
comes. 44 Truly I say to you that he will put him in charge of all his possessions.
45 But if that slave says in his heart, 'My master will be a long time in coming,'
and begins to beat the slaves, both men and women, and to eat and drink and
get drunk; 46 the master of that slave will come on a day when he does not expect
him and at an hour he does not know, and will cut him in pieces, and assign him
a place with the unbelievers. 47 And that slave who knew his master's will and did
not get ready or act in accord with his will, will receive many lashes, 48 but the
one who did not know it, and committed deeds worthy of a flogging, will receive
but few. From everyone who has been given much, much will be required; and to
whom they entrusted much, of him they will ask all the more.

49 'I have come to cast fire upon the earth; and how I wish it were already kindled! 50 But I have a baptism to undergo, and how distressed I am until it is
accomplished! 51 Do you suppose that I came to grant peace on earth? I tell you,
no, but rather division; 52 for from now on five members in one household will
be divided, three against two and two against three. 53 They will be divided,
father against son and son against father, mother against daughter and daughter against mother, mother-in-law against daughter-in-law and daughter-in-law
against mother-in-law.'

54 And He was also saying to the crowds, 'When you see a cloud rising in the
west, immediately you say, 'A shower is coming,' and so it turns out. 55 And when
you see a south wind blowing, you say, 'It will be a hot day,' and it turns out that
way. 56 You hypocrites! You know how to analyze the appearance of the earth and
the sky, but why do you not analyze this present time?

57 'And why do you not even on your own initiative judge what is right?
58 For while you are going with your opponent to appear before the magistrate,
on your way there make an effort to settle with him, so that he may not drag you
before the judge, and the judge turn you over to the officer, and the officer throw
you into prison. 59 I say to you, you will not get out of there until you have paid
the very last cent.'"

1. Without trying to interpret the images in Jesus' words, what do you think Jesus is saying in verses 35–40?

   - What is the exhortation?

   - What is the promise?

   - What is the warning?

   - What is the unexpected "twist" in verse 37?

   - What is ambiguous about verse 38? What does that mean?

   - How does verse 40 help you understand the greater context?

2. Using a dictionary, define *steward* and *stewardship*.

3. How does Jesus answer Peter's question in verse 42? What does that indicate?

4. What is the difference between the slave in verses 43–44 and in verses 45–46? How does this describe two kinds of stewardship?

5. How does Jesus define a "good slave" or steward in verse 42?

6. What is the standard for stewardship that Jesus presents in verse 48b?

7. How does this passage connect leading and serving?

8. Circle the word "blessed" in this passage. Who does Jesus say will be blessed?

9. How does Jesus describe His ministry in verses 49–50? What is the "baptism to undergo" that Jesus had yet to face?

10. How is Jesus using the weather forecast to talk about this time in history? (vv. 54–56)

11. What were the three questions Jesus asked in this passage? (vv. 51, 56, 57) How is Jesus using these questions (and their answers) to instruct the hearers?

12. Who is our opponent in verse 58 before we acknowledge our sinful state? (Romans 1:28–30, Romans 5:10, Colossians 1:21) How has Jesus "settled with him?"

Application

Is waiting an attitude or an action? What does this week's Scripture say? How are we to wait?

STUDY TWO
Repentance and Healing

When tragedy strikes, we often look for someone to blame. The Jews mentioned recent calamities to Jesus and asked Him to judge the transgressions of the suffering. Jesus wanted to erase any doubt about who had greater guilt: all have sinned and fallen short, He told them. The right answer for everyone is repentance. Jesus illustrated His point with a barren fig tree, a metaphor for a fruitless people and their gracious God. Jesus displayed His grace again on the Sabbath by healing a woman who had not seen the sky in eighteen years. A synagogue leader took issue with this loving act and instructed Jesus in the Law. Astounded by the cold and callous hearts on display, Jesus delivered a sharp rebuke, deepening the chasm between the lost sheep and the Good Shepherd.

Luke 13:1–22

"Now on the same occasion there were some present who reported to Him about
the Galileans whose blood Pilate had mixed with their sacrifices. 2 And Jesus said
to them, 'Do you suppose that these Galileans were greater sinners than all other
Galileans because they suffered this fate? 3 I tell you, no, but unless you repent,
you will all likewise perish. 4 Or do you suppose that those eighteen on whom the
tower in Siloam fell and killed them were worse culprits than all the men who live
in Jerusalem? 5 I tell you, no, but unless you repent, you will all likewise perish.'
6 And He began telling this parable: 'A man had a fig tree which had been
planted in his vineyard; and he came looking for fruit on it and did not find any.
7 And he said to the vineyard-keeper, 'Behold, for three years I have come looking
for fruit on this fig tree without finding any. Cut it down! Why does it even use
up the ground?' 8 And he answered and said to him, 'Let it alone, sir, for this year
too, until I dig around it and put in fertilizer; 9 and if it bears fruit next year, fine;
but if not, cut it down.'

10 And He was teaching in one of the synagogues on the Sabbath. 11 And there
was a woman who for eighteen years had had a sickness caused by a spirit; and
she was bent double, and could not straighten up at all. 12 When Jesus saw her,
He called her over and said to her, 'Woman, you are freed from your sickness.'
13 And He laid His hands on her; and immediately she was made erect again and
began glorifying God. 14 But the synagogue official, indignant because Jesus had
healed on the Sabbath, began saying to the crowd in response, 'There are six days
in which work should be done; so come during them and get healed, and not on
the Sabbath day.' 15 But the Lord answered him and said, 'You hypocrites, does
not each of you on the Sabbath untie his ox or his donkey from the stall and lead
him away to water him? 16 And this woman, a daughter of Abraham as she is,
whom Satan has bound for eighteen long years, should she not have been released
from this bond on the Sabbath day?' 17 As He said this, all His opponents were
being humiliated; and the entire crowd was rejoicing over all the glorious things
being done by Him.

18 So He was saying, 'What is the kingdom of God like, and to what shall I
compare it? 19 It is like a mustard seed, which a man took and threw into his
own garden; and it grew and became a tree, and the birds of the air nested in its
branches.'

20 And again He said, 'To what shall I compare the kingdom of God? 21 It is
like leaven, which a woman took and hid in three pecks of flour until it was all
leavened.'

22 And He was passing through from one city and village to another, teaching,
and proceeding on His way to Jerusalem."

1. Based on Jesus' answer in verse 2 to the report given in verse 1, what seemed to be the popular or common view regarding the cause of suffering in the world? Do we still feel that way about suffering today?

2. What does Jesus teach in verses 2 and 4? What does He say is the most important posture before the Lord in verses 3 and 5?

3. How does Jesus move the conversation from "those people" and make it personal? (vv. 3 and 5)

4. Summarize the parable of the fig tree in verses 6–9 in your own words.

   - What is the problem?

   - What is the proposed solution?

   - What is the compromise?

   - What does this teach us about the people's spiritual condition?

   - What does this teach us about the character of God?

5. How is the woman described in this passage? (vv. 11,16) What caused her disability?

6. How did her healing occur? What part did the woman play in her healing? (vv. 12–13)

7. Where was Jesus and when did this event occur? (v. 10)

8. How did the woman respond? (v. 13) How did the religious leaders respond? (v. 14) What does their response reveal about their hearts?

9. Why did Jesus call the religious leaders hypocrites in this scene? (v. 15)

10. How do we see what Jesus values from His response? How does that instruct us?

11. What contrast is seen in verse 17?

12. What common elements of the day does Jesus use to illustrate the kingdom of God? (vv. 18–21) What characteristics of the kingdom can be seen in His comparisons?

13. Describe the movement and activity of Jesus in verse 22. What was His ultimate destination? How does this one verse sum up the ministry of Jesus? How does this convey the idea of Jesus as the Good Shepherd?

Application

What are some of the ways God uses suffering in our lives? How do you respond when suffering comes? What are the truths from God's Word that you cling to?

A DEEPER LOOK

What does the Bible say about suffering? How does your "theology of suffering" line up with what God's Word says?

Romans 8:18

2 Timothy 2:8–13

1 Corinthians 4:9–13

1 Peter 2:19

Philippians 1:29

STUDY THREE
Healing of the Man Born Blind

A friendly face, an olive tree, a stream of water, or starry sky—all images completely unknown to the man born blind and begging in the road. As the disciples tried to square this man's suffering with his or his parents' sin, Jesus worked a miracle with spit and clay, bringing sight to the man and glory to God. This work of Jesus so transformed the former beggar, he was barely recognizable to his neighbors. The Pharisees were suspicious of the man and the miracle and called his parents to testify. Their fear of earthly rejection denied them a divine opportunity. The healed man, however, used his temporary platform to teach the truth. Jesus enlightened the eyes of his heart, and the man born blind was now born again.

John 9:1–41

"As He passed by, He saw a man blind from birth. 2 And His disciples asked Him,
'Rabbi, who sinned, this man or his parents, that he would be born blind?' 3 Jesus
answered, 'It was neither that this man sinned, nor his parents; but it was so that
the works of God might be displayed in him. 4 We must work the works of Him
who sent Me as long as it is day; night is coming when no one can work. 5 While
I am in the world, I am the Light of the world.' 6 When He had said this, He

spat on the ground, and made clay of the spittle, and applied the clay to his eyes,
7 and said to him, 'Go, wash in the pool of Siloam' (which is translated, Sent). So
he went away and washed, and came back seeing. 8 Therefore the neighbors, and
those who previously saw him as a beggar, were saying, 'Is not this the one who
used to sit and beg?' 9 Others were saying, 'This is he,' still others were saying,
'No, but he is like him.' He kept saying, 'I am the one.' 10 So they were saying to
him, 'How then were your eyes opened?' 11 He answered, 'The man who is called
Jesus made clay, and anointed my eyes, and said to me, 'Go to Siloam and wash';
so I went away and washed, and I received sight.' 12 They said to him, 'Where is
He?' He said, 'I do not know.'

13 They brought to the Pharisees the man who was formerly blind. 14 Now it was
a Sabbath on the day when Jesus made the clay and opened his eyes. 15 Then the
Pharisees also were asking him again how he received his sight. And he said to
them, 'He applied clay to my eyes, and I washed, and I see.' 16 Therefore some of
the Pharisees were saying, 'This man is not from God, because He does not keep
the Sabbath.' But others were saying, 'How can a man who is a sinner perform
such signs?' And there was a division among them. 17 So they said to the blind
man again, 'What do you say about Him, since He opened your eyes?' And he
said, 'He is a prophet.'

18 The Jews then did not believe it of him, that he had been blind and had
received sight, until they called the parents of the very one who had received his
sight, 19 and questioned them, saying, 'Is this your son, who you say was born
blind? Then how does he now see?" 20 His parents answered them and said, 'We
know that this is our son, and that he was born blind; 21 but how he now sees,
we do not know; or who opened his eyes, we do not know. Ask him; he is of age,
he will speak for himself.' 22 His parents said this because they were afraid of the
Jews; for the Jews had already agreed that if anyone confessed Him to be Christ,
he was to be put out of the synagogue. 23 For this reason his parents said, 'He is
of age; ask him.'

24 So a second time they called the man who had been blind, and said to him,
'Give glory to God; we know that this man is a sinner.' 25 He then answered,
'Whether He is a sinner, I do not know; one thing I do know, that though I was
blind, now I see.' 26 So they said to him, 'What did He do to you? How did He
open your eyes?' 27 He answered them, 'I told you already and you did not listen;
why do you want to hear it again? You do not want to become His disciples too,
do you?' 28 They reviled him and said, 'You are His disciple, but we are disciples
of Moses. 29 We know that God has spoken to Moses, but as for this man, we
do not know where He is from.' 30 The man answered and said to them, 'Well,
here is an amazing thing, that you do not know where He is from, and yet He
opened my eyes. 31 We know that God does not hear sinners; but if anyone is
God-fearing and does His will, He hears him. 32 Since the beginning of time it
has never been heard that anyone opened the eyes of a person born blind. 33 If
this man were not from God, He could do nothing.' 34 They answered him, 'You
were born entirely in sins, and are you teaching us?' So they put him out. 35 Jesus
heard that they had put him out, and finding him, He said, 'Do you believe in
the Son of Man?' 36 He answered, 'Who is He, Lord, that I may believe in Him?'
37 Jesus said to him, 'You have both seen Him, and He is the one who is talking
with you.' 38 And he said, 'Lord, I believe.' And he worshiped Him. 39 And Jesus

said, 'For judgment I came into this world, so that those who do not see may see,
and that those who see may become blind.' 40 Those of the Pharisees who were
with Him heard these things and said to Him, 'We are not blind too, are we?'
41 Jesus said to them, 'If you were blind, you would have no sin; but since you
say, 'We see,' your sin remains."

1. Who did Jesus and His disciples encounter while they were in Jerusalem? How long had he been in that condition?

2. What cause and effect relationship did the disciples propose in verse 2 that had been already revealed as the prevalent thought of the day? How did Jesus clearly and correctly refute their assumption in verse 3?

3. What was missing in the disciples' clinical assessment of the blind man before them?

4. What is Jesus referring to by metaphor in verses 4–5? What did He call Himself?

5. How did the miracle of the man's sight restoration take place? What did Jesus do? What did the man do? How did the people respond? (vv. 6–10)

6. How did the man describe what happened in verse 11?

7. Who enters the scene in verse 13? What detail is revealed about the healing in verse 14?

8. Describe the division in verse 16. How does 2 Corinthians 4:4 provide accurate commentary on this?

9. How should their knowledge of the Old Testament have helped the Pharisees' understanding of who Jesus was in this circumstance? (See Isaiah 29:18, 35:5, 42:6–7, and Psalms 146:8).

10. From whom did the Pharisees ask for input in verse 17 and what did he say?

11. How does the conversation twist in verse 18 and whom do the Pharisees call to speak into their next disagreement?

12. What did they say and why did they say it? (vv. 20–23)

13. How many times had the Pharisees asked the question they posed again in verse 26? What tongue-in-cheek challenge does the man issue in verse 27?

14. Summarize the man's "mini-sermon" in verses 30–33. What do we learn about God's grace and power?

15. How do the Pharisees respond to the man in verse 34?

16. What did Jesus ask the man in verse 35? What did the man call Jesus? How did Jesus shine more light on who He was in verse 37? How did the man respond in verse 38?

17. What does Jesus explain about His mission in verse 39?

18. How do Proverbs 3:7–8 and Proverbs 26:12 help interpret the exchange in verses 40–41?

Application

What does the progress of this man's faith—from darkness to dim shadows to bright revelation (John 9:38)—say about how we grow in our "spiritual sight?"

How does fear hinder our faith?

A DEEPER LOOK

How is the power of personal testimony illustrated here? What does the Bible say about telling the story of God's work in our lives?

Psalms 66:16

Psalms 71:15–16

Daniel 1:12–14

Philippians 1:12–14

Hebrews 10:24–25

1 John 1:1–4

STUDY FOUR
The Good Shepherd

Thieves and robbers disguise themselves and devise other means to inherit the kingdom, leading their sheep down a destructive path. But once the Good Shepherd speaks, all doubt is removed about Whom to follow. Sheep are eager to obey a Shepherd who knows them and leads them out of harm's way. Not only is Jesus the true Shepherd, He calls Himself the door of the sheepfold as well. Jesus was proclaiming that He is the only way to salvation. You are safe for all eternity when you enter His way and listen to His voice. But, there is a fork dividing this path with a choice to be made, and many Jews remained blind and deaf to His call. For those who still wandered and wondered where to go, Jesus had two words: "I am."

John 10:1–21

"'Truly, truly, I say to you, he who does not enter by the door into the fold of
the sheep, but climbs up some other way, he is a thief and a robber. 2 But he who
enters by the door is a shepherd of the sheep. 3 To him the doorkeeper opens, and
the sheep hear his voice, and he calls his own sheep by name and leads them out.
4 When he puts forth all his own, he goes ahead of them, and the sheep follow
him because they know his voice. 5 A stranger they simply will not follow, but will
flee from him, because they do not know the voice of strangers.' 6 This figure of
speech Jesus spoke to them, but they did not understand what those things were
which He had been saying to them.

7 So Jesus said to them again, 'Truly, truly, I say to you, I am the door of the
sheep. 8 All who came before Me are thieves and robbers, but the sheep did not
hear them. 9 I am the door; if anyone enters through Me, he will be saved, and
will go in and out and find pasture. 10 The thief comes only to steal and kill and
destroy; I came that they may have life, and have it abundantly.

11 'I am the good shepherd; the good shepherd lays down His life for the
sheep. 12 He who is a hired hand, and not a shepherd, who is not the owner of
the sheep, sees the wolf coming, and leaves the sheep and flees, and the wolf
snatches them and scatters them. 13 He flees because he is a hired hand and is
not concerned about the sheep. 14 I am the good shepherd, and I know My own
and My own know Me, 15 even as the Father knows Me and I know the Father;
and I lay down My life for the sheep. 16 I have other sheep, which are not of this
fold; I must bring them also, and they will hear My voice; and they will become
one flock with one shepherd. 17 For this reason the Father loves Me, because I lay
down My life so that I may take it again. 18 No one has taken it away from Me,
but I lay it down on My own initiative. I have authority to lay it down, and I have
authority to take it up again. This commandment I received from My Father.'

19 A division occurred again among the Jews because of these words. 20 Many
of them were saying, 'He has a demon and is insane. Why do you listen to Him?'
21 Others were saying, 'These are not the sayings of one demon-possessed. A
demon cannot open the eyes of the blind, can he?'"

1. Who are the thieves and robbers that Jesus speaks of in verse 1? How does Scripture talk about the irresponsible "shepherds" of God's people? (see Isaiah 56:9–12, Jeremiah 23:1–4, Jeremiah 25:34–37, Ezekiel 34:1–4)

2. What is the contrast between the true Shepherd and the thieves in verses John 10:1–5?

3. What are the characteristics of the Shepherd of sheep in verses 2–5? How do the sheep respond to the Shepherd?

4. What does Jesus call Himself in verses 7 and 9? How does that image depict Jesus' role in salvation? What promises does Jesus give in verses 9–10?

5. Read verses 11–15 out loud. What did Jesus say about Himself? How did He describe and distinguish Himself?

6. What "other sheep" is Jesus referring to in verse 16? (see Ephesians 2:11–22)

7. How does Jesus describe His relationship with His Father in verses 15 and 17?

8. So what does that say about the Father's commandment and Jesus' submission to it? (v. 18)

9. What freedom does Jesus say He has in verse 18? What does that tell us about His death on the cross? What does that tell us about His love for us?

10. What happened as a result of Jesus' words? (v. 19) What were the divisions of thought among the Jews?

11. What attributes of God do you see in this passage? (John 10:1–21)

Application

What are the things that steal, kill, and destroy your faith?

A DEEPER LOOK

What does the Bible say about God's people as sheep?

Psalms 95:7

Isaiah 40:11

Psalms 100:3

Isaiah 53:6

STUDY FIVE
Jesus Asserts His Deity

The worries of the world can overwhelm us. We can be deceived by the smooth lies of enemies all around. We misplace our trust, make the same mistakes, and fail to follow the Voice that is for us. And yet, in the midst of this turmoil, we find a promise: no one can snatch us from the hand of Jesus. We are forever secure in the firm grasp of God. The Door opens one way, and once we are inside, nothing can carry us away. Jesus spoke this way of His sheep to the disbelieving Jews, who did not understand because they did not know His voice. They only heard blasphemy in Jesus' words and responded by picking up stones. His hour had not yet come, but the stage was set for the final act. No greater love would be seen soon enough in the last and best sacrifice of the Good Shepherd for His sheep.

John 10:22–39

"**22** At that time the Feast of the Dedication took place at Jerusalem; **23** it was
winter, and Jesus was walking in the temple in the portico of Solomon. **24** The
Jews then gathered around Him, and were saying to Him, 'How long will You

keep us in suspense? If You are the Christ, tell us plainly.' **25** Jesus answered them,
'I told you, and you do not believe; the works that I do in My Father's name,
these testify of Me. **26** But you do not believe because you are not of My sheep.
27 My sheep hear My voice, and I know them, and they follow Me; **28** and I give
eternal life to them, and they will never perish; and no one will snatch them out
of My hand. **29** My Father, who has given them to Me, is greater than all; and no
one is able to snatch them out of the Father's hand. **30** I and the Father are one.'
31 The Jews picked up stones again to stone Him. **32** Jesus answered them, 'I
showed you many good works from the Father; for which of them are you stoning
Me?' **33** The Jews answered Him, 'For a good work we do not stone You, but for
blasphemy; and because You, being a man, make Yourself out to be God.' **34** Jesus
answered them, 'Has it not been written in your Law, 'I said, you are gods'? **35** If
he called them gods, to whom the word of God came (and the Scripture cannot
be broken), **36** do you say of Him, whom the Father sanctified and sent into the
world, 'You are blaspheming,' because I said, 'I am the Son of God'? **37** If I do not
do the works of My Father, do not believe Me; **38** but if I do them, though you
do not believe Me, believe the works, so that you may know and understand that
the Father is in Me, and I in the Father.' **39** Therefore they were seeking again to
seize Him, and He eluded their grasp."

1. What is the setting in verses 22–23?

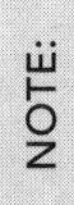

The Feast of Dedication is now known as Hanukkah, the Festival of Lights. It marks the rededication of the temple in 164 BC after the Maccabean revolt, and was not prescribed by Mosaic Law.

2. What was Jesus doing? Who confronted Him and what did they want to know? (vv. 23–24)

3. What does Jesus say are the ways He revealed Himself to them? (v. 25) Why are they unable to believe? (v. 26)

4. How do the events—and the outcome—of verse 29 reflect Jesus' words in verse 18?

5. How do verses 29–30 depict the deity of Jesus and His relationship to God?

6. What is the response of the Jews in verse 31? What reason did they give to justify this action? (v. 33)

7. Read Philippians 2:6–7 and write it below. What is the difference between the Jews' accusation against Jesus in verse 33 and the truth about Jesus from God's Word?

8. What are the good works Jesus had done up until now? (v. 32)

9. Read Psalms 82. The "gods" referred to in this psalm by Jesus in verses 34–35 represent human rulers, those God put in places of power and authority. How does this psalm help you interpret what Jesus is saying? How does Jesus use this Scripture to refute their accusation of blasphemy? (v. 34–36)

10. What does Jesus point to again about His ministry to provide confirmation to the Jews of His identity? (vv. 37–38)

11. What does verse 38 reveal about Jesus' desire for these rebellious children of Israel?

Application

What details in this passage speak to the eternal security you have in Christ, your Good Shepherd?

WRAPPING UP

Our Good Shepherd—Jesus—is a complete and thoughtful Provider. He knows what we need and only denies when what we desire would keep us from Him. He gives us rest when we are weary; He gently guides us in ways that refresh our hearts and restore our souls. All for the sake of His name.

We have no need to fear—neither evil or death—because Jesus is always by our side, watching over and comforting us, whatever comes our way. We do not wander without purpose. There is a plan and intention straight from the heart of God for every step we take.

He is a lavish Host and generous in every way. He blesses us with honor as His beloved children. Be it spiritual or physical danger, Jesus is our great Defender. Every enemy stands powerless in His presence.

Our Shepherd's care is everlasting and faithful. He pours out His mercy and goodness on us daily, infinitely. All this, and what do we have to look forward to? The joy of spending eternity in the beauty and glory of a perfect relationship with the One who made us and loves us more than we can imagine.

Notes

~ Map of Ministry Beyond Galilee ~

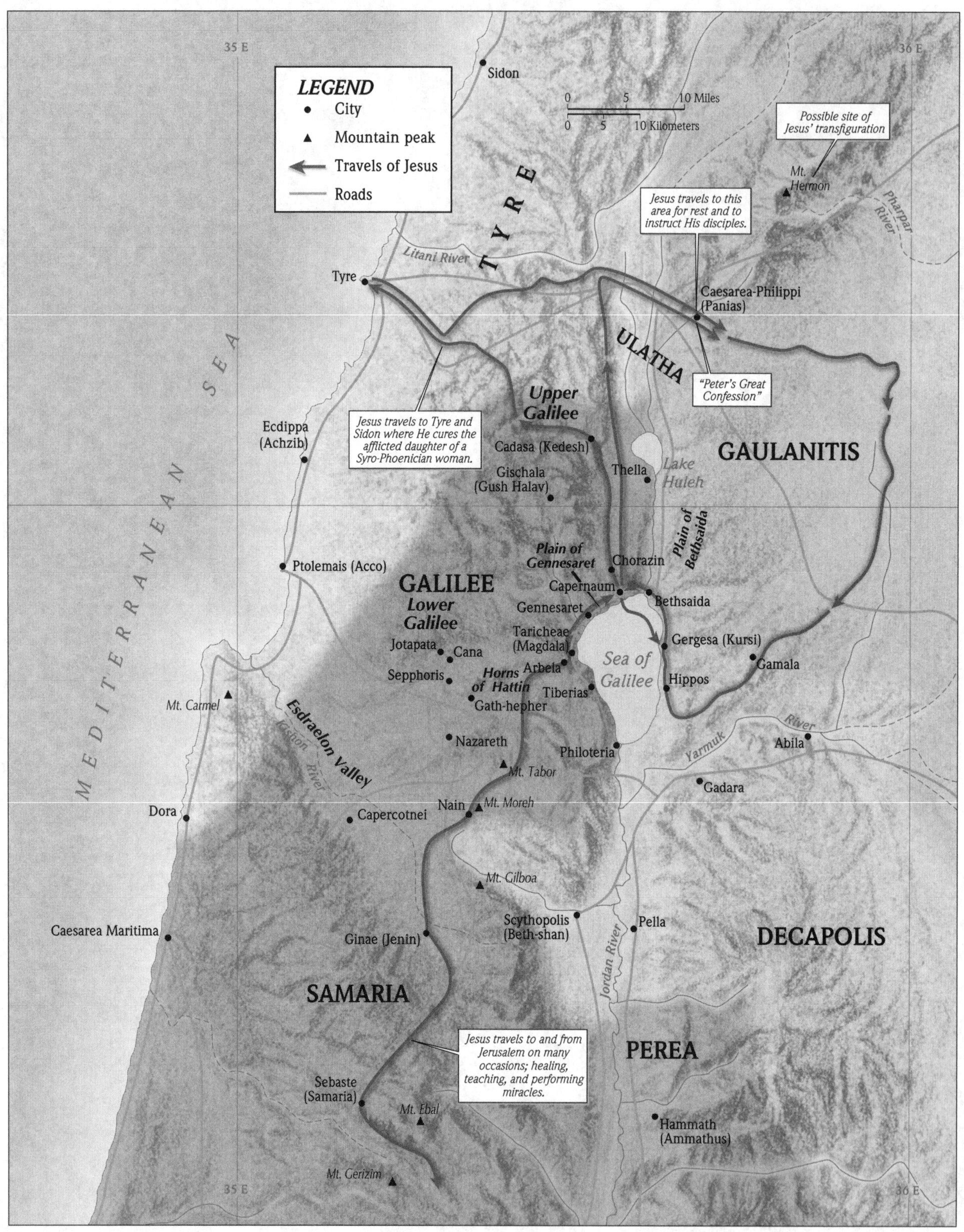

WEEK 16

JESUS, THE NARROW DOOR

"Enter through the narrow gate; for the gate is wide and the way is broad that leads to destruction, and there are many who enter through it. For the gate is small and the way is narrow that leads to life, and there are few who find it."
MATTHEW 7:13–14

The tolerance of the current culture translates "the narrow door" as narrow-minded. The world works so hard to be inclusive and accepting that the idea of narrow sounds "holier-than-thou," as if our lives must pass God's white-glove test before we can enter His kingdom. Satan distorts the truth, deceiving some into believing that Christianity is only for the very good—or at least for those who aren't very bad. And not many can achieve what is required.

When Jesus taught about the narrow door or gate, He was talking about Himself. He meant there is only one Way to God, and it's through Him. It may feel more comfortable to think that all options are available but, without Jesus, our only alternative is death. The good news too many choose to ignore is, while the door is not wide, any who respond in faith are welcome to walk through it. It is a narrow entrance, but it is open to everyone. But it isn't open forever.

Scripture is clear: there is a difference between being near Jesus and knowing Jesus. Hearing His teaching is not the same as obeying His commands. Discipleship is about more than just showing up and looking holy. It's about knowing Who you are following and loving Him with all of your heart.

The narrow door is open wide and—like a Father longing for His lost son's return—Jesus welcomes anyone and everyone. But, a deadline is set and a decision must be made. Every angel is waiting to rejoice.

STUDY ONE
The First Will Be Last

Guests at a banquet illustrate Jesus' point about the narrow door of salvation. The room is full, people of every nation have gathered, from lowly servants to royal rulers. But there is some confusion about omissions on the guest list. Jesus explained that going to church, doing good deeds, and dropping coins in a panhandler's pocket won't earn you an invitation to His table. You can't beg or buy your way into the presence of Jesus. All you have to do is believe. The resistance of the Jews is heartbreaking to Jesus, who came to wrap all of Israel in His grace. But they rejected His loving-kindness and chose desolation instead.

John 10:40–42
"**40** And He went away again beyond the Jordan to the place where John was first
baptizing, and He was staying there. **41** Many came to Him and were saying,
'While John performed no sign, yet everything John said about this man was
true.' **42** Many believed in Him there."

Luke 13:23–14:6
"**23** And someone said to Him, 'Lord, are there just a few who are being saved?'
And He said to them, **24** 'Strive to enter through the narrow door; for many, I tell
you, will seek to enter and will not be able. **25** Once the head of the house gets
up and shuts the door, and you begin to stand outside and knock on the door,
saying, 'Lord, open up to us!' then He will answer and say to you, 'I do not know
where you are from.' **26** Then you will begin to say, 'We ate and drank in Your
presence, and You taught in our streets'; **27** and He will say, 'I tell you, I do not
know where you are from; depart from Me, all you evildoers.' **28** In that place
there will be weeping and gnashing of teeth when you see Abraham and Isaac and
Jacob and all the prophets in the kingdom of God, but yourselves being thrown
out. **29** And they will come from east and west and from north and south, and
will recline at the table in the kingdom of God. **30** And behold, some are last who
will be first and some are first who will be last.'

31 Just at that time some Pharisees approached, saying to Him, 'Go away,
leave here, for Herod wants to kill You.' **32** And He said to them, 'Go and tell
that fox, 'Behold, I cast out demons and perform cures today and tomorrow,
and the third day I reach My goal.' **33** Nevertheless I must journey on today and
tomorrow and the next day; for it cannot be that a prophet would perish outside
of Jerusalem. **34** O Jerusalem, Jerusalem, the city that kills the prophets and stones
those sent to her! How often I wanted to gather your children together, just as
a hen gathers her brood under her wings, and you would not have it! **35** Behold,
your house is left to you desolate; and I say to you, you will not see Me until the
time comes when you say, 'Blessed is He who comes in the name of the Lord!'

1 It happened that when He went into the house of one of the leaders of the
Pharisees on the Sabbath to eat bread, they were watching Him closely. **2** And
there in front of Him was a man suffering from dropsy. **3** And Jesus answered and
spoke to the lawyers and Pharisees, saying, 'Is it lawful to heal on the Sabbath, or
not?' **4** But they kept silent. And He took hold of him and healed him, and sent
him away. **5** And He said to them, 'Which one of you will have a son or an ox fall
into a well, and will not immediately pull him out on a Sabbath day?' **6** And they
could make no reply to this."

1. Where did Jesus go when He left Jerusalem? (v. 40)

The appearance of John the Baptist (Matthew 3:1, Mark 1:9, Luke 3:21, and John 1:19) marks the beginning of the ministry of Jesus to Israel. Scholars say this mention of Jesus' return "to the place where John was first baptizing" places a closing bracket around the public ministry of Jesus.

2. What does verse 41 say the people recognized about John the Baptist and Jesus?

3. What was the response to Jesus in verse 42 (compared with the last encounter Jesus had with the Jews in John 9 and 10)?

4. What question was Jesus asked in Luke 13:23?

5. Read verse 22 for the context of Jesus' "audience." To what does Jesus compare salvation in verse 24? What does that image imply about faith? How would the act of simply believing be like "striving" to a people who had been under the Law for generations?

6. Peter presents this same idea in 2 Peter 1:5–11. How does Peter help us understand what Jesus is calling us to?

7. What is Jesus trying to communicate to His hearers—and to us—through His parable in verses 24–30? What was the urgency of that day? What is the urgency of this day? (2 Corinthians 6:2)

8. What prevents people from entering the "house" in verse 25? (Proverbs 28:26, Titus 1:16)

9. What assumption do the people make in verse 26? What has given them a false sense of security?

10. How do Jesus' words in verse 27 emphasize the importance of having a relationship with Him?

11. What is "that place" in verse 28? Who is "they" in verse 29? Note where they are and what they are doing. So what must be true of them? (v. 24)

12. How does Romans 1:16 help explain verse 30?

13. How might the Pharisees' warning in verse 31 been a temptation to the man (humanity of) Jesus?

14. How does Jesus respond in verse 32? What is His goal, literal and spiritual, in verse 33?

15. How is Jerusalem described in verse 34? How does verse 34 describe the tension between the Jews and their Messiah, Jesus?

16. What is the scene in Luke 14:1–2?

NOTE: *Dropsy* is an old term for edema, a pooling of fluid often in the legs, hands, or feet. It can often be a symptom of congestive heart failure.

17. Who does Jesus speak to in verse 3? What does He do in verse 4?

18. Jesus asks two questions in verses 3 and 5. What do you think He was trying to accomplish with His questions?

19. How did the Pharisees respond in verses 4 and 6? Why do you think they responded that way? If you were to put words in the mouths of these religious leaders, what would be an appropriate response to Jesus in this moment?

Application

What is the difference between knowing *about* Jesus and having a personal relationship *with* Jesus? How does living a life apart from a relationship with Jesus leave us exhausted and frustrated?

A DEEPER LOOK

Notice how Jesus used Scripture to teach, challenge, correct, and encourage. What does this tell us about His view of Scripture? And how does this instruct us about daily living?

Matthew 4:1–11

Luke 4:16–20

Mark 7:6–13

John 5:39, 46

STUDY TWO
Dinner Guests and Discipleship

Pride and power plays were being served at this dinner party, and Jesus used the opportunity to teach about feasting instead on the humility and generosity God provides. Honor isn't about selecting the best seat or inviting society's upper crust; honor is found in alleyways and street corners, in the empty cup of a beggar, and the useless legs of the lame. Jesus explained that blessing comes from blessing those who have no way to reciprocate. When you bring in the outcast, welcome the rejected, and esteem the slave, your humility reaps the praise of heaven. This was, after all, what Jesus came to do. There is a seat at the table for all who love Him above wealth, fame, even family and friends. But there is a cost to count, too. True disciples may experience poverty in the ways that the world fears, but a future reward awaits.

Luke 14:7–35

"**7** And He began speaking a parable to the invited guests when He noticed how they had been picking out the places of honor at the table, saying to them, **8** 'When you are invited by someone to a wedding feast, do not take the place of honor, for someone more distinguished than you may have been invited by him, **9** and he who invited you both will come and say to you, 'Give your place to this man,' and then in disgrace you proceed to occupy the last place. **10** But when you are invited, go and recline at the last place, so that when the one who has invited you comes, he may say to you, 'Friend, move up higher'; then you will have honor in the sight of all who are at the table with you. **11** For everyone who exalts himself will be humbled, and he who humbles himself will be exalted.'

12 And He also went on to say to the one who had invited Him, 'When you give a luncheon or a dinner, do not invite your friends or your brothers or your relatives or rich neighbors, otherwise they may also invite you in return and that will be your repayment. **13** But when you give a reception, invite the poor, the crippled, the lame, the blind, **14** and you will be blessed, since they do not have the means to repay you; for you will be repaid at the resurrection of the righteous.'

15 When one of those who were reclining at the table with Him heard this, he said to Him, 'Blessed is everyone who will eat bread in the kingdom of God!'

16 But He said to him, 'A man was giving a big dinner, and he invited many; **17** and at the dinner hour he sent his slave to say to those who had been invited, 'Come; for everything is ready now.' **18** But they all alike began to make excuses. The first one said to him, 'I have bought a piece of land and I need to go out and look at it; please consider me excused.' **19** Another one said, 'I have bought five yoke of oxen, and I am going to try them out; please consider me excused.' **20** Another one said, 'I have married a wife, and for that reason I cannot come.' **21** And the slave came back and reported this to his master. Then the head of the household became angry and said to his slave, 'Go out at once into the streets and lanes of the city and bring in here the poor and crippled and blind and lame.' **22** And the slave said, 'Master, what you commanded has been done, and still there is room.' **23** And the master said to the slave, 'Go out into the highways and along the hedges, and compel them to come in, so that my house may be filled. **24** For I tell you, none of those men who were invited shall taste of my dinner.'

25 Now large crowds were going along with Him; and He turned and said to
them, 26 'If anyone comes to Me, and does not hate his own father and mother
and wife and children and brothers and sisters, yes, and even his own life, he
cannot be My disciple. 27 Whoever does not carry his own cross and come after
Me cannot be My disciple. 28 For which one of you, when he wants to build a
tower, does not first sit down and calculate the cost to see if he has enough to
complete it? 29 Otherwise, when he has laid a foundation and is not able to finish,
all who observe it begin to ridicule him, 30 saying, 'This man began to build and
was not able to finish.' 31 Or what king, when he sets out to meet another king in
battle, will not first sit down and consider whether he is strong enough with ten
thousand men to encounter the one coming against him with twenty thousand?
32 Or else, while the other is still far away, he sends a delegation and asks for terms
of peace. 33 So then, none of you can be My disciple who does not give up all his
own possessions.

34 'Therefore, salt is good; but if even salt has become tasteless, with what will
it be seasoned? 35 It is useless either for the soil or for the manure pile; it is thrown
out. He who has ears to hear, let him hear.'"

1. What was Jesus' motive for teaching the guests in verse 7?

2. How did He instruct them? (vv. 8–10) What is the counterintuitive, core truth of His teaching in verse 11?

3. What did Jesus rebuke the host for in verse 12? What is the path to blessing in verses 13–14? What does that mean for us today?

4. Jesus responds to the man from verse 15 (and to what was in the hearts of the Jews at this dinner) with a parable about the kingdom of God. Read the parable in verses 16–24.

   What instruction is given in verses 16–17? By whom and to whom?

   Describe the three groups of people in verses 18–20.

How did each group respond to the invitation? What can you discern about their priorities?

How did the man respond to the rejection of His invitation? (vv. 21–24)

From the context given in verse 15, who is the "man" and who is the "slave?"

What does this parable teach us about His kingdom? (Isaiah 25:6–9, Revelation 19:6–9)

5. Based on what we've seen so far in Scripture, how do the Jewish religious leaders view the "poor, crippled, blind, and lame?" How does Jesus see them? (vv. 13, 23)

6. Who was Jesus with in verse 25?

7. What conditions does Jesus outline for discipleship in verses 26–27? What is He saying about commitment to Him? (see Romans 6 for Paul's teaching on the same topic)

8. What is Jesus saying is important to consider first before following Him in verses 28–29?

9. What do verses 31–32 help illustrate about the realities of spiritual warfare in our walk with Christ?

10. According to Jesus, what must we be willing to do in verse 33? Do you think He means this literally or metaphorically? What would that look like?

11. In light of Jesus' exhortation in verses 25–33, what is He warning against in verses 34–35?

Application

How do you feel when your service or good deeds go unacknowledged? What might that say about your motives?

A DEEPER LOOK

Is discipleship a necessary part of your life in Christ? What does the Bible say about this?

Romans 12:1–2

Philippians 1:6

Romans 14:7–8

1 Peter 1:15–16

1 Corinthians 11:1

1 John 2:6

Ephesians 5:1–2

STUDY THREE
Lost and Found

Going back home was the last thing he ever thought he would do. He had demanded his inheritance, and now, he had lost it all. He was face down in regret and despair, feeding pigs and abandoned by the friends who had been drawn to the gleam of gold coins that flowed like water through his hands. On the horizon, he could see a distant figure moving steadily toward him. He quickened his pace and the figure quickened his. The man blinked his eyes in disbelief—*the figure was his father, and he was running to meet him*. The joy of their reunion moved to the banquet hall, where music, dancing, and feasting on the fattened calf celebrated the son's return. His brother, however, remained outside—cut off by pride, bitterness, and anger. Whether we are lost in selfishness or self-righteousness, the Father longs for all to come to Him. The "lost" stories of Jesus teach that He pursues us with love, wraps us in grace, and restores us with joy.

Luke 15:1–32

"Now all the tax collectors and the sinners were coming near Him to listen to
Him. 2 Both the Pharisees and the scribes began to grumble, saying, 'This man
receives sinners and eats with them.'
3 So He told them this parable, saying, 4 'What man among you, if he has a
hundred sheep and has lost one of them, does not leave the ninety-nine in the
open pasture and go after the one which is lost until he finds it? 5 When he has
found it, he lays it on his shoulders, rejoicing. 6 And when he comes home, he
calls together his friends and his neighbors, saying to them, 'Rejoice with me, for
I have found my sheep which was lost!' 7 I tell you that in the same way, there
will be more joy in heaven over one sinner who repents than over ninety-nine
righteous persons who need no repentance.

8 'Or what woman, if she has ten silver coins and loses one coin, does not light a
lamp and sweep the house and search carefully until she finds it? 9 When she has
found it, she calls together her friends and neighbors, saying, 'Rejoice with me,
for I have found the coin which I had lost!' 10 In the same way, I tell you, there is
joy in the presence of the angels of God over one sinner who repents.'

11 And He said, 'A man had two sons. 12 The younger of them said to his father,
'Father, give me the share of the estate that falls to me.' So he divided his wealth
between them. 13 And not many days later, the younger son gathered everything
together and went on a journey into a distant country, and there he squandered
his estate with loose living. 14 Now when he had spent everything, a severe famine
occurred in that country, and he began to be impoverished. 15 So he went and
hired himself out to one of the citizens of that country, and he sent him into his
fields to feed swine. 16 And he would have gladly filled his stomach with the pods
that the swine were eating, and no one was giving anything to him. 17 But when
he came to his senses, he said, 'How many of my father's hired men have more
than enough bread, but I am dying here with hunger! 18 I will get up and go to
my father, and will say to him, 'Father, I have sinned against heaven, and in your
sight; 19 I am no longer worthy to be called your son; make me as one of your
hired men.' 20 So he got up and came to his father. But while he was still a long
way off, his father saw him and felt compassion for him, and ran and embraced

him and kissed him. 21 And the son said to him, 'Father, I have sinned against
heaven and in your sight; I am no longer worthy to be called your son.' 22 But the
father said to his slaves, 'Quickly bring out the best robe and put it on him, and
put a ring on his hand and sandals on his feet; 23 and bring the fattened calf, kill
it, and let us eat and celebrate; 24 for this son of mine was dead and has come to
life again; he was lost and has been found.' And they began to celebrate.

25 "Now his older son was in the field, and when he came and approached the
house, he heard music and dancing. 26 And he summoned one of the servants and
began inquiring what these things could be. 27 And he said to him, 'Your brother
has come, and your father has killed the fattened calf because he has received him
back safe and sound.' 28 But he became angry and was not willing to go in; and
his father came out and began pleading with him. 29 But he answered and said
to his father, 'Look! For so many years I have been serving you and I have never
neglected a command of yours; and yet you have never given me a young goat, so
that I might celebrate with my friends; 30 but when this son of yours came, who
has devoured your wealth with prostitutes, you killed the fattened calf for him.'
31 And he said to him, 'Son, you have always been with me, and all that is mine
is yours. 32 But we had to celebrate and rejoice, for this brother of yours was dead
and has begun to live, and was lost and has been found.'"

1. Who is in the presence of Jesus in verses 1–2?

2. What were the sinners doing in verse 1? What were the Pharisees doing in verse 2? What is the motive for being with Jesus for each of these groups?

3. What is lost in verses 3–10?

4. What does the woman do in verse 8 in order to find her coin? How does this emphasize our perseverance with our lost loved ones and neighbors?

5. What is the response of the woman and man in each parable to their loss? How do they respond when they find it?

6. How does Jesus interpret the parable in verses 7 and 10?

7. Compare the Pharisees' response to sinners in verse 2 to heaven's response in verses 7 and 10. Record your observations below.

8. What did the younger son ask for? What did the son choose to do? What was the result? (vv. 12–13)

9. What series of events in verses 14–16 results in the son's response in verse 17? (see 2 Peter 3:9 and 1 Timothy 2:4)

10. What evidence is given of the heart change in the younger son?

11. What do we learn in verse 20 about the father's experience during the son's absence?

12. Did the father respond directly to his son's speech? (vv. 21–22) What does this indicate about the son's confession and the father's heart? What does he do in verses 22–24?

13. Where was the older son during the party? How did he respond to the events of the day? How does the father respond to him? (vv. 25–28)

14. How did the father respond to his older son? What consistency is seen in the way the father responds to his children? (vv. 28, 31–32)

15. How does the older brother's sense of justice get in the way of experiencing joy? How is he also "lost?"

16. How does the brother describe the prodigal in verse 30? How does the father describe him in verse 32? What is each trying to communicate?

17. What does the father say in verse 32 that they were compelled to do and why?

Application

How does the father's response to his son's request speak to the idea of "helicopter parenting"—the 21st-century attempt to micromanage our children's choices, experiences, and lives? (vv. 12–13) How is this father the antithesis to this modern parenting phenomenon? How does this speak to you?

A DEEPER LOOK

From the details of the story, describe the possible appearance of the prodigal son upon his return to his father. Compare this to verses 22–24.

How does Scripture tell us we appear in the eyes of the Lord before we receive the righteousness of Jesus?

Isaiah 64:6

Zechariah 3:3–5

Jude 1:23

And after?

Isaiah 61:10

2 Corinthians 4:16–18

Revelation 7:9

STUDY FOUR
The Unrighteous Steward

Money is a weapon and a tool, a snare and a release, a blessing and a burden. Jesus wanted His disciples to learn how to use this necessary resource in a way that pleased Him and benefitted others. *Regardless of what you have,* He said, *faithful stewardship is the key.* The dilemma of the wasteful manager illustrated the consequences for neglecting to care for what you've been given, and the opportunity to learn from mistakes. This parable echoes the exhortation to honor others: the manager gives up his profit to collect what belonged to his master. And he gained favor in the process. If you are a lover of money, Jesus said you cannot love Him. If you cannot be obedient in a small thing, you will not be entrusted with more. How we use money is just one more way we love and serve the Giver of every gift.

Luke 16:1–18
" Now He was also saying to the disciples, 'There was a rich man who had a manager, and this manager was reported to him as squandering his possessions. 2 And
he called him and said to him, 'What is this I hear about you? Give an accounting
of your management, for you can no longer be manager.' 3 The manager said to
himself, 'What shall I do, since my master is taking the management away from
me? I am not strong enough to dig; I am ashamed to beg. 4 I know what I shall
do, so that when I am removed from the management people will welcome me
into their homes.' 5 And he summoned each one of his master's debtors, and he
began saying to the first, 'How much do you owe my master?' 6 And he said,
'A hundred measures of oil.' And he said to him, 'Take your bill, and sit down
quickly and write fifty.' 7 Then he said to another, 'And how much do you owe?'
And he said, 'A hundred measures of wheat.' He said to him, 'Take your bill, and
write eighty.' 8 And his master praised the unrighteous manager because he had
acted shrewdly; for the sons of this age are more shrewd in relation to their own
kind than the sons of light. 9 And I say to you, make friends for yourselves by

means of the wealth of unrighteousness, so that when it fails, they will receive you
into the eternal dwellings.
10 'He who is faithful in a very little thing is faithful also in much; and he who
is unrighteous in a very little thing is unrighteous also in much. 11 Therefore if
you have not been faithful in the use of unrighteous wealth, who will entrust the
true riches to you? 12 And if you have not been faithful in the use of that which
is another's, who will give you that which is your own? 13 No servant can serve
two masters; for either he will hate the one and love the other, or else he will be
devoted to one and despise the other. You cannot serve God and wealth.'
14 Now the Pharisees, who were lovers of money, were listening to all these
things and were scoffing at Him. 15 And He said to them, 'You are those who
justify yourselves in the sight of men, but God knows your hearts; for that which
is highly esteemed among men is detestable in the sight of God.
16 'The Law and the Prophets were proclaimed until John; since that time the
gospel of the kingdom of God has been preached, and everyone is forcing his way
into it. 17 But it is easier for heaven and earth to pass away than for one stroke of
a letter of the Law to fail.
18 'Everyone who divorces his wife and marries another commits adultery,
and he who marries one who is divorced from a husband commits adultery."

1. Who is in Jesus' audience in this scene? (vv. 1, 14)

2. What is the conflict in this story in verses 1–3?

3. Describe what the manager did to "redeem" himself in an attempt to leave on good terms and secure his future. (vv. 4–7)

4. What did the master do in verse 8?

5. How is Jesus encouraging the disciples to use wealth for eternal purposes in verse 9?

6. What are the promises and abiding principles in verses 10–12?

7. What is the warning of verse 13? How can we guard our hearts?

8. Why did the Pharisees respond as they did in verse 14? How does Jesus rebuke them? (vv. 14–17)

9. How does Jesus describe His authority and the authority of God's Word in this passage? How does Galatians 3:23–26 help explain the purpose of the Law and interpret verse 17?

10. Jesus addresses another kind of "stewardship" in verse 18. What is the issue and how does this verse demonstrate His authority over it?

NOTE: The Pharisees divorced at will; no reason had to be given (although women were not allowed the same "privilege"). God's view of divorce is laid out in other passages in Scripture (Deuteronomy 24:1–4, Malachi 2:16, Matthew 5:31–32, 19:1–12, Mark 10:1–12, and 1 Corinthians 7:8–16). In this particular, small section, Jesus was stating that marriage is a permanent commitment—a covenant made before Him—and how we view the marriage relationship is another illustration of how willing we are to obey His call to kingdom living.

Application

As usual, Jesus is setting up a contrast in this story: the time and attention given to cultivating earthly wealth vs. the time and attention given to seeking eternal things. How can money be used in a purposeful, eternal way? How can money be used to test our character?

STUDY FIVE
The Rich Man and Lazarus

As usual, Jesus upended expectations with His teaching, revealing how the things of earth look very different through the eyes of heaven. Here, we see splendor and poverty, feasting and emptiness, health and sickness, joy and want. And when accounts are settled at the end of life, the lean side of the equation is the one who enters heaven. Lazarus (the only character ever named in Jesus' parables) was neglected on earth, so poor he was hardly considered human. The rich man never shared even a crumb with Lazarus, but he most likely wasn't the only one who passed him by. This story is designed to examine our hearts: "Where is the Lazarus in your life?" Jesus was teaching that who we are on earth does not always determine who we are in heaven. There it's too late to reverse these "fortunes." The Narrow Door has closed.

Luke 16:19–17:10

"**19** 'Now there was a rich man, and he habitually dressed in purple and fine linen, joyously living in splendor every day. **20** And a poor man named Lazarus was laid at his gate, covered with sores, **21** and longing to be fed with the crumbs which were falling from the rich man's table; besides, even the dogs were coming and licking his sores. **22** Now the poor man died and was carried away by the angels to Abraham's bosom; and the rich man also died and was buried. **23** In Hades he lifted up his eyes, being in torment, and saw Abraham far away and Lazarus in his bosom. **24** And he cried out and said, 'Father Abraham, have mercy on me, and send Lazarus so that he may dip the tip of his finger in water and cool off my tongue, for I am in agony in this flame.' **25** But Abraham said, 'Child, remember that during your life you received your good things, and likewise Lazarus bad things; but now he is being comforted here, and you are in agony. **26** And besides all this, between us and you there is a great chasm fixed, so that those who wish to come over from here to you will not be able, and that none may cross over from there to us.' **27** And he said, 'Then I beg you, father, that you send him to my father's house— **28** for I have five brothers—in order that he may warn them, so that they will not also come to this place of torment.' **29** But Abraham said, 'They have Moses and the Prophets; let them hear them.' **30** But he said, 'No, father Abraham, but if someone goes to them from the dead, they will repent!' **31** But he said to him, 'If they do not listen to Moses and the Prophets, they will not be persuaded even if someone rises from the dead.'

1 He said to His disciples, 'It is inevitable that stumbling blocks come, but woe to him through whom they come! **2** It would be better for him if a millstone were hung around his neck and he were thrown into the sea, than that he would cause one of these little ones to stumble. **3** Be on your guard! If your brother sins, rebuke him; and if he repents, forgive him. **4** And if he sins against you seven times a day, and returns to you seven times, saying, 'I repent,' forgive him.'

5 The apostles said to the Lord, 'Increase our faith!' **6** And the Lord said, 'If you had faith like a mustard seed, you would say to this mulberry tree, 'Be uprooted and be planted in the sea'; and it would obey you.

7 'Which of you, having a slave plowing or tending sheep, will say to him when he has come in from the field, 'Come immediately and sit down to eat'? **8** But will he not say to him, 'Prepare something for me to eat, and properly clothe yourself and serve me while I eat and drink; and afterward you may eat and drink'? **9** He does not thank the slave because he did the things which were commanded, does he? **10** So you too, when you do all the things which are commanded you, say, 'We are unworthy slaves; we have done only that which we ought to have done.'"

1. Read verses 19–21. Record the description of the rich man and Lazarus in Jesus' story.

   Was there ever any interaction between the two men? (1 John 3:17)

NOTE: The name "Lazarus" means "God helps."

2. Describe the two experiences after the death of each man. (vv. 22–23)

3. How might these two men and their life situations have appeared to the world and society they lived in?

   What can be discerned from the context about heaven's perspective on each of these men? (see James 2:5)

4. What appeal does the rich man now make? (v. 24) How did the rich man still view Lazarus, even as their situations had been reversed for eternity? (v. 24)

5. What is Abraham's response in verses 25–26? This is not a commentary on rewards and punishment for good or bad behavior in life. Rather, it's a reminder of a choice the rich man made. What was that choice? (review Luke 12:16–21 for direction)

6. What does the rich man ask for next in verses 27–28? What does this reveal about his family? Why is his request denied? (vv. 29–31)

7. Who does verse 31 point to and how is it prophetic?

8. Who is Jesus speaking to in Luke 17:1?

9. What are the two warnings in verse 1? How does verse 2 highlight the seriousness of this offense?

10. What is the process of dealing with sin in a relationship based on verses 3–4? What is our responsibility on both sides of the sin?

11. What did the disciples ask Jesus for in verse 5?

    What did He say in the preceding verses that could have prompted that response?

    How does Jesus encourage them in verse 6?

12. How does the example in verses 7–10 talk about the expectations for those who follow Jesus?

13. In verse 10, Jesus teaches that obedience is the duty of the Christian. Deuteronomy 11:1 and 2 John 1:6 connect obedience to love for God. How are these two attributes compatible or complementary?

Application

Why do we tend to believe that obeying commands like "love one another," "serve one another," "forgive one another," and the like are exceptional or extraordinary? Do you think that God is under obligation to reward you for your obedience?

A DEEPER LOOK

How might the following Old Testament passages help point the rich man's family in the passage today (or the Pharisees within earshot of Jesus) to grasp the meaning of this story?

Deuteronomy 24:10–22

Amos 5:11–12

Ezekiel 18:12–13

Amos 8:4–6

Ezekiel 33:14–16

Zechariah 7:9–12

WRAPPING UP

Many times, Christians are looking for an emotional experience in their walk with Jesus. Yet Jesus told us that discipleship isn't about feelings. We follow Him even when the road is rough and the way is dim, and joy and blessing seem far away.

Jesus described discipleship many different ways this week, especially in Luke 14. These images and His teaching help give us a deeper understanding of how we are called to live—with Jesus as the Lord of our family, possessions, relationships, work, ministry, and future plans.

This is the "narrow door" Jesus speaks about—a daily choice, despite our feelings and circumstances—to follow Him on the path of righteousness.

Notes

~ Map of Jesus in Judea and Jerusalem ~

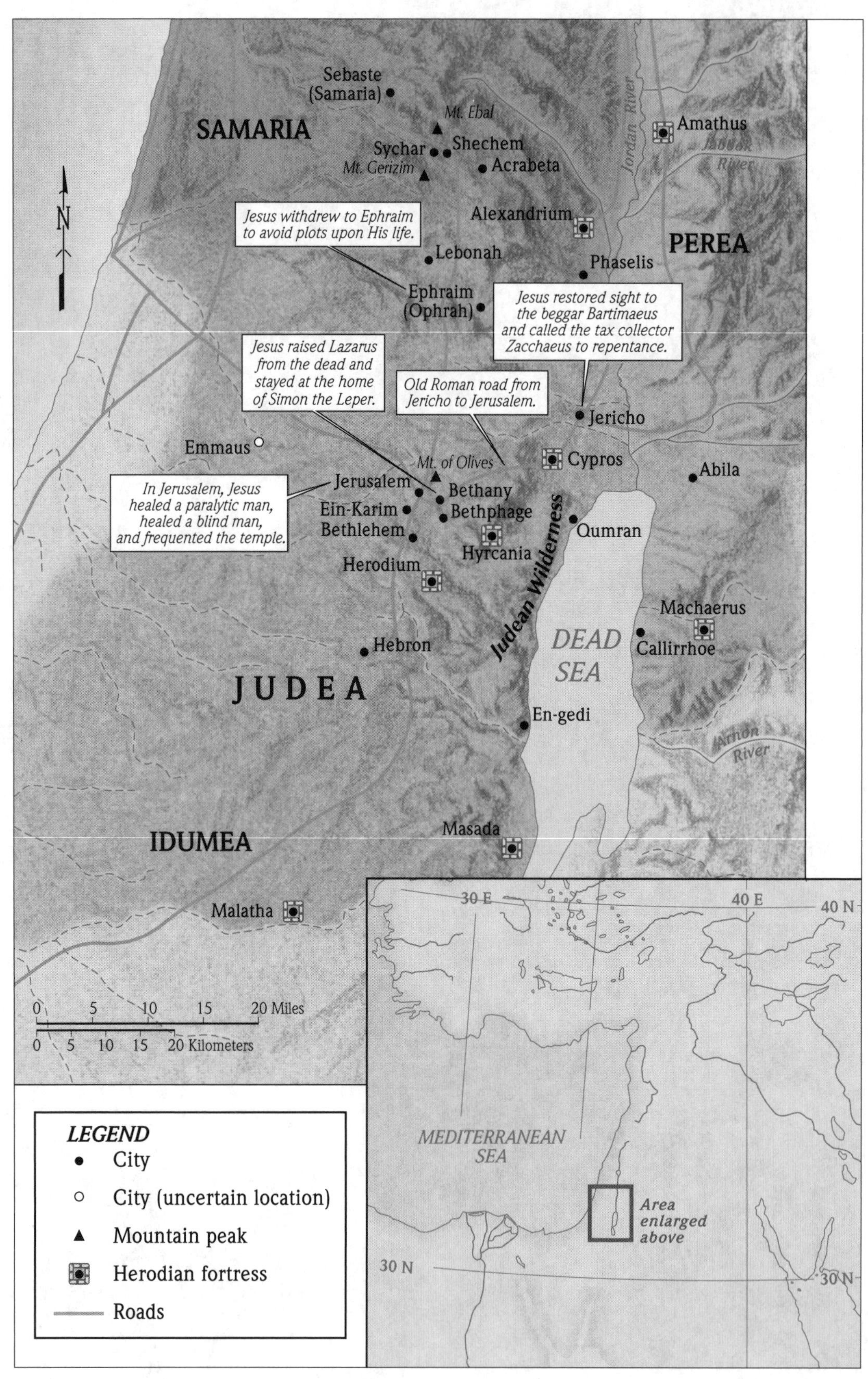

JESUS, THE RESURRECTION AND THE LIFE

"Jesus said to her, 'I am the resurrection and the life; he who believes in Me will live even if he dies, and everyone who lives and believes in Me will never die. Do you believe this?'"
JOHN 11:25–26

Whether the interaction is peaceful or strained, every conversation Jesus had during His time on earth was designed to give life to those around Him. A rebuke could restore life to the heart; a blessing could bring life to the discouraged, and living words of truth could resurrect the darkest soul from eternal death.

In every relationship Jesus had—from long-term friendships to a momentary exchange—the Messiah offered a resurrection: *Come out of your old self, the flesh that rejects the Law, the body that brings you death, and walk instead with Me as a new creation, cleansed and forgiven, more alive than you can possibly imagine.*

This week is bookended with such transformations: one man, dead in the grave, was resurrected and given back to his family. Another, dead in his sins, embraced life-giving forgiveness and was restored to his community. Both were merciful acts of love, public displays of the extravagant grace of Jesus, the great I AM.

Yet, with all Jesus desired to give, we see many still clinging to what their eyes could see. The rulers and religious were blinded by their greed and pride, too high-minded to accept Jesus' simple offer of life. Jesus holds children as the example of uncomplicated faith, just strong enough to grasp His gift. Ironically, a man known for his small stature had the child-like faith to understand what was at stake. So he gave up everything, and lost nothing. No longer first in this world, but nearer to glory than he had ever been.

STUDY ONE
The Death and Resurrection of Lazarus

The deity and humanity of Jesus appear side-by-side in this story: only the fully human, fully divine Son of God could be grieved by death, knowing He was moments from reversing the curse on His friend and bringing him back to life. Before this miracle took place, however, Jesus laid a foundation that would build faith. His delay appeared insensitive and His decisions defied logic, but when we follow a sovereign Lord, we can trust Him when things don't make sense. Here we also see a different Martha from our last encounter. Her faith is stronger, but Jesus needed to sharpen her focus—from the promise to the Person of the resurrection. Lazarus' resurrection was real, but it also served as a symbol: we are bound by sin in death until we respond to the call of Jesus. Then, like the believing Jews, we can go and tell of the great things He has done!

John 11:1–46

"Now a certain man was sick, Lazarus of Bethany, the village of Mary and her
sister Martha. 2 It was the Mary who anointed the Lord with ointment, and
wiped His feet with her hair, whose brother Lazarus was sick. 3 So the sisters sent
word to Him, saying, 'Lord, behold, he whom You love is sick.' 4 But when Jesus
heard this, He said, 'This sickness is not to end in death, but for the glory of God,
so that the Son of God may be glorified by it.' 5 Now Jesus loved Martha and her
sister and Lazarus. 6 So when He heard that he was sick, He then stayed two days
longer in the place where He was. 7 Then after this He said to the disciples, 'Let
us go to Judea again.' 8 The disciples said to Him, 'Rabbi, the Jews were just now
seeking to stone You, and are You going there again?' 9 Jesus answered, 'Are there
not twelve hours in the day? If anyone walks in the day, he does not stumble,
because he sees the light of this world. 10 But if anyone walks in the night, he
stumbles, because the light is not in him.' 11 This He said, and after that He said
to them, 'Our friend Lazarus has fallen asleep; but I go, so that I may awaken him
out of sleep.' 12 The disciples then said to Him, 'Lord, if he has fallen asleep, he
will recover.' 13 Now Jesus had spoken of his death, but they thought that He was
speaking of literal sleep. 14 So Jesus then said to them plainly, 'Lazarus is dead,
15 and I am glad for your sakes that I was not there, so that you may believe; but
let us go to him.' 16 Therefore Thomas, who is called Didymus, said to his fellow
disciples, 'Let us also go, so that we may die with Him.'

17 So when Jesus came, He found that he had already been in the tomb four
days. 18 Now Bethany was near Jerusalem, about two miles off; 19 and many of the
Jews had come to Martha and Mary, to console them concerning their brother.
20 Martha therefore, when she heard that Jesus was coming, went to meet Him,
but Mary stayed at the house. 21 Martha then said to Jesus, 'Lord, if You had been
here, my brother would not have died. 22 Even now I know that whatever You
ask of God, God will give You.' 23 Jesus said to her, 'Your brother will rise again.'
24 Martha said to Him, 'I know that he will rise again in the resurrection on the
last day.' 25 Jesus said to her, 'I am the resurrection and the life; he who believes
in Me will live even if he dies, 26 and everyone who lives and believes in Me will
never die. Do you believe this?' 27 She said to Him, 'Yes, Lord; I have believed
that You are the Christ, the Son of God, even He who comes into the world.'

28 When she had said this, she went away and called Mary her sister, saying
secretly, 'The Teacher is here and is calling for you.' 29 And when she heard it, she
got up quickly and was coming to Him.

30 Now Jesus had not yet come into the village, but was still in the place
where Martha met Him. 31 Then the Jews who were with her in the house, and
consoling her, when they saw that Mary got up quickly and went out, they followed her, supposing that she was going to the tomb to weep there. 32 Therefore,
when Mary came where Jesus was, she saw Him, and fell at His feet, saying to
Him, 'Lord, if You had been here, my brother would not have died.' 33 When
Jesus therefore saw her weeping, and the Jews who came with her also weeping,
He was deeply moved in spirit and was troubled, 34 and said, 'Where have you
laid him?' They said to Him, 'Lord, come and see.' 35 Jesus wept. 36 So the Jews
were saying, 'See how He loved him!' 37 But some of them said, 'Could not this
man, who opened the eyes of the blind man, have kept this man also from dying?'

38 So Jesus, again being deeply moved within, came to the tomb. Now it was
a cave, and a stone was lying against it. 39 Jesus said, 'Remove the stone.' Martha,

the sister of the deceased, said to Him, 'Lord, by this time there will be a stench,
for he has been dead four days.' **40** Jesus said to her, 'Did I not say to you that if
you believe, you will see the glory of God?' **41** So they removed the stone. Then
Jesus raised His eyes, and said, 'Father, I thank You that You have heard Me. **42** I
knew that You always hear Me; but because of the people standing around I said
it, so that they may believe that You sent Me.' **43** When He had said these things,
He cried out with a loud voice, 'Lazarus, come forth.' **44** The man who had died
came forth, bound hand and foot with wrappings, and his face was wrapped
around with a cloth. Jesus said to them, 'Unbind him, and let him go.'

45 Therefore many of the Jews who came to Mary, and saw what He had
done, believed in Him. **46** But some of them went to the Pharisees and told them
the things which Jesus had done."

1. What do we learn about the characters, background, and location for this story in verses 1–2?

2. How did the sisters describe Lazarus to Jesus? (v. 3) What did Jesus say the purposes of the sickness were? (v. 4)

3. What is the relationship between Jesus and the sisters and Lazarus according to verses 3 and 5?

4. What surprising decisions did Jesus make in verses 6–7? How did the disciples respond in verse 8?

5. What does verse 11 say had transpired since the time Martha and Mary sent Jesus a message about their brother? How does Jesus describe death in verses 11–13?

6. Jesus outlines another purpose for Lazarus' death in verses 14–15. What is it?

7. What does Thomas believe is going to happen to Jesus? (v. 16) What does his statement tell us about Thomas?

8. What promise does Jesus make in verse 23? Is there a timeline on the fulfillment of this promise?

9. Who does Jesus say that He is in verses 25–26? What promises are associated with these proclamations? Martha confesses three truths about Jesus in verse 27. What are they?

10. What did Martha do right after her confession of Christ? (v. 28) How is her action similar to Andrew's in John 1:40–42? How did Mary respond? (v. 29)

11. Read vv. 30–36 out loud. Describe the scene in your own words.

12. How did Mary approach Jesus? (v. 32) What other times do we see Mary in this posture? (Luke 10:39, John 12:3)

13. How does Jesus feel about death? (vv. 33, 38) What is your response to the idea that Jesus was "enebrimesato" at death?

NOTE: The phrase "deeply moved" is *enebrimesato* in Greek and means "angered" or "outraged." It is the same word translated as "sternly warned" in Matthew 9:30 and Mark 1:43.

14. Record the evidence of Jesus' humanity in this passage.

15. How did the Jews interpret the tears of Jesus in verses 36–37? What did they wrongly assume about Jesus?

16. What was Martha's concern in verse 39? What was Jesus' reply in verse 40?

17. Describe the order of events in verses 41–44. What was the outcome for Lazarus? How did the people respond in verses 45–46?

18. Contrast Jesus' miracle with Elisha's in 2 Kings 4:32–36. How does the contrast emphasize Jesus' claim in verse 25?

Application

Has the Lord ever "delayed" in answering your prayers or responding to your need? How did this strengthen your faith?

A DEEPER LOOK

What does the Bible promise about death?

Psalms 23:4

Isaiah 57:1–2

Psalms 116:15

Ecclesiastes 7:1

1 Corinthians 15:54–57

1 Thessalonians 4:13–14

2 Corinthians 5:1–8

Revelation 14:3

STUDY TWO
Ten Lepers Cleansed

Even after one of His most public and dramatic miracles, Jesus remained a divisive figure in Israel. Many believed in Him after Lazarus' resurrection. But many others stirred up strife. We learn the result of that stirring in the passage today. The priests and Pharisees came together and schemed, their own words a prophecy and promise for the children of God. These threats of death sent the life-giving Messiah into the wilderness, but His work continued. Ten lepers, also cast out from community, sought deliverance from their isolating condition, and Jesus had compassion on them all. But only one of them returned to give thanks for His healing. Jesus pronounced the man completely well, healed not only from disease but also the sickness of sin. This believing foreigner stands in stark contrast to the skeptical Pharisees, whose expectations for the kingdom kept them from seeing Who was right before their eyes.

John 11:47–54
"**47** Therefore the chief priests and the Pharisees convened a council, and were
saying, 'What are we doing? For this man is performing many signs. **48** If we let
Him go on like this, all men will believe in Him, and the Romans will come and
take away both our place and our nation.' **49** But one of them, Caiaphas, who was
high priest that year, said to them, 'You know nothing at all, **50** nor do you take
into account that it is expedient for you that one man die for the people, and that
the whole nation not perish.' **51** Now he did not say this on his own initiative,
but being high priest that year, he prophesied that Jesus was going to die for the
nation, **52** and not for the nation only, but in order that He might also gather
together into one the children of God who are scattered abroad. **53** So from that
day on they planned together to kill Him.

54 Therefore Jesus no longer continued to walk publicly among the Jews,
but went away from there to the country near the wilderness, into a city called
Ephraim; and there He stayed with the disciples."

Luke 17:11–21
"**11** While He was on the way to Jerusalem, He was passing between Samaria and
Galilee. **12** As He entered a village, ten leprous men who stood at a distance met
Him; **13** and they raised their voices, saying, 'Jesus, Master, have mercy on us!'
14 When He saw them, He said to them, 'Go and show yourselves to the priests.'

And as they were going, they were cleansed. [15] Now one of them, when he saw
that he had been healed, turned back, glorifying God with a loud voice, [16] and
he fell on his face at His feet, giving thanks to Him. And he was a Samaritan.
[17] Then Jesus answered and said, 'Were there not ten cleansed? But the nine—
where are they? [18] Was no one found who returned to give glory to God, except
this foreigner?' [19] And He said to him, 'Stand up and go; your faith has made
you well.'
[20] Now having been questioned by the Pharisees as to when the kingdom
of God was coming, He answered them and said, 'The kingdom of God is not
coming with signs to be observed; [21] nor will they say, 'Look, here it is!' or, 'There
it is!' For behold, the kingdom of God is in your midst.'"

1. How did the Jews respond to the resurrection of Lazarus in verse 47? What do verses 47–48 reveal was the ultimate concern for the religious leaders?

2. What can be gleaned about Caiaphas' character from his remarks in verse 49? What was Caiaphas' proposal regarding Jesus in verse 50?

3. What was the greater purpose of Jesus' death? (v. 52)

4. What was the official outcome to the meeting in verse 53? What did Jesus do in response to their intent? (v. 54)

5. Where was Jesus in Luke 17:11? Who did He encounter and what did they do? (vv. 12–13) According to Leviticus 13:45–46, what was a leper supposed to "cry out?" What did these lepers cry out in verse 13?

6. What was Jesus' command in verse 14? (see Leviticus 14:1–11) How did the lepers respond and what happened to them?

7. What is the exception we see in verses 15–16? How did Jesus respond to the man who returned?

8. What is different about what Jesus said to the ten lepers and what He said to the one? How is that an additional blessing? (vv. 14, 19)

9. What does verse 20 say the Pharisees were questioning Jesus about?

10. What was Jesus saying about Himself in verses 20–21?

11. What or who is the ultimate sign that the kingdom of God is here? (v. 21)

Application

In what areas of your life do you under-appreciate the blessings of God? Stop right now and make a list of ten blessings God has given you. Then take time to thank Him for his marvelous gifts.

A DEEPER LOOK

What are we called to give thanks for, according to God's Word?

Psalms 35:9

1 Corinthians 15:57

Psalms 118:21

Philippians 1:3

Romans 6:17

1 Thessalonians 5:18

STUDY THREE
The Rich Young Ruler

Leaving can be hard. Especially if you think where you are headed is not as good as where you have been. Then again, sometimes we leave because we believe the next thing is "it"—the next job, home, church, or spouse. This is the theme of the discussions Jesus had in this passage. A challenge about divorce and sending a wife away revealed the hardness of the Pharisees' hearts. A question about doing good to gain life led to a command to leave the world behind, an impossible task for anyone weighed down with more than they need. The disciples had already left everything behind to follow Jesus; now they wondered if it was worth it. Jesus assured them their sacrifice would be richly rewarded. And in the midst of talk about gain and loss stood a child, a surprising picture of a faithful follower. This isn't the first time Jesus called what is insignificant in this world precious in His sight. Being last in order to be first is a hard calling, but great honor awaits all who chose to live as the least of these.

Mathew 19:1–30

"When Jesus had finished these words, He departed from Galilee and came into
the region of Judea beyond the Jordan; 2 and large crowds followed Him, and He
healed them there.

3 Some Pharisees came to Jesus, testing Him and asking, 'Is it lawful for a
man to divorce his wife for any reason at all?' 4 And He answered and said, 'Have
you not read that He who created them from the beginning made them male and
female, 5 and said, 'For this reason a man shall leave his father and mother and
be joined to his wife, and the two shall become one flesh'? 6 So they are no longer
two, but one flesh. What therefore God has joined together, let no man separate.'
7 They said to Him, 'Why then did Moses command to give her a certificate of
divorce and send her away?' 8 He said to them, 'Because of your hardness of heart
Moses permitted you to divorce your wives; but from the beginning it has not
been this way. 9 And I say to you, whoever divorces his wife, except for immoral-
ity, and marries another woman commits adultery.'

10 The disciples said to Him, 'If the relationship of the man with his wife is
like this, it is better not to marry.' 11 But He said to them, 'Not all men can accept
this statement, but only those to whom it has been given. 12 For there are eunuchs
who were born that way from their mother's womb; and there are eunuchs who
were made eunuchs by men; and there are also eunuchs who made themselves
eunuchs for the sake of the kingdom of heaven. He who is able to accept this, let
him accept it.'

13 Then some children were brought to Him so that He might lay His hands
on them and pray; and the disciples rebuked them. 14 But Jesus said, 'Let the

children alone, and do not hinder them from coming to Me; for the kingdom of
heaven belongs to such as these.' **15** After laying His hands on them, He departed
from there.

16 And someone came to Him and said, 'Teacher, what good thing shall I do
that I may obtain eternal life?' **17** And He said to him, 'Why are you asking Me
about what is good? There is only One who is good; but if you wish to enter into
life, keep the commandments.' **18** Then he said to Him, 'Which ones?' And Jesus
said, 'You shall not commit murder; You shall not commit adultery; You shall not
steal; You shall not bear false witness; **19** Honor your father and mother; and You
shall love your neighbor as yourself.' **20** The young man said to Him, 'All these
things I have kept; what am I still lacking?' **21** Jesus said to him, 'If you wish to
be complete, go and sell your possessions and give to the poor, and you will have
treasure in heaven; and come, follow Me.' **22** But when the young man heard this
statement, he went away grieving; for he was one who owned much property.

23 And Jesus said to His disciples, 'Truly I say to you, it is hard for a rich man
to enter the kingdom of heaven. **24** Again I say to you, it is easier for a camel to go
through the eye of a needle, than for a rich man to enter the kingdom of God.'
25 When the disciples heard this, they were very astonished and said, 'Then who
can be saved?' **26** And looking at them Jesus said to them, 'With people this is
impossible, but with God all things are possible.'

27 Then Peter said to Him, 'Behold, we have left everything and followed
You; what then will there be for us?' **28** And Jesus said to them, 'Truly I say to
you, that you who have followed Me, in the regeneration when the Son of Man
will sit on His glorious throne, you also shall sit upon twelve thrones, judging the
twelve tribes of Israel. **29** And everyone who has left houses or brothers or sisters
or father or mother or children or farms for My name's sake, will receive many
times as much, and will inherit eternal life. **30** But many who are first will be last;
and the last, first."

1. Where is Jesus in this passage and what was happening? (vv. 1–2)

2. Based on verse 2 and verse 3, what continues to be the relationship between Jesus and the people and Jesus and the religious leaders?

3. In answer to the question about divorce, what does Jesus teach about marriage? (vv. 4–6)

4. What did Jesus say was the original reason for the concession of divorce? (vv. 7–8)

5. What do verses 13–15 tell us Jesus thinks about children? (see Mark 10:13–16 for more details) What does verse 14 teach about the faith of children?

6. Read verses 16–17. What was the man asking and how did Jesus respond?

7. What might be the meaning behind the man's question in verse 18?

8. How does Jesus present the Gospel to the young man in verse 21?

9. What does the man's response reveal about his heart? (v. 22)

10. How does Paul's "resume" in Philippians 3:4–6 help us understand this man's mindset? How would Paul advise this man, based on Philippians 3:7–11?

11. What was the challenge Jesus presented in verses 23–25? What was the hope in verse 26?

12. What reassurance was Peter looking for from Jesus in verse 27? What reassurance did Jesus give in verses 28–29?

13. How do Jesus' words in verse 29 speak to our motive for serving Him? How does verse 30 inform us about how we are to live our lives now?

Application

What are some of the blessings of wealth? What can be some of the burdens?

STUDY FOUR
Laborers in the Vineyard

Our reaction to this parable is a measure of our generosity. It also tests our understanding of grace. Does a need for perceived fairness eclipse the methods God might use to draw all men to His Son? Our Savior's kindness can soften or harden our hearts; the response depends on how we interpret grace in action. Jesus will display His active grace on the cross, a future event He predicted here for His disciples once again. The mother of James and John doesn't seem to grasp the weight of His words and thoughtlessly asked for a special favor. Jesus responded by re-focusing His friends on the status of a servant. *Choosing to be last may mean we are overlooked on earth*, He said, *but in the eyes of heaven, it's the best seat in the house.*

Matthew 20:1–34

"'For the kingdom of heaven is like a landowner who went out early in the morning to hire laborers for his vineyard. **2** When he had agreed with the laborers for
a denarius for the day, he sent them into his vineyard. **3** And he went out about
the third hour and saw others standing idle in the market place; **4** and to those he
said, 'You also go into the vineyard, and whatever is right I will give you.' And
so they went. **5** Again he went out about the sixth and the ninth hour, and did
the same thing. **6** And about the eleventh hour he went out and found others
standing around; and he said to them, 'Why have you been standing here idle all
day long?' **7** They said to him, 'Because no one hired us.' He said to them, 'You
go into the vineyard too.'

8 'When evening came, the owner of the vineyard said to his foreman, 'Call
the laborers and pay them their wages, beginning with the last group to the first.'
9 When those hired about the eleventh hour came, each one received a denarius.
10 When those hired first came, they thought that they would receive more; but
each of them also received a denarius. **11** When they received it, they grumbled
at the landowner, **12** saying, 'These last men have worked only one hour, and you
have made them equal to us who have borne the burden and the scorching heat
of the day.' **13** But he answered and said to one of them, 'Friend, I am doing you
no wrong; did you not agree with me for a denarius? **14** Take what is yours and
go, but I wish to give to this last man the same as to you. **15** Is it not lawful for
me to do what I wish with what is my own? Or is your eye envious because I am
generous?' **16** So the last shall be first, and the first last.'

17 As Jesus was about to go up to Jerusalem, He took the twelve disciples aside
by themselves, and on the way He said to them, 18 'Behold, we are going up to
Jerusalem; and the Son of Man will be delivered to the chief priests and scribes,
and they will condemn Him to death, 19 and will hand Him over to the Gentiles
to mock and scourge and crucify Him, and on the third day He will be raised up.'

20 Then the mother of the sons of Zebedee came to Jesus with her sons, bowing
down and making a request of Him. 21 And He said to her, 'What do you wish?'
She said to Him, 'Command that in Your kingdom these two sons of mine may
sit one on Your right and one on Your left.' 22 But Jesus answered, 'You do not
know what you are asking. Are you able to drink the cup that I am about to
drink?' They said to Him, 'We are able.' 23 He said to them, 'My cup you shall
drink; but to sit on My right and on My left, this is not Mine to give, but it is for
those for whom it has been prepared by My Father.'

24 And hearing this, the ten became indignant with the two brothers. 25 But
Jesus called them to Himself and said, 'You know that the rulers of the Gentiles
lord it over them, and their great men exercise authority over them. 26 It is not
this way among you, but whoever wishes to become great among you shall be
your servant, 27 and whoever wishes to be first among you shall be your slave;
28 just as the Son of Man did not come to be served, but to serve, and to give His
life a ransom for many.'

29 As they were leaving Jericho, a large crowd followed Him. 30 And two blind men
sitting by the road, hearing that Jesus was passing by, cried out, 'Lord, have mercy
on us, Son of David!' 31 The crowd sternly told them to be quiet, but they cried
out all the more, 'Lord, Son of David, have mercy on us!' 32 And Jesus stopped and
called them, and said, 'What do you want Me to do for you?' 33 They said to Him,
'Lord, we want our eyes to be opened.' 34 Moved with compassion, Jesus touched
their eyes; and immediately they regained their sight and followed Him."

1. What is the kingdom of heaven compared to in the parable? (v. 1)

NOTE: A denarius was an average day's wage for a laborer in the time of Jesus.

2. What does the landowner promise to pay the laborers? (vv. 2, 4, 5, 9)

3. What is the vineyard in the parable?

4. Describe how the landowner treated the laborers in verses 8–10?

5. How do the laborers respond to the landowner's generosity? (vv. 11–12)

6. How do you respond when grace is poured out into another's life? (vv. 14–15)

7. Why is it so easy for us to sympathize with the workers who were hired first? (vv. 2, 10–12)

8. What is Jesus saying to the workers in His rebuke? (vv. 13–15)

9. What do we learn about God in this parable? What do we learn about grace?

10. What additional details about His death did Jesus give in verse 19?

11. What was the first response to Jesus' prediction of His death? (vv. 20–21)

12. Read Isaiah 51:17. What "cup" was Jesus referring to in verse 23? What does this mean?

13. What does verse 24 reveal about the heart of the other ten disciples?

14. What contrast does Jesus make in verses 25–26?

15. How does Jesus define leadership in verses 25–28?

16. How do verses 20–28 illustrate Jesus' words in verse 16 and Matthew 19:30?

17. What happened in verses 29–30? What did the two men call Jesus in verse 30?

18. Compare verses 29–34 to the passages we just studied in verses 17–28. Who was truly blind in this passage?

Application

As the "hired hands" of the sovereign Landowner of the kingdom of God, how can we count on Him treating us, regardless of when we came to know Jesus as Savior?

STUDY FIVE
Zaccheus Converted

The branches of a sycamore tree turned out to be a front row seat for a heart transformation that children have sung about for generations. Tax collectors gained their wealth by wicked means, making them public enemy number one. And Zaccheus was their chief. But his encounter with the grace of Jesus softened his heart. He responded to the angry crowd with humility and true repentance, proving that the eye of the needle isn't so narrow when your hands are empty and your heart is full. Jesus brought another lost sheep into His fold, and proclaimed this encounter an illustration of one of His purposes for coming to earth. Then Jesus told a story about patience, stewardship, and faithfulness. Jesus was headed to fulfill another purpose—death so that we might live—and knew His followers would need instruction on how to flourish in the in-between. Responsibility, no matter how much or little you have, is connected to the Father's pleasure and your preparation for heaven. So live generously, act faithfully, and serve fervently.

Luke 19:1–28

"He entered Jericho and was passing through. 2 And there was a man called by the name of Zaccheus; he was a chief tax collector and he was rich. 3 Zaccheus was trying to see who Jesus was, and was unable because of the crowd, for he was small in stature. 4 So he ran on ahead and climbed up into a sycamore tree in order to see Him, for He was about to pass through that way. 5 When Jesus came to the place, He looked up and said to him, 'Zaccheus, hurry and come down, for today I must stay at your house.' 6 And he hurried and came down and received Him gladly. 7 When they saw it, they all began to grumble, saying, 'He has gone to be the guest of a man who is a sinner.' 8 Zaccheus stopped and said to the Lord, 'Behold, Lord, half of my possessions I will give to the poor, and if I have defrauded anyone of anything, I will give back four times as much.' 9 And Jesus said to him, 'Today salvation has come to this house, because he, too, is a son of Abraham. 10 For the Son of Man has come to seek and to save that which was lost.'

11 While they were listening to these things, Jesus went on to tell a parable, because He was near Jerusalem, and they supposed that the kingdom of God was going to appear immediately. 12 So He said, 'A nobleman went to a distant country to receive a kingdom for himself, and then return. 13 And he called ten of his slaves, and gave them ten minas and said to them, 'Do business with this until I come back.' 14 But his citizens hated him and sent a delegation after him, saying, 'We do not want this man to reign over us.' 15 When he returned, after receiving the kingdom, he ordered that these slaves, to whom he had given the money, be called to him so that he might know what business they had done. 16 The first appeared, saying, 'Master, your mina has made ten minas more.' 17 And he said to him, 'Well done, good slave, because you have been faithful in a very little thing, you are to be in authority over ten cities.' 18 The second came, saying, 'Your mina, master, has made five minas.' 19 And he said to him also, 'And you are to be over five cities.' 20 Another came, saying, 'Master, here is your mina, which I kept put away in a handkerchief; 21 for I was afraid of you, because you are an exacting man; you take up what you did not lay down and reap what you did not sow.' 22 He said to him, 'By your own words I will judge you, you worthless slave. Did you know that I am an exacting man, taking up what I did not lay down and reaping what I did not sow? 23 Then why did you not put my money in the bank, and having come, I would have collected it with interest?' 24 Then he said to the bystanders, 'Take the mina away from him and give it to the one who has the ten minas.' 25 And they said to him, 'Master, he has ten minas already.' 26 I tell you that to everyone who has, more shall be given, but from the one who does not have, even what he does have shall be taken away. 27 But these enemies of mine, who did not want me to reign over them, bring them here and slay them in my presence.'

28 After He had said these things, He was going on ahead, going up to Jerusalem."

1. Who do we meet and where is he in verses 1–2? What is Zaccheus' job according to verse 2? From what we know about tax collectors, what can be inferred about Zaccheus and his popularity?

2. How does Zaccheus illustrate Matthew 19:23–24?

3. What do verses 3–4 tell us about Zaccheus' desire to see Jesus?

NOTE: Zaccheus means "just" or "pure."

4. Based on his position/role in the community, what do you think it might have been like for him to be in a crowd of people?

5. How did Jesus respond to Zaccheus? (v. 5) How did Zaccheus respond to Jesus? (v 6) How did the people respond to Zaccheus and Jesus? (v.7)

6. Read Zaccheus' response in verse 8. Why do you think he responded this way? Read Leviticus 5:16 and Numbers 5:5–7 for Mosaic law about defrauding others.

7. Read Jesus' words in verses 9–10. How does this story illustrate Jesus' heart and primary purpose on earth?

8. What does verse 11 say about the reasons Jesus told the parable in verses 12–27?

NOTE: A mina is approximately three months' average wages.

9. What was the nobleman's instruction to his slaves? (v. 13) How did they respond? (vv. 14–24)

10. What does this parable teach us about stewardship and faithfulness as we wait for Christ's return?

11. What does this parable teach about those who reject Jesus? (vv. 14, 27)

Application

What opportunities has God given you to steward or invest to bring Him glory? If Jesus returned today, how would you account for the way you have stewarded what He's given you?

A DEEPER LOOK

What does the Bible say we are to spend our time doing while we wait for the glorious appearing of Jesus?

Ephesians 2:10

1 Peter 2:12

Philippians 1:9–10

2 Peter 3:11–14

Titus 2:12–14

Jude 21–23

James 5:7–9

What are you doing to discern and carry out those things?

WRAPPING UP

Hearing Jesus call Himself "the Resurrection and the Life" in the face of heart-wrenching loss must have been a comfort to Martha. Her brother was four days dead in the tomb, the effects of death having firmly taken hold. Yet there was relief in her voice, *"Yes, Lord, I have believed..."* She knew her Savior was able to bring back what had been lost. So when Lazarus emerged, whole and healthy, able to participate in the second life he had been graciously given (John 12:2), there was cause for rejoicing!

Lazarus is a picture of who we are before and after meeting our Savior. We are born dead. From conception we are a spiritual "flat line," walking and breathing, but not living. The cross accomplished all that was needed for our resurrection, and now there is no greed, pride, anger, disease, or past or future sin that can separate us from His perfect love. There is no life without Jesus, whether on earth or in heaven, because life isn't just something Jesus gives us. *It's who He is.* Jesus has defeated death, and now no obstacle stands between us and eternity with Him. That is cause for rejoicing!

~ A Map of Passion Week ~

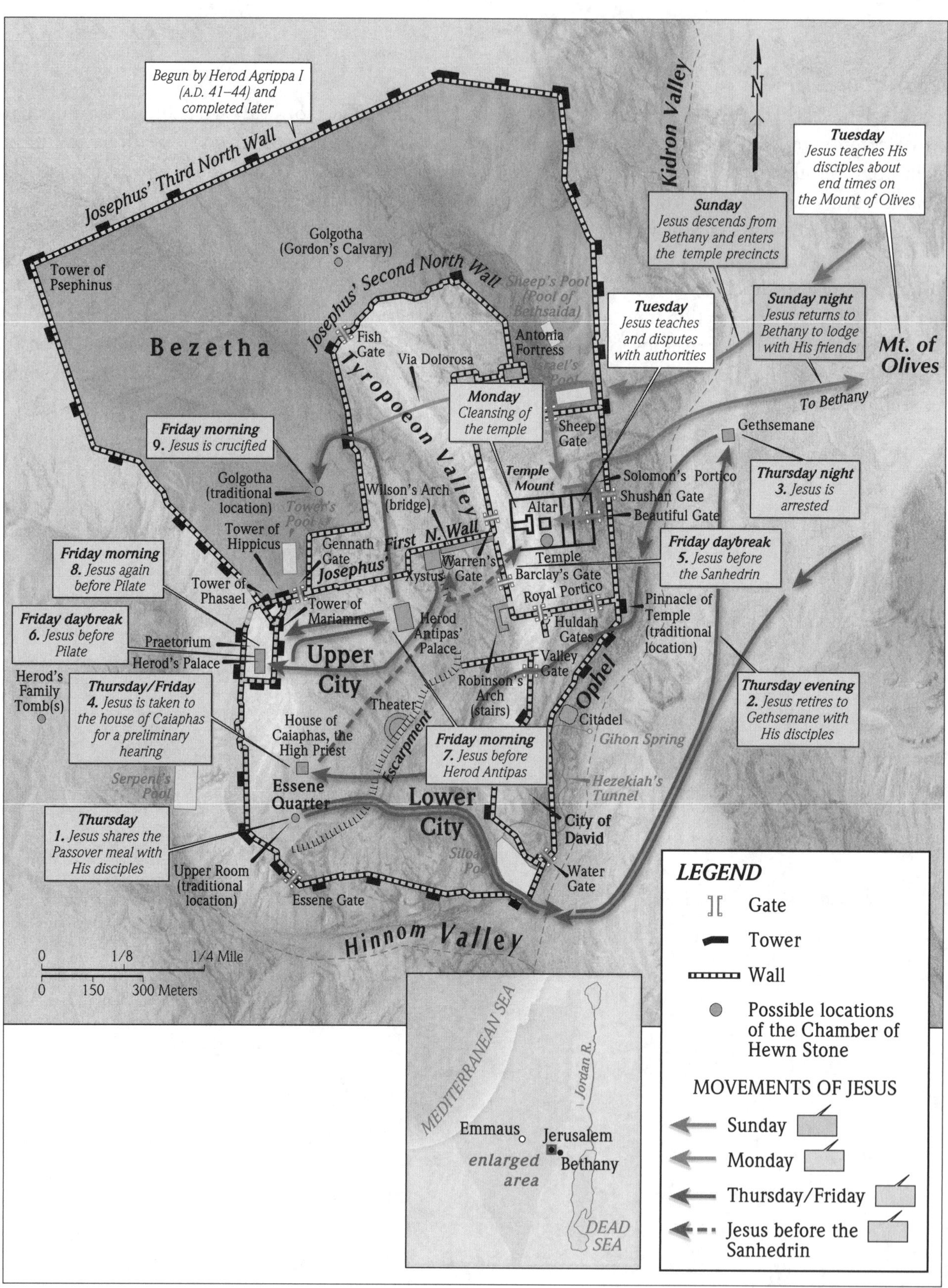

WEEK 18

JESUS, SON OF DAVID

"The crowds going ahead of Him, and those who followed, were shouting, 'Hosanna to the Son of David; BLESSED IS HE WHO COMES IN THE NAME OF THE LORD; Hosanna in the highest!'"
MATTHEW 21:9

More than 3,000 years ago, God made a promise to a king. A king that came out of nowhere, literally—plucked by God's prophet from a sheep pasture in a little town called Bethlehem. After years of running, hiding, and fighting enemies on all sides, this anointed one of Israel became the beneficiary of God's grace: the LORD made a covenant with King David, promising him peace, security, prosperity, and a dynasty. (2 Samuel 7)

But this last provision was different from every royal line in history; we can even see proof of the sovereign lineage in Matthew 1 and Luke 3. King David's kingdom would be everlasting, culminating in the rule and reign of the greatest Son who ever lived: Jesus.

Even though He lived on earth more than 1,000 years after the earthly king, Jesus is called the "Son of David" because of this covenant and prophecy. The LORD told David, "Your throne shall be established forever." (2 Samuel 7:16) This was an irrevocable, eternal promise from the Maker of heaven and earth. Nothing could alter or affect what God ordained for the future of mankind.

This week we see Jesus arrive in the Holy City as the long-expected Messiah, come to set His people free. But Jesus knows this isn't a truly triumphant entry. Praises rang out from a fickle and faithless crowd, and the Pharisees' arrogance kept hearts hard and eyes blind. Despite all this, Jesus fulfilled the ancient covenant with Israel as the Shoot from the stump of Jesse, divinely descended from David, covering His people with His love, at every cost to Him.

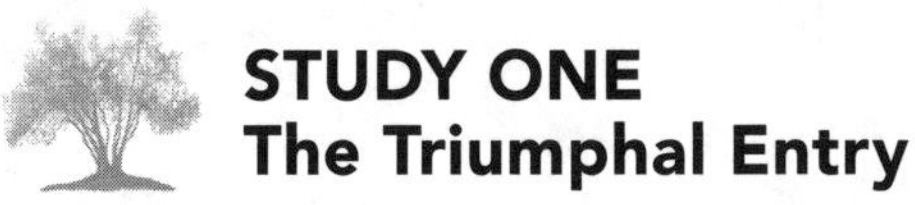

STUDY ONE
The Triumphal Entry

Lazarus was experiencing his fifteen minutes of fame. Known around the region as "the one who was raised from the dead," it's likely he couldn't walk down the street without being recognized. Since his miraculous resurrection, Lazarus was a symbol of what Jesus had come to mean to the people: they believed in Jesus' power and wanted the help and comfort it could provide, but most stopped short of receiving the true healing He offered. The crowd clamored for relief when Jesus entered Jerusalem, but only one in this passage understood what Jesus had come to do. At great sacrifice, Mary poured out her love at the feet of Jesus, an act of worship that lingered in the air—for some, the aroma of life, but for others, the stench of death to come.

John 11:55–12:19

"55 Now the Passover of the Jews was near, and many went up to Jerusalem out of the country before the Passover to purify themselves. 56 So they were seeking for Jesus, and were saying to one another as they stood in the temple, 'What do you think; that He will not come to the feast at all?' 57 Now the chief priests and the Pharisees had given orders that if anyone knew where He was, he was to report it, so that they might seize Him.

1 Jesus, therefore, six days before the Passover, came to Bethany where Lazarus was, whom Jesus had raised from the dead. 2 So they made Him a supper there, and Martha was serving; but Lazarus was one of those reclining at the table with Him. 3 Mary then took a pound of very costly perfume of pure nard, and anointed the feet of Jesus and wiped His feet with her hair; and the house was filled with the fragrance of the perfume. 4 But Judas Iscariot, one of His disciples, who was intending to betray Him, said, 5 'Why was this perfume not sold for three hundred denarii and given to poor people?' 6 Now he said this, not because he was concerned about the poor, but because he was a thief, and as he had the money box, he used to pilfer what was put into it. 7 Therefore Jesus said, 'Let her alone, so that she may keep it for the day of My burial. 8 For you always have the poor with you, but you do not always have Me.'

9 The large crowd of the Jews then learned that He was there; and they came, not for Jesus' sake only, but that they might also see Lazarus, whom He raised from the dead. 10 But the chief priests planned to put Lazarus to death also; 11 because on account of him many of the Jews were going away and were believing in Jesus.

12 On the next day the large crowd who had come to the feast, when they heard that Jesus was coming to Jerusalem, 13 took the branches of the palm trees and went out to meet Him, and began to shout, 'Hosanna! Blessed is He who comes in the name of the Lord, even the King of Israel.' 14 Jesus, finding a young donkey, sat on it; as it is written, 15 'Fear not, daughter of Zion; behold, your King is coming, seated on a donkey's colt.' 16 These things His disciples did not understand at the first; but when Jesus was glorified, then they remembered that these things were written of Him, and that they had done these things to Him. 17 So the people, who were with Him when He called Lazarus out of the tomb and raised him from the dead, continued to testify about Him. 18 For this reason also the people went and met Him, because they heard that He had performed this sign. 19 So the Pharisees said to one another, 'You see that you are not doing any good; look, the world has gone after Him.'"

1. How do verses 55–57 set the tone for this scene?

2. Describe in your own words the scene in verses 1–3. Who is mentioned? What are they doing?

NOTE: The amount of perfume poured out on Jesus is equal to about eleven ounces. Imagine the scent of eleven ounces of spilled perfume in your home!

3. What details in verse 3 indicate the lavishness of Mary's act toward Jesus?

4. Who enters the scene in verse 4 and what do we learn about him in verses 4–6?

5. Another example of sacrificial worship can be found in Luke 21:1–4. How are these offerings similar? How are they different?

6. Contrast the people inside the home with Jesus (vv. 1–8) with the people outside the house looking for Jesus (vv. 9–11). What is the difference about their motives, devotion, and understanding of who Jesus was?

7. How are the words of the crowd in John 12:12–13 different from Jesus' previous instruction seen in Mark 1:43–44, 5:43, and 7:36?

NOTE: *Hosanna* means, "Save, please" or "Give salvation now." See also Psalms 118:25–26

8. Read Zechariah 9:9. How was their purpose being fulfilled in this moment?

9. What if Jesus had done as the people wanted that day? What if He had ascended to an earthly throne to rule and reign? What if Jesus was only the Conquering King and not also the Suffering Servant? (Hebrews 9:22, Romans 5:8)

10. When did all the pieces fall into place for the disciples? (v. 16)

11. What seemingly prophetic words did the religious leaders speak in verse 19?

Application

The Jews were praising and following Jesus because of things they had seen Him do. (vv. 17–18) Are you able to follow Jesus when He feels far off? How does your remembrance of His past faithfulness help you in your current trials?

STUDY TWO
The Hour Has Come

When Jesus cast out the thieves and robbers who stole sacred space in the temple of God, He made room for those who had true need. Children sang praises to the Son of David as He healed the blind and lame, demonstrating compassion and love and that He truly is worthy of worship. Jesus' encounter with a fruitless fig tree exemplified the hearts of the Israelites who criticized the wonderful works Jesus performed. A temple filled with impurity is like a tree with leaves but no fruit—everything looks as it should from a distance but, on close examination, it's obvious the life is gone. Apart from a growing relationship with Christ, we too are dead in our sins and empty works. Our only hope is Jesus, who restores and transforms us from the inside out, giving life that lasts forever.

Matthew 21:12–22

"12 And Jesus entered the temple and drove out all those who were buying and
selling in the temple, and overturned the tables of the money changers and the
seats of those who were selling doves. 13 And He said to them, 'It is written, 'My
house shall be called a house of prayer'; but you are making it a robbers' den.'
14 And the blind and the lame came to Him in the temple, and He healed
them. 15 But when the chief priests and the scribes saw the wonderful things
that He had done, and the children who were shouting in the temple, 'Hosanna

to the Son of David,' they became indignant 16 and said to Him, 'Do You hear
what these children are saying?' And Jesus said to them, 'Yes; have you never read,
'Out of the mouth of infants and nursing babies You have prepared praise for
Yourself'?' 17 And He left them and went out of the city to Bethany, and spent
the night there.

18 Now in the morning, when He was returning to the city, He became hungry.
19 Seeing a lone fig tree by the road, He came to it and found nothing on it except
leaves only; and He said to it, 'No longer shall there ever be any fruit from you.'
And at once the fig tree withered.

20 Seeing this, the disciples were amazed and asked, 'How did the fig tree
wither all at once?' 21 And Jesus answered and said to them, 'Truly I say to you,
if you have faith and do not doubt, you will not only do what was done to the
fig tree, but even if you say to this mountain, 'Be taken up and cast into the sea,'
it will happen. 22 And all things you ask in prayer, believing, you will receive.'"

John 12:20–26

"20 Now there were some Greeks among those who were going up to worship
at the feast; 21 these then came to Philip, who was from Bethsaida of Galilee,
and began to ask him, saying, 'Sir, we wish to see Jesus.' 22 Philip came and told
Andrew; Andrew and Philip came and told Jesus. 23 And Jesus answered them,
saying, 'The hour has come for the Son of Man to be glorified. 24 Truly, truly, I
say to you, unless a grain of wheat falls into the earth and dies, it remains alone;
but if it dies, it bears much fruit. 25 He who loves his life loses it, and he who
hates his life in this world will keep it to life eternal. 26 If anyone serves Me, he
must follow Me; and where I am, there My servant will be also; if anyone serves
Me, the Father will honor him."

1. What did Jesus call the temple in verse 13 and why?

2. How did the people respond to Jesus in verses 14–16? How did the Pharisees respond?

3. Notice the kinds of people who surround Jesus in verses 14–15. What does this tell us about the Son of David?

4. What does the Bible say about fig trees? See Deuteronomy 8:7–10, Judges 9:11, 1 Kings 4:25, Hosea 9:10, and Nahum 3:12.

5. How is Israel a picture of a barren fig tree in Matthew 21:12–13? What does Jesus say a fruitful "fig tree" can accomplish in verses 21–22? What does this living parable say to you about your fruit and your faith?

6. Look back at John 12:19. Who comes looking for Jesus in John 12:20–21 and how does this illustrate those words?

7. What significant moment in history did Jesus announce in verse 23? How was that the answer to the Greeks' request?

8. Jesus lays out some difficult commands with glorious results in John 12:24–26. What are they?

9. How did Jesus describe His glorification in verse 24?

10. Jesus taught this same idea in Matthew 10:39, Matthew 16:25, Mark 8:34–36, Luke 9:24, and Luke 14:26. What does this repetition indicate about this instruction?

Application

Where might Jesus discover fruitfulness in your life?

STUDY THREE
Jesus Foretells His Death

Jesus fulfilled another prophecy here that no one would embrace: the prophecy of rejection. Jesus foretold His death—specifically death by crucifixion—and the people were indignant: *Who are you and how can you say these things?* Jesus wanted to light their way with Truth, but darkness, like a well-worn blanket, had wrapped their minds in a false and fragile comfort. Isaiah promised no one would see, believe, or repent, yet Jesus persisted in His message of hope. The people so longed for the approval of men, they could not see that true salvation came only through the favor of God in Christ. He had come to save the world; they were still trying to save themselves.

John 12:27–50

"**27** 'Now My soul has become troubled; and what shall I say, 'Father, save Me from this hour'? But for this purpose I came to this hour. **28** Father, glorify Your name.' Then a voice came out of heaven: 'I have both glorified it, and will glorify it again.' **29** So the crowd of people who stood by and heard it were saying that it had thundered; others were saying, 'An angel has spoken to Him.' **30** Jesus answered and said, 'This voice has not come for My sake, but for your sakes. **31** Now judgment is upon this world; now the ruler of this world will be cast out. **32** And I, if I am lifted up from the earth, will draw all men to Myself.' **33** But He was saying this to indicate the kind of death by which He was to die. **34** The crowd then answered Him, 'We have heard out of the Law that the Christ is to remain forever; and how can You say, 'The Son of Man must be lifted up'? Who is this Son of Man?' **35** So Jesus said to them, 'For a little while longer the Light is among you. Walk while you have the Light, so that darkness will not overtake you; he who walks in the darkness does not know where he goes. **36** While you have the Light, believe in the Light, so that you may become sons of Light.'

These things Jesus spoke, and He went away and hid Himself from them. **37** But though He had performed so many signs before them, yet they were not believing in Him. **38** This was to fulfill the word of Isaiah the prophet which he spoke: 'Lord, who has believed our report? And to whom has the arm of the Lord been revealed?' **39** For this reason they could not believe, for Isaiah said again, **40** 'He has blinded their eyes and He hardened their heart, so that they would not see with their eyes and perceive with their heart, and be converted and I heal them.' **41** These things Isaiah said because he saw His glory, and he spoke of Him. **42** Nevertheless many even of the rulers believed in Him, but because of the Pharisees they were not confessing Him, for fear that they would be put out of the synagogue; **43** for they loved the approval of men rather than the approval of God.

44 And Jesus cried out and said, 'He who believes in Me, does not believe in Me but in Him who sent Me. **45** He who sees Me sees the One who sent Me. **46** I have come as Light into the world, so that everyone who believes in Me will not remain in darkness. **47** If anyone hears My sayings and does not keep them, I do not judge him; for I did not come to judge the world, but to save the world. **48** He who rejects Me and does not receive My sayings, has one who judges him; the word I spoke is what will judge him at the last day. **49** For I did not speak on My own initiative, but the Father Himself who sent Me has given Me a commandment as to what to say and what to speak. **50** I know that His commandment is eternal life; therefore the things I speak, I speak just as the Father has told Me.'"

1. What was troubling Jesus in verse 27? How does this speak to the two natures of Jesus? (His humanity and His deity)

2. What conflict do we see Jesus acknowledge in verses 27–28? How does He resolve this "tension" in these same verses? What remained His ultimate goal? (v. 28)

3. How does God answer Jesus' prayer in verse 28? What did Jesus say was the purpose of this event in verse 30?

4. What do verses 31–32 tell us Jesus' death will accomplish?

5. What is Jesus saying about Himself and the crowd in verses 35–36?

6. What is the issue in verse 37? How do verses 38–40 help explain that?

7. What does the writer John reveal about Israel's rulers in verse 42? What was their obstacle to embracing Jesus in verses 41–43?

8. Read verses 44–50. How does Jesus speak about His unity and connection with and distinction from the Father?

9. How does verse 44 tell us Jesus delivered those words? What does that say about their importance?

Application

Jesus—Son of David, Son of Man, and Son of God—expressed a range of emotion to His Father in this passage. How does that encourage you in how honest you are with God about your struggles on this earth? How does Jesus' primary purpose expressed in verse 28 shape your perspective?

STUDY FOUR
Pharisaism Exposed

The Pharisees set a trap for Jesus and ended up ensnaring themselves. Their question about taxes turned to how to honor your leaders. Their question about the Law turned to loving God and others. And when Jesus asked a question about the lineage of the Messiah from a familiar psalm penned by David, their response was silence. Jesus took advantage of this space in the conversation and called out the behavior of the religious leaders to the crowd. *The scribes and Pharisees tell you how to live*, Jesus said, *but neglect to live that way themselves. They let you carry all the burdens and expect you to stand aside while they seek admiration and take the most prominent seat at the table. They are not your teachers or your fathers*, Jesus explained. Those who humble themselves and selflessly serve are the ones who lead the way.

Matthew 22:15–22

"15 Then the Pharisees went and plotted together how they might trap Him in
what He said. 16 And they sent their disciples to Him, along with the Herodians,
saying, 'Teacher, we know that You are truthful and teach the way of God in
truth, and defer to no one; for You are not partial to any. 17 Tell us then, what do
You think? Is it lawful to give a poll-tax to Caesar, or not?' 18 But Jesus perceived
their malice, and said, 'Why are you testing Me, you hypocrites? 19 Show Me the
coin used for the poll-tax.' And they brought Him a denarius. 20 And He said to
them, 'Whose likeness and inscription is this?' 21 They said to Him, 'Caesar's.'
Then He said to them, 'Then render to Caesar the things that are Caesar's; and
to God the things that are God's.' 22 And hearing this, they were amazed, and
leaving Him, they went away."

Matthew 22:34–46

"34 But when the Pharisees heard that Jesus had silenced the Sadducees, they
gathered themselves together. 35 One of them, a lawyer, asked Him a question,
testing Him, 36 'Teacher, which is the great commandment in the Law?' 37 And
He said to him, 'You shall love the Lord your God with all your heart, and with
all your soul, and with all your mind.' 38 This is the great and foremost commandment. 39 The second is like it, 'You shall love your neighbor as yourself.'
40 On these two commandments depend the whole Law and the Prophets.'

41 Now while the Pharisees were gathered together, Jesus asked them a question: 42 'What do you think about the Christ, whose son is He?' They said to
Him, 'The son of David.' 43 He said to them, 'Then how does David in the Spirit
call Him 'Lord,' saying,

44 'The Lord said to my Lord,
'Sit at My right hand,
Until I put Your enemies beneath Your feet'?
45 If David then calls Him 'Lord,' how is He his son?' 46 No one was able to
answer Him a word, nor did anyone dare from that day on to ask Him another
question."

Matthew 23:1–12

"Then Jesus spoke to the crowds and to His disciples, 2 saying: 'The scribes and
the Pharisees have seated themselves in the chair of Moses; 3 therefore all that
they tell you, do and observe, but do not do according to their deeds; for they say
things and do not do them. 4 They tie up heavy burdens and lay them on men's
shoulders, but they themselves are unwilling to move them with so much as a
finger. 5 But they do all their deeds to be noticed by men; for they broaden their
phylacteries and lengthen the tassels of their garments. 6 They love the place of
honor at banquets and the chief seats in the synagogues, 7 and respectful greetings in the market places, and being called Rabbi by men. 8 But do not be called
Rabbi; for One is your Teacher, and you are all brothers. 9 Do not call anyone
on earth your father; for One is your Father, He who is in heaven. 10 Do not be
called leaders; for One is your Leader, that is, Christ. 11 But the greatest among
you shall be your servant. 12 Whoever exalts himself shall be humbled; and whoever humbles himself shall be exalted."

1. What do verses 15–17 say was the purpose of the Pharisees' and/or Herodians' questions?

NOTE: For information about Herodians, use the Quick Reference Dictionary at biblestudytools.com

2. How did Jesus describe their intentions in verse 18?

3. What was the "double bind" the Jews were trying to put Jesus in? (vv. 17–18)

NOTE: A likeness of Tiberias Caesar was on every denarius. On one side was inscribed in Latin the words, "Good and High Priest." On the other side, "Son of the Divine Augustus."

4. How did Jesus escape that trap? How did the Pharisees respond? (vv. 18–22)

5. What question is the lawyer asking in Matthew 22:36? What does Jesus' answer in verses 37–40 reveal as the whole purpose or "big idea" behind the Law? (see Deuteronomy 6:4–5, Leviticus 19:18)?

6. Who asks a question in verse 41? What did He ask?

7. What does Scripture say about Jesus being the Son of David or in the line of David? See 2 Samuel 7:12–14, Isaiah 9: 2–7, 11:1, 10; Jeremiah 23:5–6, and Matthew 1:1.

8. In verse 43, how did Jesus say the Pharisees' answer was incomplete? (Psalms 110:1?)

9. Who is "Him" in verses 43 and 45?

10. Scripture tells us the questions of the Pharisees were always intended to trap or test Jesus. Knowing the character of Jesus, what might be the purpose of the questions Jesus asked?

11. Who does Jesus speak to in Matthew 23:1?

12. What is Jesus' indictment of the religious leaders in verses 2–3?

13. What does Jesus reveal is the motive behind this in verses 4–7?

14. Read Exodus 13:16, Numbers 15: 37–41, Deuteronomy 6:8, 11:18, and 22:12, to help you interpret verse 5. What is Jesus saying these religious leaders had done with those commands?

15. What instruction/warning does Jesus give in verses 8–12?

16. Underline the word "One" in the Matthew 23 passage. Who is the "One" Jesus was referring to?

17. What does Jesus say He exalts in verses 11–12? What is He indirectly saying about the Pharisees?

Application

How is loving others "like" loving God? (see Philippians 2:3–4, 1 John 3:16–18, and 1 John 4:7–8, 11)

A DEEPER LOOK

Whose "likeness" is stamped on our hearts and lives? What does that tell us we are to "give" to God?

Genesis 1:26–27

Colossians 3:10

Ephesians 4:24

James 3:9

STUDY FIVE
Jesus Laments over Jerusalem

Serpents and vipers. Sons of hell. Lawless fools and blind guides. Dead men's bones. Strong words from the Son of David about the self-proclaimed righteous religious of the day. Jesus continued His hostile indictment of the Pharisees in the hearing of the people. More than just inadequate leaders, the scribes and Pharisees represented the status quo of the nation spiritually. Jesus was trying to open their eyes to the reality of their shallow faith. The people were following leaders who were going nowhere and serving only themselves. They carefully measured their spice offerings but refused to show mercy to others, and every relationship withered. They paid close attention to their appearance but neglected to clean their hearts, unaware that no amount of soap and water could make the nation pure. Jesus does not rejoice over these sins; He laments. He wanted to be a refuge for His people but, for now, they chose their own way.

Matthew 23:13–39

"13 'But woe to you, scribes and Pharisees, hypocrites, because you shut off the
kingdom of heaven from people; for you do not enter in yourselves, nor do you
allow those who are entering to go in. 14 [Woe to you, scribes and Pharisees, hypocrites, because you devour widows' houses, and for a pretense you make long
prayers; therefore you will receive greater condemnation.]
15 'Woe to you, scribes and Pharisees, hypocrites, because you travel around
on sea and land to make one proselyte; and when he becomes one, you make him
twice as much a son of hell as yourselves.
16 'Woe to you, blind guides, who say, 'Whoever swears by the temple, that
is nothing; but whoever swears by the gold of the temple is obligated.' 17 You
fools and blind men! Which is more important, the gold or the temple that
sanctified the gold? 18 And, 'Whoever swears by the altar, that is nothing, but
whoever swears by the offering on it, he is obligated.' 19 You blind men, which
is more important, the offering, or the altar that sanctifies the offering? 20 Therefore, whoever swears by the altar, swears both by the altar and by everything
on it. 21 And whoever swears by the temple, swears both by the temple and by
Him who dwells within it. 22 And whoever swears by heaven, swears both by the
throne of God and by Him who sits upon it.
23 'Woe to you, scribes and Pharisees, hypocrites! For you tithe mint and dill
and cummin, and have neglected the weightier provisions of the law: justice and
mercy and faithfulness; but these are the things you should have done without
neglecting the others. 24 You blind guides, who strain out a gnat and swallow a
camel!
25 'Woe to you, scribes and Pharisees, hypocrites! For you clean the outside
of the cup and of the dish, but inside they are full of robbery and self-indulgence.
26 You blind Pharisee, first clean the inside of the cup and of the dish, so that the
outside of it may become clean also.
27 'Woe to you, scribes and Pharisees, hypocrites! For you are like white-
washed tombs which on the outside appear beautiful, but inside they are full of
dead men's bones and all uncleanness. 28 So you, too, outwardly appear righteous
to men, but inwardly you are full of hypocrisy and lawlessness.
29 'Woe to you, scribes and Pharisees, hypocrites! For you build the tombs of
the prophets and adorn the monuments of the righteous, 30 and say, 'If we had

been living in the days of our fathers, we would not have been partners with them
in shedding the blood of the prophets.' 31 So you testify against yourselves, that
you are sons of those who murdered the prophets. 32 Fill up, then, the measure
of the guilt of your fathers. 33 You serpents, you brood of vipers, how will you
escape the sentence of hell?

34 'Therefore, behold, I am sending you prophets and wise men and scribes;
some of them you will kill and crucify, and some of them you will scourge in
your synagogues, and persecute from city to city, 35 so that upon you may fall the
guilt of all the righteous blood shed on earth, from the blood of righteous Abel
to the blood of Zechariah, the son of Berechiah, whom you murdered between
the temple and the altar. 36 Truly I say to you, all these things will come upon
this generation.

37 'Jerusalem, Jerusalem, who kills the prophets and stones those who are sent to
her! How often I wanted to gather your children together, the way a hen gathers
her chicks under her wings, and you were unwilling. 38 Behold, your house is
being left to you desolate! 39 For I say to you, from now on you will not see Me
until you say, 'Blessed is He who comes in the name of the Lord!'"

1. What are the "woes" in this passage, in your own words? (vv. 13–15, 16–22, 23–26, 27–36)

2. Look up the word "woe" and write the definition below. What was the intent behind the rebuke of Jesus?

3. Can you hear the "wake-up call" in Jesus' words? What specific offenses is He pointing out?

4. What labels did Jesus give the religious leaders throughout His pronouncement?

5. Jesus moves from condemnation to compassion in verses 37–39. How does Jesus describe His compassion for His people in verse 37? What does Jesus say is the only obstacle to His compassion?

6. What is the warning and hope in verses 38–39?

Application

How might a Christian's life be a hindrance or stumbling block to those who are seeking the kingdom of God?

WRAPPING UP

Thousands of years passed between the Lord's covenant to David and the coming of His Son, Jesus, but the thread of that promise is seen throughout the Word of God. Meditate on the beautiful truths that God will accomplish His will in our lives, that salvation through the Son of David was a sovereign plan from before time began, and that, one day, He will return for His children.

Psalms 132:11: "The Lord has sworn to David a truth from which He will not turn back: 'Of the fruit of your body I will set upon your throne.'"

Isaiah 11:1: "Then a shoot will spring from the stem of Jesse, And a branch from his roots will bear fruit."

Jeremiah 23:5: "'Behold, the days are coming,' declares the Lord, 'When I will raise up for David a righteous Branch; And He will reign as king and act wisely and do justice and righteousness in the land.'"

Romans 1:3: "…concerning His Son, who was born of a descendant of David according to the flesh…"

2 Timothy 2:8: "Remember Jesus Christ, risen from the dead, descendant of David, according to my gospel…"

Revelation 22:16: "I, Jesus, have sent My angel to testify to you these things for the churches. I am the root and the descendant of David, the bright morning star."

~ Map of Passion Week ~

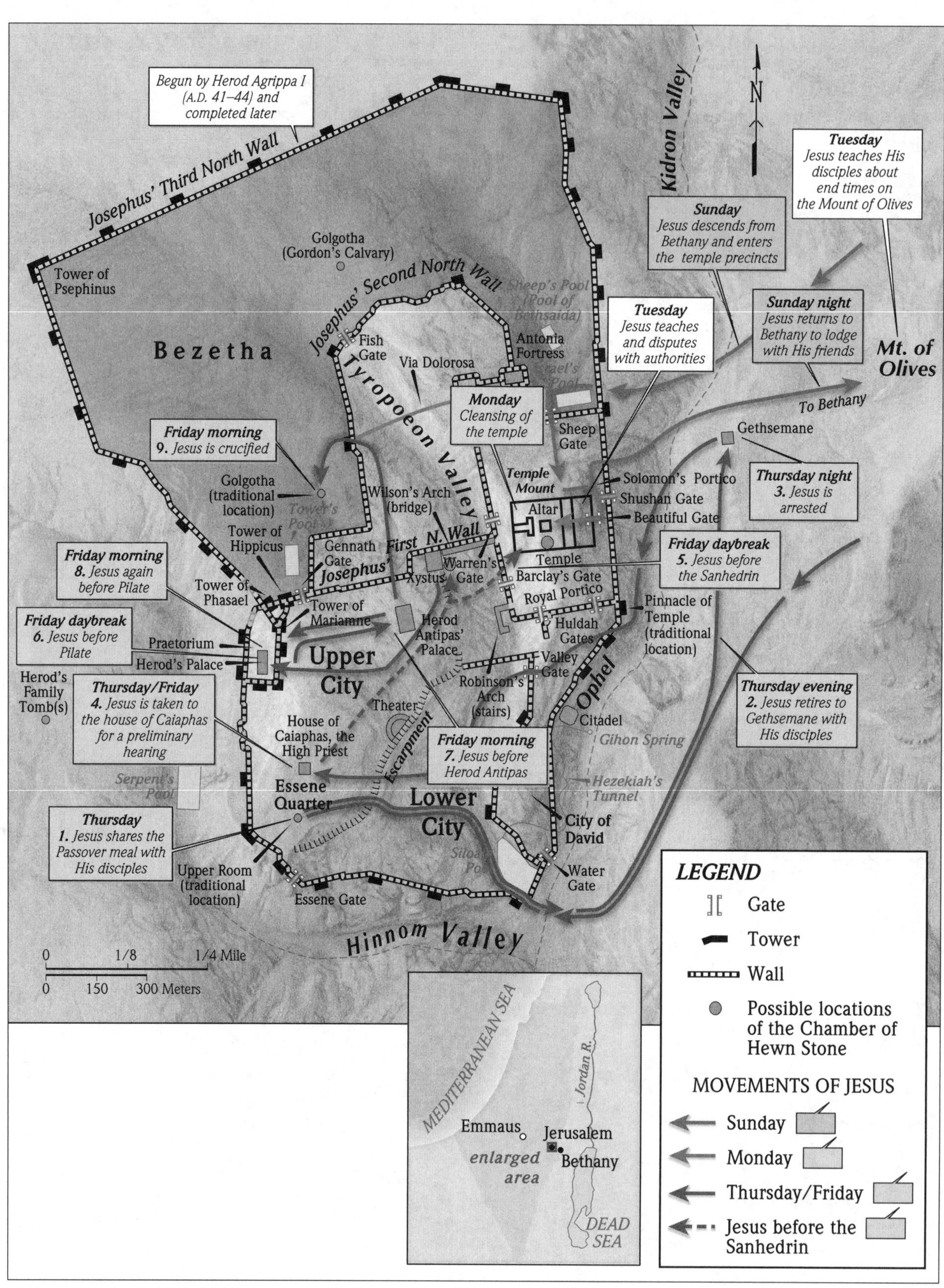

WEEK 19

JESUS, THE JUDGE

"But when the Son of Man comes in His glory, and all the angels with Him, then He will sit on His glorious throne. All the nations will be gathered before Him; and He will separate them from one another, as the shepherd separates the sheep from the goats."
Matthew 25:31–32

You don't have to live very long before you encounter injustice in the world. Something happens in your life or the life of someone you love that doesn't make sense or simply is not fair. It's a maddening experience. Which makes thinking of Jesus as Judge more challenging to our finite, human minds. Because judges aren't always just, and the "justice system" isn't always fair, what might that mean about Jesus?

What a blessing that Scripture so clearly helps us answer this question! Look at the words of Isaiah as he describes our righteous Judge, Jesus: *"And He will delight in the fear of the Lord, And He will not judge by what His eyes see, Nor make a decision by what His ears hear; But with righteousness He will judge the poor, And decide with fairness for the afflicted of the earth; And He will strike the earth with the rod of His mouth, And with the breath of His lips He will slay the wicked."* (Isaiah 11:3–4)

In this week's study, we see Jesus as the authority and Judge over all things, and Scripture tells us we can trust that He will be gracious as He examines our hearts and motives. His scales always balance in favor of His people.

Courtroom judges must consider the facts of a case, and busybodies make assumptions based on rumors. But Jesus is not deceived by hypocrisy or half-truths. His judgments are based on His righteousness—a divine discernment that acts on behalf of all who are oppressed and afflicted by the wickedness of the world. In other words, Jesus is for us. And those who side with Him will always win.

STUDY ONE
The Olivet Discourse

The passages this week come from Matthew 24–25, a section of Scripture known as The Olivet Discourse. The title of this teaching is based on Jesus' location (see verse 3). He and the disciples had a perfect view of the temple from their mountainside seats. The disciples came privately to ask Jesus two questions that had more depth and significance than they understood at the time. These men did not yet grasp that their Savior would be crucified, so they had no concept of a resurrection or a future return. Yet Jesus lived each day with the bigger picture and end in mind, so while He answered their immediate questions, much of what He said is yet to come. Just like the disciples, discernment and faith on our part bring understanding and insight into the truths spoken by the Word made flesh.

Matthew 24:1–14

"Jesus came out from the temple and was going away when His disciples came
up to point out the temple buildings to Him. 2 And He said to them, 'Do you
not see all these things? Truly I say to you, not one stone here will be left upon
another, which will not be torn down.'

3 As He was sitting on the Mount of Olives, the disciples came to Him privately, saying, 'Tell us, when will these things happen, and what will be the sign
of Your coming, and of the end of the age?'

4 And Jesus answered and said to them, 'See to it that no one misleads you.
5 For many will come in My name, saying, 'I am the Christ,' and will mislead
many. 6 You will be hearing of wars and rumors of wars. See that you are not
frightened, for those things must take place, but that is not yet the end. 7 For
nation will rise against nation, and kingdom against kingdom, and in various
places there will be famines and earthquakes. 8 But all these things are merely the
beginning of birth pangs.

9 'Then they will deliver you to tribulation, and will kill you, and you will be
hated by all nations because of My name. 10 At that time many will fall away and
will betray one another and hate one another. 11 Many false prophets will arise
and will mislead many. 12 Because lawlessness is increased, most people's love will
grow cold. 13 But the one who endures to the end, he will be saved. 14 This gospel
of the kingdom shall be preached in the whole world as a testimony to all the
nations, and then the end will come."

1. What were the disciples impressed with in verse 1? (see Mark 13:1 for additional details) What future event did Jesus speak about in verse 2?

2. Where is Jesus in verse 3? What did the disciples ask? Because they did not fully understand Jesus' death and resurrection yet, did they really understand what they were asking? (Mark 9:31–32, John 2:22, and John 12:16)

3. What did Jesus warn His disciples would be "the beginning of birth pangs" in verses 4–8? How were they to respond? (vv. 4, 6)

4. How does the instruction of Jude 17–25 help illuminate this passage?

NOTE: Jesus is speaking to His disciples but also to all future followers of Jesus. (see 2 Timothy 3:1–5, 10–14)

5. Jesus gives a more precise timeline for the events in Matthew 24:9–14. What future persecution are the disciples to expect?

6. What is the exhortation in verse 13? What does verse 14 tell us will happen despite tribulation, false prophets, and lawlessness?

7. Read Revelation 6 for Scripture's description of the beginning of the tribulation and write your observations below.

8. Look up "tribulation" and write the definition below. We usually expect to be "delivered *from*" such things. What does it mean to be "delivered *to*?" (Matthew 24:9)

Application

What does Scripture say about how Christians are to respond to persecution? See Matthew 5:11–12, Romans 9:33, Philippians 4:6–7, James 1:2–4, and 1 Peter 2:23. What is your response to the promise of persecution?

STUDY TWO
Peril and Glory

The theme of this extended teaching is complex, but many elements refer to the end times and the establishment of Jesus' kingdom on earth. We know the disciples experienced persecution and tribulation—history records all but one of the Twelve being martyred for their faith—but there is a "great tribulation" yet to come that John writes about in Revelation 6–18. Jesus' warnings in this passage in Matthew are clear and relevant even for our days: beware of false teachers and be vigilant over your hearts and minds. The return of Jesus will be as obvious as lightning in the sky—times ten—so don't settle for anyone "less than." All creation will cooperate in proclaiming His coming. All this will usher in a time of mourning for those who Jesus will judge, and joy for those who long to see His glory.

Matthew 24:15–31
"**15** 'Therefore when you see the abomination of desolation which was spoken
of through Daniel the prophet, standing in the holy place (let the reader understand), **16** then those who are in Judea must flee to the mountains. **17** Whoever
is on the housetop must not go down to get the things out that are in his house.
18 Whoever is in the field must not turn back to get his cloak. **19** But woe to those
who are pregnant and to those who are nursing babies in those days! **20** But pray
that your flight will not be in the winter, or on a Sabbath. **21** For then there will
be a great tribulation, such as has not occurred since the beginning of the world
until now, nor ever will. **22** Unless those days had been cut short, no life would
have been saved; but for the sake of the elect those days will be cut short. **23** Then
if anyone says to you, 'Behold, here is the Christ,' or 'There He is,' do not believe
him. **24** For false Christs and false prophets will arise and will show great signs
and wonders, so as to mislead, if possible, even the elect. **25** Behold, I have told
you in advance. **26** So if they say to you, 'Behold, He is in the wilderness,' do not
go out, or, 'Behold, He is in the inner rooms,' do not believe them. **27** For just as
the lightning comes from the east and flashes even to the west, so will the coming
of the Son of Man be. **28** Wherever the corpse is, there the vultures will gather.

29 'But immediately after the tribulation of those days the sun will be darkened,
and the moon will not give its light, and the stars will fall from the sky, and the
powers of the heavens will be shaken. **30** And then the sign of the Son of Man will
appear in the sky, and then all the tribes of the earth will mourn, and they will
see the Son of Man coming on the clouds of the sky with power and great glory.
31 And He will send forth His angels with a great trumpet and they will gather
together His elect from the four winds, from one end of the sky to the other."

1. What is the "sign" in verse 15? What does He say this sign in the temple precedes? (vv. 21–22)

2. What does Jesus say should be the response to the abomination of desolation? (vv. 16–20)

3. What other "signs" in Matthew 24:23–26 does Jesus say will occur before the end of the age? (Matthew 24:3, 14)

4. What does Jesus say about His return in verse 27? What is different about the coming of false prophets and the return of the true Christ?

5. For any who are not vigilant in watching for the return of Jesus, the righteous Judge, what picture of judgment does verse 28 give? (see also Revelation 19:11–21)

6. How does creation respond to the return of Jesus, the Son of Man? (vv. 29–31) See also Isaiah 13:9–10, Isaiah 34:4, Joel 2:30–31, Haggai 2:6, and Zechariah 14:6.

7. What is the response of the tribes of earth to Jesus' return? (v. 30) See also Philippians 2:10–11 and Revelation 1:7.

8. How does Jesus respond to His people? (v. 31) See also 1 Thessalonians 4:17, 1 John 3:2, and Revelation 22:4.

9. Read Revelation 19:11–21. How does this passage expand on what else happens when the Son of Man returns in verse 31?

Application

Think about the trials besetting you, the conflicts in your relationships, the stress and tension you are enduring, your goals, concerns, and needs. Hold all these things up in the light that Matthew 24:30–31 provides. Describe the perspective "that day" gives to the troubles and urgencies in "this day."

A DEEPER LOOK

Read the passages below and discover what is said in Scripture about the abomination of desolation. The accurate interpretation of this phrase is "the abomination that causes desolation." Scripture often connects the word *abomination* to something God detests, like idolatry. (see Deuteronomy 29:16–17, 1 Kings 11:6–7)

Daniel 9:27

2 Thessalonians 2:3–4

Daniel 11:31–32

Revelation 21:27

Daniel 12:11

STUDY THREE
Be Ready

While God's Word gives us signs and hope for the end of all time, this passage clearly proclaims the final word on when we can expect Jesus to return: "no one knows." Not the angels, not even Jesus Himself. Only our Father in heaven has knowledge of the point in history when the end will signal the beginning. By God's grace, we can picture what it might look like and watch for warnings along the way. While Scripture encourages us to anticipate that day with joy, we are called to do something vital in the meantime: *live*. And live "as if." As if this day was your last day, as if this was your last chance, as if your words of life were the last words your lost neighbor, friend, or family member might hear. We can be distracted by the things we don't know, but blessed is the one who chooses instead to be ready and faithful.

Matthew 24:32–51
"**32** 'Now learn the parable from the fig tree: when its branch has already become
tender and puts forth its leaves, you know that summer is near; **33** so, you too,
when you see all these things, recognize that He is near, right at the door. **34** Truly
I say to you, this generation will not pass away until all these things take place.
35 Heaven and earth will pass away, but My words will not pass away.
36 'But of that day and hour no one knows, not even the angels of heaven, nor
the Son, but the Father alone. **37** For the coming of the Son of Man will be just
like the days of Noah. **38** For as in those days before the flood they were eating
and drinking, marrying and giving in marriage, until the day that Noah entered

the ark, 39 and they did not understand until the flood came and took them all
away; so will the coming of the Son of Man be. 40 Then there will be two men in
the field; one will be taken and one will be left. 41 Two women will be grinding
at the mill; one will be taken and one will be left.

42 'Therefore be on the alert, for you do not know which day your Lord is coming.
43 But be sure of this, that if the head of the house had known at what time of the
night the thief was coming, he would have been on the alert and would not have
allowed his house to be broken into. 44 For this reason you also must be ready; for
the Son of Man is coming at an hour when you do not think He will.

45 'Who then is the faithful and sensible slave whom his master put in charge
of his household to give them their food at the proper time? 46 Blessed is that
slave whom his master finds so doing when he comes. 47 Truly I say to you that
he will put him in charge of all his possessions. 48 But if that evil slave says in his
heart, 'My master is not coming for a long time,' 49 and begins to beat his fellow
slaves and eat and drink with drunkards; 50 the master of that slave will come on a
day when he does not expect him and at an hour which he does not know, 51 and
will cut him in pieces and assign him a place with the hypocrites; in that place
there will be weeping and gnashing of teeth."

1. What assurance does Jesus give concerning the appearance of "these things" in verses 33–35?

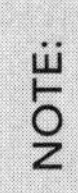

The term "this generation" has been much discussed by scholars over time. *The Amazing Life of Jesus Christ* focuses on the truth that these things *will* take place as Jesus said, rather than trying to determine when.

2. How is the authority of Jesus described in verse 35? (Isaiah 40:8)

3. How do you see the sovereignty of God in this passage? (vv. 36–41)

4. Make a list of all the signs of the end of the age presented so far this week. Despite all the visible evidence, what do verses 38 and 42 tell us about our knowledge and limitations?

5. Based on Jesus' analogy of Noah to His coming (v. 37), what might "the days" be like when He returns to judge? (vv. 38–41)

6. What is the difference in the two slaves in verses 45–51? What is the outcome of each? What is the message of the parable?

7. How is Jesus' delay an expression of grace? (Romans 9:22–24)

Application

If you believe in the imminent return of Jesus Christ, how should that affect how you live each day?

A DEEPER LOOK

How does Jesus encourage believers to be prepared and live expectantly as they await His return? What hope does Scripture give us as we long for His return?

Hosea 12:6

1 Peter 1:3–4

Romans 8:18

Revelation 3:1–3

1 Thessalonians 5:2–11

Revelation 16:15

STUDY FOUR
Ten Virgins and Talents

Knowing a picture paints a thousand words, Jesus told His disciples a parable to illustrate the difference between waiting faithfully and faithlessly. Five virgins made wise decisions and five made foolish decisions as they waited for their bridegroom to arrive. The result for those who were ready was celebration and joy, but those who were lazy and unprepared got lost in the darkness. Slaves entrusted with their master's possessions depict believers' responsibility in the world. Two slaves invested with abundant return, but the one who held back lost it all. We are entrusted with the Gospel and called to participate in good works on earth (Ephesians 2:10). God's judgment awaits those who ignore this privilege. Playing it safe isn't always what pleases God, especially when it comes to growing His kingdom.

Matthew 25:1–30
"'Then the kingdom of heaven will be comparable to ten virgins, who took their
lamps and went out to meet the bridegroom. 2 Five of them were foolish, and
five were prudent. 3 For when the foolish took their lamps, they took no oil with
them, 4 but the prudent took oil in flasks along with their lamps. 5 Now while
the bridegroom was delaying, they all got drowsy and began to sleep. 6 But at
midnight there was a shout, 'Behold, the bridegroom! Come out to meet him.'
7 Then all those virgins rose and trimmed their lamps. 8 The foolish said to the
prudent, 'Give us some of your oil, for our lamps are going out.' 9 But the prudent answered, 'No, there will not be enough for us and you too; go instead to the
dealers and buy some for yourselves.' 10 And while they were going away to make
the purchase, the bridegroom came, and those who were ready went in with him
to the wedding feast; and the door was shut. 11 Later the other virgins also came,
saying, 'Lord, lord, open up for us.' 12 But he answered, 'Truly I say to you, I do
not know you.' 13 Be on the alert then, for you do not know the day nor the hour.

14 'For it is just like a man about to go on a journey, who called his own slaves and
entrusted his possessions to them. 15 To one he gave five talents, to another, two,
and to another, one, each according to his own ability; and he went on his journey. 16 Immediately the one who had received the five talents went and traded
with them, and gained five more talents. 17 In the same manner the one who had
received the two talents gained two more. 18 But he who received the one talent
went away, and dug a hole in the ground and hid his master's money.

19 'Now after a long time the master of those slaves came and settled accounts
with them. 20 The one who had received the five talents came up and brought five
more talents, saying, 'Master, you entrusted five talents to me. See, I have gained
five more talents.' 21 His master said to him, 'Well done, good and faithful slave.
You were faithful with a few things, I will put you in charge of many things; enter
into the joy of your master.'

22 'Also the one who had received the two talents came up and said, 'Master,
you entrusted two talents to me. See, I have gained two more talents.' 23 His
master said to him, 'Well done, good and faithful slave. You were faithful with
a few things, I will put you in charge of many things; enter into the joy of your
master.'

24 "And the one also who had received the one talent came up and said,
'Master, I knew you to be a hard man, reaping where you did not sow and

gathering where you scattered no seed. 25 And I was afraid, and went away and
hid your talent in the ground. See, you have what is yours.'
26 "But his master answered and said to him, 'You wicked, lazy slave, you
knew that I reap where I did not sow and gather where I scattered no seed.
27 Then you ought to have put my money in the bank, and on my arrival I would
have received my money back with interest. 28 Therefore take away the talent
from him, and give it to the one who has the ten talents.'
29 'For to everyone who has, more shall be given, and he will have an abundance; but from the one who does not have, even what he does have shall be
taken away. 30 Throw out the worthless slave into the outer darkness; in that place
there will be weeping and gnashing of teeth."

1. What do we learn about the characters in this parable in verses 1–2?

2. What character trait distinguishes the prudent from the foolish virgins? (vv. 3–4)

3. Who is responsible for being prepared to receive the bridegroom? (vv. 8–9) What is the implication for your spiritual life and walk with Christ?

4. How did the bridegroom respond to the wise virgins? Foolish virgins? (vv. 10–12) What is the most important thing you can do to prepare for the return of Jesus? (Romans 10:9–10)

5. The parable of the talents illustrates what it means to wait with readiness. What do you learn about the man and his slaves in verses 14–18?

6. What standard of "good and faithful" did the Master use with each slave?

What was different and the same about His expectations for each? (vv. 21, 23, 29)

7. What emotion motivated the last slave and how did it affect the outcome and his relationship with his master? (v. 25)

8. Who did the third slave blame for his lack of productivity? (vv. 24–25)

9. Discerning the principles in this parable, what is God's opinion of those who neglect to use the talents they are given? What does Jesus want His followers to learn from this parable?

10. How does James 2:14–26 help further explain or interpret this parable in terms of your daily walk with Christ?

Application

The "wicked, lazy slave" in verses 24–28 was fearful and risk adverse. Are you willing to take risks for the Kingdom of God?

A DEEPER LOOK

How does Scripture compare wisdom and foolishness?

Proverbs 3:35

Proverbs 10:8

Proverbs 10:14, 20–23

Proverbs 11:29

Proverbs 12:15

Proverbs 15:5

Proverbs 13:20

Proverbs 28:26

Proverbs 14:3, 29

STUDY FIVE
The Judgment

This is a scene of separation: those who are received, honored, and accepted by Jesus on the right; those who are rejected, cursed, and forever lost on the left. This is a picture of blessing and judgment from the righteous Judge, who called His children "sheep" and His enemies "goats" for good reason. Sheep are sensitive animals, inclined to follow a leader and congregate in close relationship. They are vulnerable to predators and loyal to their shepherd. Goats are rebellious. They tend to escape enclosures and live in isolation, leaving even their young exposed and alone. The "goats" in this passage failed to see opportunities to love others, while the "sheep" responded to need without hesitation. Both made heart-directed decisions with very different results. Judas made a choice in his heart about Jesus long ago, and here we see that seed take root and grow. No doubt Judas would have placed himself with the sheep, but Jesus knew Judas had moved into Satan's fold.

Matthew 25:31–46
"**31** 'But when the Son of Man comes in His glory, and all the angels with Him,
then He will sit on His glorious throne. **32** All the nations will be gathered before
Him; and He will separate them from one another, as the shepherd separates the
sheep from the goats; **33** and He will put the sheep on His right, and the goats
on the left.
34 'Then the King will say to those on His right, 'Come, you who are blessed
of My Father, inherit the kingdom prepared for you from the foundation of the
world. **35** For I was hungry, and you gave Me something to eat; I was thirsty,
and you gave Me something to drink; I was a stranger, and you invited Me in;
36 naked, and you clothed Me; I was sick, and you visited Me; I was in prison,
and you came to Me.' **37** Then the righteous will answer Him, 'Lord, when did
we see You hungry, and feed You, or thirsty, and give You something to drink?
38 And when did we see You a stranger, and invite You in, or naked, and clothe
You? **39** When did we see You sick, or in prison, and come to You?' **40** The King
will answer and say to them, 'Truly I say to you, to the extent that you did it to

one of these brothers of Mine, even the least of them, you did it to Me.'
41 'Then He will also say to those on His left, 'Depart from Me, accursed
ones, into the eternal fire which has been prepared for the devil and his angels;
42 for I was hungry, and you gave Me nothing to eat; I was thirsty, and you gave
Me nothing to drink; 43 I was a stranger, and you did not invite Me in; naked,
and you did not clothe Me; sick, and in prison, and you did not visit Me.' 44 Then
they themselves also will answer, 'Lord, when did we see You hungry, or thirsty, or
a stranger, or naked, or sick, or in prison, and did not take care of You?' 45 Then
He will answer them, 'Truly I say to you, to the extent that you did not do it
to one of the least of these, you did not do it to Me.' 46 These will go away into
eternal punishment, but the righteous into eternal life.'"

Luke 21:37–22:6

"37 Now during the day He was teaching in the temple, but at evening He would
go out and spend the night on the mount that is called Olivet. 38 And all the
people would get up early in the morning to come to Him in the temple to listen
to Him.

1 Now the Feast of Unleavened Bread, which is called the Passover, was approaching. 2 The chief priests and the scribes were seeking how they might put Him to
death; for they were afraid of the people.
3 And Satan entered into Judas who was called Iscariot, belonging to the
number of the twelve. 4 And he went away and discussed with the chief priests
and officers how he might betray Him to them. 5 They were glad and agreed to
give him money. 6 So he consented, and began seeking a good opportunity to
betray Him to them apart from the crowd."

1. What future event is taking place in verses 31–34?

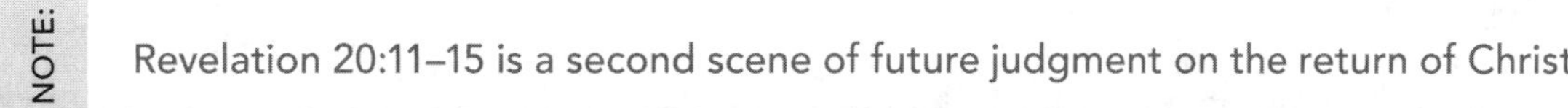

2. In what way is this a picture of Jesus as Judge? (vv. 34–40) How does He judge the "sheep" and the "goats?" (v. 46)

3. Define the word *judge*—noun and verb. Now use a thesaurus and look up synonyms for judge. What do you learn about the person and the act? How does this help you understand Jesus as Judge?

4. What actions did Jesus judge in this scene?

5. How does Jesus exalt our demonstrations of compassion to others? (v. 40) How does that spur you on to love and good deeds?

6. Contrast the words of Jesus to the sheep (vv. 34, 46) and the goats (vv. 41, 46). What is their identity? What is their destiny?

7. How does Scripture explain the cause/effect relationship of salvation and good works? See Galatians 5:22–23, Ephesians 2:8–9, Colossians 2:6–7, and 1 John 4:19.

8. How does Luke 21:37–38 describe "a day in the life" of Jesus at this point in His ministry?

9. What time of year does Luke tell us it is in Luke 22:1? What were the religious leaders doing at this time and why? (v. 2)

10. What happens in Luke 22:3 to indicate this was a battle/conspiracy beyond mere human conflict?

11. How was Judas Iscariot connected to the death of Jesus? (vv. 3, 6; see also Matthew 26:14–16)

NOTE:

30 pieces of silver was the price for a wounded slave (see Exodus 21:32)

12. What does Scripture tell us was Jesus' understanding of Judas and the Jews' motives and desires? See John 6:70 and John 8:44.

13. What were the religious leaders glad about in Luke 22:5?

Application

Have you ever been betrayed by a friend? Based on Matthew 5:44, what should your response be to betrayal? Have you ever betrayed a friend? What steps from Matthew 5:23–24 must you take to bring about healing and reconciliation? Read Psalms 55:12–14 for fresh insight into the pain of betrayal.

A DEEPER LOOK

How does Psalms 7 describe God as Judge? How does Scripture describe Jesus' authority to judge?

John 5:22, 27, 30

Romans 2:16

Acts 10: 38–42

1 Corinthians 4:5

Acts 17: 30–31

WRAPPING UP

The prophet Micah gives another comforting picture of Jesus as Judge and the response His judgment elicits on a grand scale. Micah 4:3 says, "*And He will judge between many peoples And render decisions for mighty, distant nations. Then they will hammer their swords into plowshares And their spears into pruning hooks; Nation will not lift up sword against nation, And never again will they train for war.*"

This verse tells us that when Jesus returns to judge "many peoples" and "strong nations," the response is peace. No more swords or spears or weapons of war. Instead, the perfect, righteous Judge—Jesus—inspires rest on every side. There will be no need for treaties or détente, no United Nations or Geneva Conventions. All will respond with soft hearts and firm resolve, transforming their defenses into tools that cultivate the gift of life.

Let this future truth direct your response to our strong and gracious Judge. Every decision Jesus makes is right and good—now and forever—and we can trust Him to provide peace in our hearts today and in our world when He returns.

Notes

~ Map of Passion Week ~

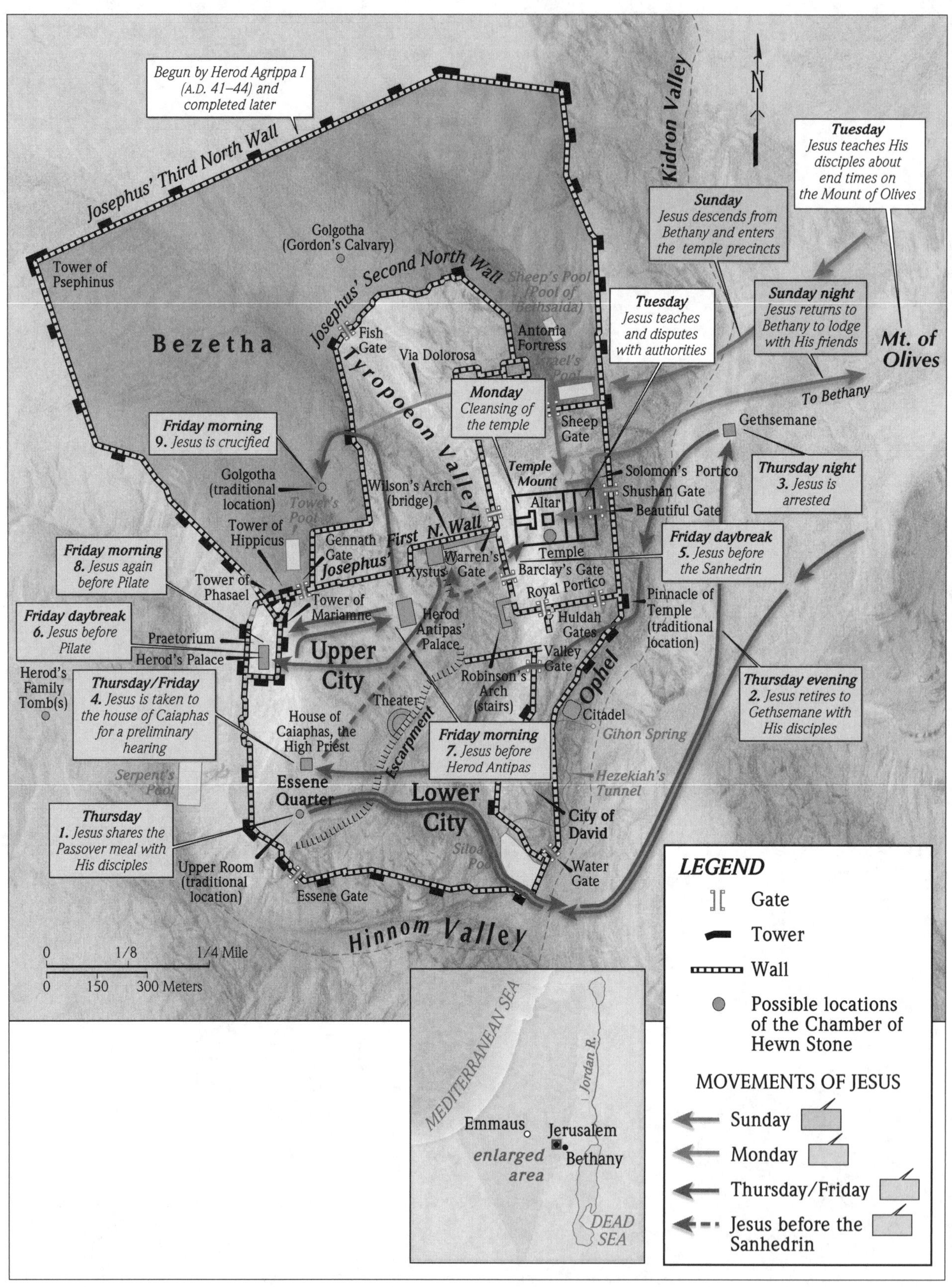

JESUS, THE WAY, THE TRUTH, AND THE LIFE

"Jesus said to him, 'I am the way, and the truth, and the life; no one comes to the Father but through Me.'"
JOHN 14:6

The sun was setting, and the meal had been prepared. Jesus and His friends gathered around a table and began to take part in the most significant unfolding of events in the history of the world.

What a moment that must have been: the All-Knowing One gazed into the eyes and hearts of each of His followers, and saw everything that was to come in the hours—and centuries—ahead. The disciples, some still scrambling for power, others blinded by pride, were unaware they were in the presence of the final Passover Lamb.

And the one who had become a servant of Satan was sitting among them like a shadow, waiting for night to fall.

Jesus knew the hour had come, and He spent every last minute teaching truth: Serve others like a slave. Abide in Me and bear fruit. Lay down your life. Take heart and have courage. Trust in the Helper to come.

In "a little while," Jesus said, He would leave, and the disciples panicked: *Where are you going and how can we get there?,* they asked. The Savior patiently assured these men that they already knew where to go because He was, in fact, the Way.

Jesus died to bring us into an immediate and eternal relationship with our heavenly Father. As Jesus said, He is the only Way to the only kind of Life worth living. He is perfect Truth because He fulfilled every letter of the Law the Jews had studied since childhood. And He is I AM—God Himself, the Holy One, infinitely powerful and graciously humble, condescending to His creation and giving life to all who believe.

STUDY ONE
The Lord's Supper

It was unheard of. A superior washing the feet of his servants? Peter verbalized their collective shock, acknowledging Jesus as "Lord" and Master over everyone in the room, and therefore, above such a menial act. Yet even in these final hours, Jesus continued on His path of humility, placing their spiritual poverty above His majesty. Jesus commended this posture to His followers, exhorting them to loving service in His name. As the bread and cup were passed around the table, Jesus instructed the disciples to regularly remember the ultimate sacrifice the elements symbolized. His body and blood would be broken and poured out. This meal was a prelude and memorial to the suffering He would endure and the gift He would freely give.

Luke 22:7–16
“7 Then came the first day of Unleavened Bread on which the Passover lamb had
to be sacrificed. 8 And Jesus sent Peter and John, saying, ‘Go and prepare the Passover for us, so that we may eat it.’ 9 They said to Him, ‘Where do You want us to
prepare it?’ 10 And He said to them, ‘When you have entered the city, a man will
meet you carrying a pitcher of water; follow him into the house that he enters.
11 And you shall say to the owner of the house, ‘The Teacher says to you, ‘Where
is the guest room in which I may eat the Passover with My disciples?’ 12 And he
will show you a large, furnished upper room; prepare it there.’ 13 And they left
and found everything just as He had told them; and they prepared the Passover.

14 When the hour had come, He reclined at the table, and the apostles with Him.
15 And He said to them, ‘I have earnestly desired to eat this Passover with you
before I suffer; 16 for I say to you, I shall never again eat it until it is fulfilled in
the kingdom of God.’”

John 13:1–20
“ Now before the Feast of the Passover, Jesus knowing that His hour had come
that He would depart out of this world to the Father, having loved His own who
were in the world, He loved them to the end. 2 During supper, the devil having
already put into the heart of Judas Iscariot, the son of Simon, to betray Him,
3 Jesus, knowing that the Father had given all things into His hands, and that He
had come forth from God and was going back to God, 4 got up from supper, and
laid aside His garments; and taking a towel, He girded Himself.

5 Then He poured water into the basin, and began to wash the disciples’ feet and
to wipe them with the towel with which He was girded. 6 So He came to Simon
Peter. He said to Him, ‘Lord, do You wash my feet?’ 7 Jesus answered and said
to him, ‘What I do you do not realize now, but you will understand hereafter.’
8 Peter said to Him, ‘Never shall You wash my feet!’ Jesus answered him, ‘If I do
not wash you, you have no part with Me.’ 9 Simon Peter said to Him, ‘Lord, then
wash not only my feet, but also my hands and my head.’ 10 Jesus said to him, ‘He
who has bathed needs only to wash his feet, but is completely clean; and you are
clean, but not all of you.’ 11 For He knew the one who was betraying Him; for
this reason He said, ‘Not all of you are clean.’

12 So when He had washed their feet, and taken His garments and reclined at
the table again, He said to them, ‘Do you know what I have done to you? 13 You
call Me Teacher and Lord; and you are right, for so I am. 14 If I then, the Lord
and the Teacher, washed your feet, you also ought to wash one another’s feet.
15 For I gave you an example that you also should do as I did to you. 16 Truly,
truly, I say to you, a slave is not greater than his master, nor is one who is sent
greater than the one who sent him. 17 If you know these things, you are blessed if
you do them. 18 I do not speak of all of you. I know the ones I have chosen; but
it is that the Scripture may be fulfilled, ‘He who eats My bread has lifted up his

heel against Me.' **19** From now on I am telling you before it comes to pass, so that
when it does occur, you may believe that I am He. **20** Truly, truly, I say to you,
he who receives whomever I send receives Me; and he who receives Me receives
Him who sent Me.'"

Luke 22:17–23

"**17** And when He had taken a cup and given thanks, He said, 'Take this and
share it among yourselves; **18** for I say to you, I will not drink of the fruit of the
vine from now on until the kingdom of God comes.' **19** And when He had taken
some bread and given thanks, He broke it and gave it to them, saying, 'This is
My body which is given for you; do this in remembrance of Me.' **20** And in the
same way He took the cup after they had eaten, saying, 'This cup which is poured
out for you is the new covenant in My blood. **21** But behold, the hand of the one
betraying Me is with Mine on the table. **22** For indeed, the Son of Man is going
as it has been determined; but woe to that man by whom He is betrayed!' **23** And
they began to discuss among themselves which one of them it might be who was
going to do this thing."

1. Read Exodus 12 for details of this feast mentioned by Luke. With the Passover serving as the backdrop of this passage, what is significant about the explanation in Luke 22:7?

2. How does Luke 22:8–13 demonstrate Jesus' omniscience?

3. Imagine Jesus in that moment, knowing what He knows about "the hour" that had come. Describe the emotional experience Jesus might have had, a man sitting at a table with His dear friends. (vv. 14–16, John 13:1–2)

4. What are the future events Jesus was aware of in John 13:1–3? With that in mind, what does Jesus do in verses 4–5? What is surprising about that?

5. What was Jesus communicating in washing His disciples' feet? Did Jesus wash Judas' feet? (see John 13:21–30)

6. When did Jesus say the disciples would understand His actions? (John 13:7)

7. What example did Jesus encourage His disciples to replicate? (see Philippians 2:1–11)

8. What promise did Jesus make in Luke 22:17–18? (see Revelation 19:6–9)

9. How is the Lord's Supper established in this scene and why? (vv. Luke 22:19–20) What does the bread symbolize? What does the cup symbolize?

10. What new covenant was Jesus referring to in Luke 22:20? (Jeremiah 31:31–34, Hebrews 9:11–15)

11. Why are we commanded to remember what Jesus did for us? (see 1 Corinthians 11:26, Ephesians 2: 12–14)

12. With His promise of sacrifice still hanging in the air, what startling announcement does Jesus make in Luke 22:21–22?

Application

Think on a favorite meal or occasion that you've gathered around the table with the people you love most. What emotions come to mind when you personalize and then reflect on this scene in Scripture?

A DEEPER LOOK

Based on the Scriptures below, why do you think it wasn't obvious to the disciples who would betray Jesus? What does this say about our ability to hide our true motives from God?

1 Samuel 16:7

Isaiah 29:13, 15

Proverbs 26:24–26

2 Corinthians 11:13–15

STUDY TWO
Jesus Comforts His Disciples

The mood in the room moved from feasting with friends to growing tension over an uncertain future. Arguments among the disciples signaled the unrest and, into their distraction, Jesus spoke a warning about a demand from the demonic realm. Known as "the Rock," Peter affirmed his unwavering loyalty. Jesus prophesied that failure was certain, but restoration would follow. The unknowns caused angst that required a special comfort from the Savior, who painted a picture of heavenly dwellings and a glorious future return. Jesus also promised a Helper—the Spirit of truth who would teach their minds and guide their hearts. Jesus was leaving, but in His place He would give peace. His words left their heads spinning, but these truths would eventually become the building blocks of a faith that could withstand any test.

Luke 22:24–38

"**24** And there arose also a dispute among them as to which one of them was
regarded to be greatest. **25** And He said to them, 'The kings of the Gentiles lord
it over them; and those who have authority over them are called 'Benefactors.'
26 But it is not this way with you, but the one who is the greatest among you must
become like the youngest, and the leader like the servant. **27** For who is greater,
the one who reclines at the table or the one who serves? Is it not the one who
reclines at the table? But I am among you as the one who serves.

28 'You are those who have stood by Me in My trials; **29** and just as My Father
has granted Me a kingdom, I grant you **30** that you may eat and drink at My table
in My kingdom, and you will sit on thrones judging the twelve tribes of Israel.

31 'Simon, Simon, behold, Satan has demanded permission to sift you like
wheat; **32** but I have prayed for you, that your faith may not fail; and you, when
once you have turned again, strengthen your brothers.' **33** But he said to Him,
'Lord, with You I am ready to go both to prison and to death!' **34** And He said,
'I say to you, Peter, the rooster will not crow today until you have denied three
times that you know Me.'

35 And He said to them, 'When I sent you out without money belt and bag
and sandals, you did not lack anything, did you?' They said, 'No, nothing.' **36** And

He said to them, 'But now, whoever has a money belt is to take it along, likewise also a bag, and whoever has no sword is to sell his coat and buy one. 37 For I tell you that this which is written must be fulfilled in Me, 'And He was numbered with transgressors'; for that which refers to Me has its fulfillment.' 38 They said, 'Lord, look, here are two swords.' And He said to them, 'It is enough.'"

John 14:1–31

"'Do not let your heart be troubled; believe in God, believe also in Me. 2 In My Father's house are many dwelling places; if it were not so, I would have told you; for I go to prepare a place for you. 3 If I go and prepare a place for you, I will come again and receive you to Myself, that where I am, there you may be also. 4 And you know the way where I am going.' 5 Thomas said to Him, 'Lord, we do not know where You are going, how do we know the way?' 6 Jesus said to him, 'I am the way, and the truth, and the life; no one comes to the Father but through Me.

7 If you had known Me, you would have known My Father also; from now on you know Him, and have seen Him.' 8 Philip said to Him, 'Lord, show us the Father, and it is enough for us.' 9 Jesus said to him, 'Have I been so long with you, and yet you have not come to know Me, Philip? He who has seen Me has seen the Father; how can you say, 'Show us the Father'? 10 Do you not believe that I am in the Father, and the Father is in Me? The words that I say to you I do not speak on My own initiative, but the Father abiding in Me does His works. 11 Believe Me that I am in the Father and the Father is in Me; otherwise believe because of the works themselves. 12 Truly, truly, I say to you, he who believes in Me, the works that I do, he will do also; and greater works than these he will do; because I go to the Father. 13 Whatever you ask in My name, that will I do, so that the Father may be glorified in the Son. 14 If you ask Me anything in My name, I will do it.

15 'If you love Me, you will keep My commandments.

16 'I will ask the Father, and He will give you another Helper, that He may be with you forever; 17 that is the Spirit of truth, whom the world cannot receive, because it does not see Him or know Him, but you know Him because He abides with you and will be in you.

18 'I will not leave you as orphans; I will come to you. 19 After a little while the world will no longer see Me, but you will see Me; because I live, you will live also. 20 In that day you will know that I am in My Father, and you in Me, and I in you. 21 He who has My commandments and keeps them is the one who loves Me; and he who loves Me will be loved by My Father, and I will love him and will disclose Myself to him.' 22 Judas (not Iscariot) said to Him, 'Lord, what then has happened that You are going to disclose Yourself to us and not to the world?' 23 Jesus answered and said to him, 'If anyone loves Me, he will keep My word; and My Father will love him, and We will come to him and make Our abode with him. 24 He who does not love Me does not keep My words; and the word which you hear is not Mine, but the Father's who sent Me.

25 'These things I have spoken to you while abiding with you. 26 But the Helper, the Holy Spirit, whom the Father will send in My name, He will teach you all things, and bring to your remembrance all that I said to you. 27 Peace I leave with you; My peace I give to you; not as the world gives do I give to you. Do not let your heart be troubled, nor let it be fearful. 28 You heard that I said to

you, 'I go away, and I will come to you.' If you loved Me, you would have rejoiced
because I go to the Father, for the Father is greater than I. 29 Now I have told you
before it happens, so that when it happens, you may believe. 30 I will not speak
much more with you, for the ruler of the world is coming, and he has nothing in
Me; 31 but so that the world may know that I love the Father, I do exactly as the
Father commanded Me. Get up, let us go from here."

1. The discussion from Luke 22:23 in Study One took a turn in verse 24. What are the disciples discussing now?

2. What contrast does Jesus make in verses 25–27 to define greatness for the disciples?

3. What does Jesus promise the disciples in verses 28–30? What similar promise does He make to us in 2 Timothy 2:11–13?

4. Jesus moves from speaking to all twelve disciples to one: Peter. What did Satan demand in verse 31? And how did Jesus respond? (v. 32) What was Jesus' prayer? What was His prediction? (v. 34)

5. How do Peter's own words in 1 Peter 5:10 provide evidence that Jesus' request was answered?

6. Just as Jesus' disciples were being drawn into the ultimate spiritual battle, so our life with Christ should cause us to be on the defense against the enemy. How does Ephesians 6:10–18 say we are to fight as followers of Jesus?

7. What comfort does Jesus give His disciples in John 14:1–4?

8. What does Jesus proclaim about Himself in verse 6? What are the implications for our presence in heaven? What is exclusive and inclusive about Jesus' claim?

9. How do the following verses reinforce Jesus' claim in verse 9? See 2 Corinthians 4:4, Colossians 1:15, and Hebrews 1:1–4.

10. How does Jesus connect love and obedience? (vv. 15, 21, 23–24, 31) What does that tell us our motive for following/obeying Jesus should be?

11. What promises does Jesus make to His followers in verses 12 and 16? Read Acts 2:41–43, 3:6–8, 12:24, and 19:20 as illustrations.

12. Read verses 12–14 considering the context of "greater works" and prayer. What would a prayer sound like that was formed and instructed based on verses 12–14? (see Matthew 6:10)

13. Who is "the Helper?" What do we learn about His character and purpose in this passage? (vv. 17, 26)

Application

The disciples were in the presence of Jesus in this passage, and yet pride and self-exaltation still consumed their hearts. What does this tell us about sin? (Genesis 4:7, Hebrews 12:1, 1 Peter 5:8–9)

A DEEPER LOOK

Read Revelation 21:1–22:5 and write your observations about heaven. How do you respond to what you learn?

STUDY THREE
The True Vine

A gentle Gardener. A strong, healthy Vine. And growing branches among lifeless ones, all in need of pruning so that more fruit would emerge. This is the final "I am" statement of Jesus, where He offered a vine as an image of relationship and fruitfulness in Christ. In this teaching, Jesus gave a command that is at once simple and complex: *abide*. Jesus promised to abide in His children, but the fruit of that gift will never manifest if we do not do the same. Separation brings barrenness; clinging to Him yields life. *Abide* is a simple word, but what does it look like? He told the disciples if they "keep My commandments," they "will abide in My love." Later in life, John said this another way: *"the one who says he abides in Him ought himself to walk in the same manner as He walked."* (1 John 2:6) Keeping His commandments isn't about rules or self-denial. Jesus wants our lives to mirror Him, and love is the best reflection.

John 15:1–27

"'I am the true vine, and My Father is the vinedresser. 2 Every branch in Me that
does not bear fruit, He takes away; and every branch that bears fruit, He prunes it
so that it may bear more fruit. 3 You are already clean because of the word which I
have spoken to you. 4 Abide in Me, and I in you. As the branch cannot bear fruit
of itself unless it abides in the vine, so neither can you unless you abide in Me. 5 I
am the vine, you are the branches; he who abides in Me and I in him, he bears
much fruit, for apart from Me you can do nothing. 6 If anyone does not abide
in Me, he is thrown away as a branch and dries up; and they gather them, and
cast them into the fire and they are burned. 7 If you abide in Me, and My words
abide in you, ask whatever you wish, and it will be done for you. 8 My Father is
glorified by this, that you bear much fruit, and *so* prove to be My disciples. 9 Just
as the Father has loved Me, I have also loved you; abide in My love. 10 If you keep
My commandments, you will abide in My love; just as I have kept My Father's
commandments and abide in His love. 11 These things I have spoken to you so
that My joy may be in you, and that your joy may be made full.

12 'This is My commandment, that you love one another, just as I have loved you.
13 Greater love has no one than this, that one lay down his life for his friends.
14 You are My friends if you do what I command you. 15 No longer do I call you
slaves, for the slave does not know what his master is doing; but I have called
you friends, for all things that I have heard from My Father I have made known
to you. 16 You did not choose Me but I chose you, and appointed you that you
would go and bear fruit, and that your fruit would remain, so that whatever you
ask of the Father in My name He may give to you. 17 This I command you, that
you love one another.

18 'If the world hates you, you know that it has hated Me before it hated you. 19 If
you were of the world, the world would love its own; but because you are not of
the world, but I chose you out of the world, because of this the world hates you.
20 Remember the word that I said to you, 'A slave is not greater than his master.'
If they persecuted Me, they will also persecute you; if they kept My word, they
will keep yours also. 21 But all these things they will do to you for My name's sake,
because they do not know the One who sent Me. 22 If I had not come and spoken

to them, they would not have sin, but now they have no excuse for their sin.
23 He who hates Me hates My Father also. 24 If I had not done among them the
works which no one else did, they would not have sin; but now they have both
seen and hated Me and My Father as well. 25 But they have done this to fulfill the
word that is written in their Law, 'They hated Me without a cause.'
26 'When the Helper comes, whom I will send to you from the Father, that is
the Spirit of truth who proceeds from the Father, He will testify about Me, 27 and
you will testify also, because you have been with Me from the beginning."

1. What does Jesus call Himself in verse 1? What does He call His Father? What does He call His followers in verses 2 and 5?

2. What does the Vinedresser or Gardener do? (v. 2) What are we as His disciples—the branches—called to do? (v. 4) How is our fruitfulness made possible? (v. 3)

3. How does Jesus say we glorify God? (v. 8)

4. What does verse 11 reveal is Jesus' ultimate hope for His children/disciples?

5. How does Jesus say His disciples are supposed to relate to one another? (vv. 12, 17)

6. What characteristics do we see of Jesus' love in verses 13–16?

7. How does Jesus make a distinction between slaves and friends in verse 15? What would Jesus call you?

8. What does Jesus say He has done for His friends in verse 16 and why?

9. How does Jesus set expectations for the disciples and their relationship with the world? (vv. 18–20)

10. What does Jesus say is the reason for the opposition that will come against them? (v. 21)

11. How are those who reject Jesus (and thus, God) without excuse? (vv. 22–24) See also Romans 1:18–23.

12. How did those who rejected Jesus fulfill His word? (v. 25) See Psalms 35:19 and 69:4.

13. Who are the members of the Trinity? Where do you see the Trinity in verse 26?

Application

What are some of the ways God has "pruned" you to make your life more fruitful for Him? What might need to be pruned now?

STUDY FOUR
The Holy Spirit Promised

The disciples felt overwhelmed by the promises and predictions Jesus had made. The world would hate them—even want to kill them. They would be rejected by their community and, to top it all off, Jesus was leaving. This was layer upon layer of discouraging news, so it is no surprise that their hearts were filled with sorrow. It was mysterious and might have even seemed inappropriate for Jesus to say it was better for Him to leave than stay. In the Old Testament, the Holy Spirit would come and go based on the sovereignty of

God (Numbers 11:25, Judges 14:6, 1 Samuel 10:10, Psalms 51:11). But here, Jesus promised the Spirit would take up permanent residence in the hearts of His children. And as a result, Scripture calls us "sealed." (Ephesians 4:30) The last things Jesus promised here were trouble and triumph. Jesus' words were designed to prepare His followers then, and believers still today can take heart that He has overcome.

John 16:1–33
"'These things I have spoken to you so that you may be kept from stumbling.
2 They will make you outcasts from the synagogue, but an hour is coming for
everyone who kills you to think that he is offering service to God. 3 These things
they will do because they have not known the Father or Me. 4 But these things
I have spoken to you, so that when their hour comes, you may remember that I
told you of them. These things I did not say to you at the beginning, because I
was with you.

5 'But now I am going to Him who sent Me; and none of you asks Me, 'Where
are You going?' 6 But because I have said these things to you, sorrow has filled
your heart. 7 But I tell you the truth, it is to your advantage that I go away; for if
I do not go away, the Helper will not come to you; but if I go, I will send Him
to you. 8 And He, when He comes, will convict the world concerning sin and
righteousness and judgment; 9 concerning sin, because they do not believe in Me;
10 and concerning righteousness, because I go to the Father and you no longer see
Me; 11 and concerning judgment, because the ruler of this world has been judged.
12 'I have many more things to say to you, but you cannot bear them now.
13 But when He, the Spirit of truth, comes, He will guide you into all the truth;
for He will not speak on His own initiative, but whatever He hears, He will
speak; and He will disclose to you what is to come. 14 He will glorify Me, for He
will take of Mine and will disclose it to you. 15 All things that the Father has are
Mine; therefore I said that He takes of Mine and will disclose it to you.

16 'A little while, and you will no longer see Me; and again a little while, and you
will see Me." 17 Some of His disciples then said to one another, 'What is this thing
He is telling us, 'A little while, and you will not see Me; and again a little while,
and you will see Me'; and, 'because I go to the Father'?' 18 So they were saying,
'What is this that He says, 'A little while'? We do not know what He is talking
about.' 19 Jesus knew that they wished to question Him, and He said to them,
'Are you deliberating together about this, that I said, 'A little while, and you will
not see Me, and again a little while, and you will see Me'? 20 Truly, truly, I say to
you, that you will weep and lament, but the world will rejoice; you will grieve,
but your grief will be turned into joy. 21 Whenever a woman is in labor she has
pain, because her hour has come; but when she gives birth to the child, she no
longer remembers the anguish because of the joy that a child has been born into
the world. 22 Therefore you too have grief now; but I will see you again, and your
heart will rejoice, and no one will take your joy away from you.

23 'In that day you will not question Me about anything. Truly, truly, I say to you,
if you ask the Father for anything in My name, He will give it to you. 24 Until
now you have asked for nothing in My name; ask and you will receive, so that
your joy may be made full.

25 'These things I have spoken to you in figurative language; an hour is coming
when I will no longer speak to you in figurative language, but will tell you plainly
of the Father. 26 In that day you will ask in My name, and I do not say to you that
I will request of the Father on your behalf; 27 for the Father Himself loves you,
because you have loved Me and have believed that I came forth from the Father.
28 I came forth from the Father and have come into the world; I am leaving the
world again and going to the Father.'

29 His disciples said, 'Lo, now You are speaking plainly and are not using a
figure of speech. 30 Now we know that You know all things, and have no need
for anyone to question You; by this we believe that You came from God.' 31 Jesus
answered them, 'Do you now believe? 32 Behold, an hour is coming, and has
already come, for you to be scattered, each to his own home, and to leave Me
alone; and yet I am not alone, because the Father is with Me. 33 These things I
have spoken to you, so that in Me you may have peace. In the world you have
tribulation, but take courage; I have overcome the world.'"

1. What did Jesus say was the purpose of His exhortation to His disciples? What predictions did Jesus make? How did Jesus say His exhortation would prepare the disciples for what's to come? (vv. 1–4)

2. What do we learn about the Holy Spirit and His role in verses 5–15—in the world and in His children?

3. What encouragement did Jesus offer the disciples in verse 7? Why is this better than the presence of Jesus? (see Romans 8:9, Galatians 4:6–7, Ephesians 4:30, and Philippians 2:13)

4. Read Romans 15:4. How does verse 13 connect with Paul's words for the disciples? For us?

5. With the benefit of hindsight, what are the two "little whiles" Jesus is talking about in verse 16?

6. What does Jesus promise will someday transform the sorrow and grief the disciples feel? (vv. 20, 22) How does Jesus illustrate this change? (v. 21)

7. Read Zechariah 13:7. How does Jesus predict the fulfillment of this prophecy in verse 32? Who is the One who will stand with Jesus in His "hour?"

8. How does Jesus offer comfort in advance of the need to His disciples in verse 33?

Application

Where do you need to "take heart" today? (v. 33) Note the forward-thinking, future-focused language of Jesus—in His verbs, illustrations, and perspective. How can looking toward "that day" help provide joy for this day? Or every day?

A DEEPER LOOK

What does Scripture say about standing firm in your faith (how, why, and when is it important)?

Joshua 23:6

Hebrews 6:11–12

Ephesians 6:11

1 Timothy 4:13–16

Philippians 1:27

STUDY FIVE
The High Priestly Prayer

The Lord has given us a great gift in preserving the longest prayer of Jesus in the Gospels. It is approximately 650 words, but the sanctifying work and eternal blessings His petitions continue to accomplish are immeasurable. John's timeline places this prayer before the Garden of Gethsemane, and Scripture seems to indicate Jesus spoke to His Father in the presence of His disciples. This is one more act of grace by the Suffering Servant. Jesus knew He was hours from enduring great anguish on our behalf. Yet He prayed to God in the hearing of these confused and trembling men, asking Him to keep them, unite them, and fill them with joy. His prayer was instructive. He wanted the disciples to remember that what He was about to do was bring glory to the Son and the one true God. His prayer also imparted responsibility to these men: the world would come to salvation through their faithful work in Jesus' name. This gave them vision and purpose to carry on. Now, thousands of years later, by their obedience and the work of the Holy Spirit, we stand as one in Christ.

John 17:1–26

"Jesus spoke these things; and lifting up His eyes to heaven, He said, 'Father, the
hour has come; glorify Your Son, that the Son may glorify You, 2 even as You
gave Him authority over all flesh, that to all whom You have given Him, He
may give eternal life. 3 This is eternal life, that they may know You, the only true
God, and Jesus Christ whom You have sent. 4 I glorified You on the earth, having
accomplished the work which You have given Me to do. 5 Now, Father, glorify Me
together with Yourself, with the glory which I had with You before the world was.
6 'I have manifested Your name to the men whom You gave Me out of the
world; they were Yours and You gave them to Me, and they have kept Your word.
7 Now they have come to know that everything You have given Me is from You;
8 for the words which You gave Me I have given to them; and they received them
and truly understood that I came forth from You, and they believed that You sent
Me. 9 I ask on their behalf; I do not ask on behalf of the world, but of those whom
You have given Me; for they are Yours; 10 and all things that are Mine are Yours,
and Yours are Mine; and I have been glorified in them. 11 I am no longer in the
world; and yet they themselves are in the world, and I come to You. Holy Father,
keep them in Your name, the name which You have given Me, that they may be
one even as We are. 12 While I was with them, I was keeping them in Your name
which You have given Me; and I guarded them and not one of them perished but
the son of perdition, so that the Scripture would be fulfilled.

13 But now I come to You; and these things I speak in the world so that they may
have My joy made full in themselves. 14 I have given them Your word; and the
world has hated them, because they are not of the world, even as I am not of the
world. 15 I do not ask You to take them out of the world, but to keep them from
the evil one. 16 They are not of the world, even as I am not of the world. 17 Sanctify them in the truth; Your word is truth. 18 As You sent Me into the world, I
also have sent them into the world. 19 For their sakes I sanctify Myself, that they
themselves also may be sanctified in truth.
20 'I do not ask on behalf of these alone, but for those also who believe in Me
through their word; 21 that they may all be one; even as You, Father, are in Me
and I in You, that they also may be in Us, so that the world may believe that You
sent Me.

22 The glory which You have given Me I have given to them, that they may be
one, just as We are one; 23 I in them and You in Me, that they may be perfected
in unity, so that the world may know that You sent Me, and loved them, even as
You have loved Me. 24 Father, I desire that they also, whom You have given Me,
be with Me where I am, so that they may see My glory which You have given Me,
for You loved Me before the foundation of the world.

25 'O righteous Father, although the world has not known You, yet I have
known You; and these have known that You sent Me; 26 and I have made Your
name known to them, and will make it known, so that the love with which You
loved Me may be in them, and I in them.'"

1. Jesus was looking toward the cross in John 17. What can you discern about His mood and heart as He speaks to His Father?

2. In what ways are the works of God the Father and Jesus the Son intertwined according to verses 1–5?

3. How does Jesus pray for Himself in verses 1–5?

4. Where do you see the sovereignty of God in verses 1–5?

5. Who does Jesus pray for in verses 6–12?

6. What did Jesus ask God for in His prayer? When given below, what is the purpose for these practices?

   Verses 11, 15–16:

   Verse 13:

Verses 17–19:

Verses 20–23:

Verse 24:

Verse 26:

7. How do Jesus' words in verse 15 speak to our desire or inclination to withdraw into a "holy huddle" away from the world we are called to love?

8. What language in Jesus' prayer reveals His equality with God?

9. How does Jesus' prayer for believers bring you joy?

10. How does Jesus conclude His prayer? (vv. 25–26)

11. Circle the "I" pronoun Jesus used in His prayer and the corresponding verbs. What work does Jesus say He has accomplished in verses 4, 6, 8, 12, 18, 22?

12. Use the dictionary in biblestudytools.com and look up the word *sanctification*. What does it mean? How has the truth of God's Word sanctified you? (v. 17)

Application

How do you respond to the truth that in the last hours of His earthly life, Jesus stopped and prayed for you? (v. 20)

A DEEPER LOOK

What does it mean to glorify God?

Psalms 34:3

1 Corinthians 10:31

Psalms 50:23

Philippians 2:11

Psalms 96:1–9

WRAPPING UP

Jesus showed Himself to be the Way, the Truth, and the Life through His actions, prayers, and sacrifice. The Holy Spirit imparts faith and assurance that His words about Himself are true, so there is no denying Christ's singular role in our eternal condition.

Sadly, the world often uses this declaration as a strike against Christianity. Claiming to know "*the* way" and "*the* truth" sounds exclusive, like a secret club with selective membership. It is more popular and easier to digest the idea that there are many roads to heaven, that the way is wide and all are welcome. And that is partly true: Jesus died for the sins of the world (John 3:16) and God *"desires all men to be saved and to come to the knowledge of the truth."* (1 Timothy 2:4) Exclusivity is the devil's lie, and it is a sinister roadblock on the way to the path of life.

We cannot waver from what we believe because Jesus *is* the only Way. Nor can we alter Scripture to help it go down easier because the Truth *is* often hard to hear. We must carry the message of life and hope just as Jesus did: in love and with joy.

Notes

~ Map of Passion Week ~

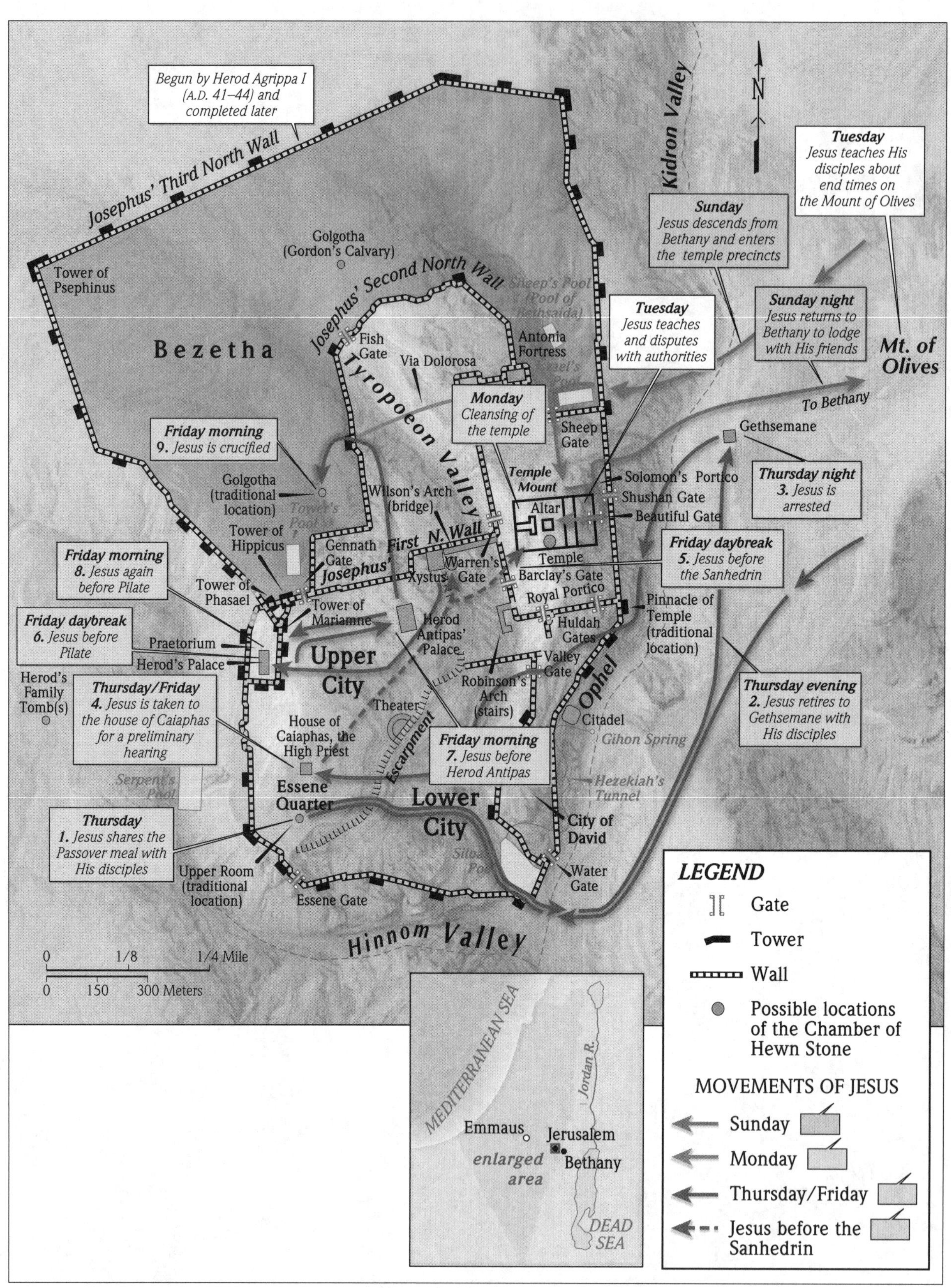

JESUS, SON OF MAN

"Then He came to the disciples and said to them, 'Are you still sleeping and resting? Behold, the hour is at hand and the Son of Man is being betrayed into the hands of sinners.'"
MATTHEW 26:45

The disciples were disoriented, weary from a long day and groggy after nodding off under an olive tree. Rubbing the sleep from their eyes, they realized they were no longer alone. One minute, Peter, James, and John were trying to stay awake while praying near Jesus in an ancient garden. Then suddenly, the darkness around them filled with men wielding swords and clubs, their torches illuminating hatred in their eyes.

Judas emerged from the crowd and kissed Jesus on the cheek, the warm greeting a betrayal in itself. Peter tried to fight, but once the disciples realized resistance was useless, they fled into the night. Jesus was alone.

The Roman and Jewish soldiers arrested Jesus, bound Him like a captive, and brought Him to the priests. Here, Jesus endured His first round of abuse as His human flesh and bones were battered by the guards. Next, the entire Jewish Council declared His very existence blasphemy. Their false grief and fists landed their offenses on the divine humanity of the Son of Man. And as dawn broke, a rooster crowed.

For hours Jesus was mocked, ridiculed, beaten, and shuffled between weak religious leaders and powerful Roman rulers searching for miracles and truth. Pilate wanted to appease the crowd and keep his hands clean, so he ordered the Savior severely flogged, not understanding that His wounds would heal.

To avoid a riot, Pilate set another prisoner free. The rabid crowd shouted their wicked indictment, written by Satan himself. Their cry—"Crucify Him!"—still echoes through the ages and into the depths of our souls. The dark demand was met as the Son of Man was nailed to a tree. The blood of Jesus was indeed on their hands, but He died so that it might be poured out over their hearts.

STUDY ONE
Jesus' Betrayal and Arrest

There probably wasn't even an hour between Peter's firm declaration of loyalty to Jesus and his first steps down the slope toward denial. Gathering His disciples in an olive grove, the Son of Man shared His very human grief with His closest friends and asked them to pray. But Peter slept through his chance to fortify himself for what was to come. Jesus petitioned His Father three times for "this cup to pass"—the cup that would taste like sorrow and sting like death—but the only answer was submission. Aligned in heart with His

Father's will, Jesus allowed the mob to seize Him. John named Peter as the one who sliced off the ear of a servant with his sword, his last act in defense of Jesus. Jesus reminded His friend that his sword was nothing compared to the power He possessed. But instead, to accomplish Scripture, the Shepherd chose suffering. And the sheep scattered.

Matthew 26:30–56

"30 After singing a hymn, they went out to the Mount of Olives.

31 Then Jesus said to them, 'You will all fall away because of Me this night, for it is written, 'I will strike down the shepherd, and the sheep of the flock shall be scattered.' 32 But after I have been raised, I will go ahead of you to Galilee.' 33 But Peter said to Him, 'Even though all may fall away because of You, I will never fall away.' 34 Jesus said to him, 'Truly I say to you that this very night, before a rooster crows, you will deny Me three times.' 35 Peter said to Him, 'Even if I have to die with You, I will not deny You.' All the disciples said the same thing too.

36 Then Jesus came with them to a place called Gethsemane, and said to His disciples, 'Sit here while I go over there and pray.' 37 And He took with Him Peter and the two sons of Zebedee, and began to be grieved and distressed. 38 Then He said to them, 'My soul is deeply grieved, to the point of death; remain here and keep watch with Me.'

39 And He went a little beyond them, and fell on His face and prayed, saying, 'My Father, if it is possible, let this cup pass from Me; yet not as I will, but as You will." 40 And He came to the disciples and found them sleeping, and said to Peter, 'So, you men could not keep watch with Me for one hour? 41 Keep watching and praying that you may not enter into temptation; the spirit is willing, but the flesh is weak.'

42 He went away again a second time and prayed, saying, 'My Father, if this cannot pass away unless I drink it, Your will be done.' 43 Again He came and found them sleeping, for their eyes were heavy. 44 And He left them again, and went away and prayed a third time, saying the same thing once more. 45 Then He came to the disciples and said to them, 'Are you still sleeping and resting? Behold, the hour is at hand and the Son of Man is being betrayed into the hands of sinners. 46 Get up, let us be going; behold, the one who betrays Me is at hand!'

47 While He was still speaking, behold, Judas, one of the twelve, came up accompanied by a large crowd with swords and clubs, who came from the chief priests and elders of the people. 48 Now he who was betraying Him gave them a sign, saying, 'Whomever I kiss, He is the one; seize Him.' 49 Immediately Judas went to Jesus and said, 'Hail, Rabbi!' and kissed Him. 50 And Jesus said to him, 'Friend, do what you have come for.' Then they came and laid hands on Jesus and seized Him.

51 And behold, one of those who were with Jesus reached and drew out his sword, and struck the slave of the high priest and cut off his ear. 52 Then Jesus said to him, 'Put your sword back into its place; for all those who take up the sword shall perish by the sword. 53 Or do you think that I cannot appeal to My Father, and He will at once put at My disposal more than twelve legions of angels? 54 How then will the Scriptures be fulfilled, which say that it must happen this way?'

[55] At that time Jesus said to the crowds, 'Have you come out with swords and
clubs to arrest Me as you would against a robber? Every day I used to sit in the
temple teaching and you did not seize Me. [56] But all this has taken place to fulfill
the Scriptures of the prophets.' Then all the disciples left Him and fled."

1. What did Jesus and the disciples do in verse 30?

2. Scholars believe Psalms 118 is the hymn Jesus and His disciples sang in verse 30. Read Psalms 118, with the context of the Last Supper and the events awaiting Jesus in mind. How does connecting the context of the scene give this psalm deeper meaning?

NOTE: The Jews also sang words from Psalms 118 when Jesus entered Jerusalem. Hosanna means "save us." (vv. 25–26)

3. What did Jesus predict and what hope did He promise in verses 31–32?

4. What evidence recorded here reveals Peter and the disciples underestimated and misunderstood what was about to take place? (vv. 33–35)

5. What did Jesus do with His disciples before His crucifixion? (v. 36) Who did He take with Him? (v. 37)

6. Jesus knew the end from the beginning. Yet we still see evidence of His human struggle in this scene. Write down the picture of the humanity of Jesus that Matthew records here.

7. Observe and record the details of Jesus' prayer to His Father. What did He ask? How many times did He ask it? What were the disciples doing?

8. How does Jesus' warning in verse 41 connect to verses 33–35?

9. Describe who is in the scene in verse 47. See John 18:1–6 for additional detail.

10. What does Jesus call Judas in verse 50? What was the sign of the betrayal (v.48)?

11. Jesus and the disciples had the same opportunity in the Garden (Hebrews 4:16), and they chose to spend their time differently. What did Jesus do in the garden? What did the disciples do in the garden? How might their actions affect their preparedness for what was to come?

12. How did the disciples respond in verse 51? (John 18:10) What did Jesus say and do? (Luke 22:51) What did Jesus say He could do? Why did He refrain? (vv. 53–54)

NOTE: Twelve legions can be up to 72,000 angels.

13. Judas is responsible for betraying Jesus to the religious leaders. How do verses 55–56 show us the extent or completeness of the betrayal and abandonment of Jesus?

14. How does Jesus demonstrate His sovereign control in this chaotic situation?

Application

In what ways do we underestimate spiritual battles and the power of Satan that is always at work against believers? How does confidence (or ignorance) make you vulnerable?

A DEEPER LOOK

Jesus alluded to a cup in His prayers. Read the passages below for background on this image. What did the cup represent? Why would Jesus want "this cup (to) pass from Me?"

Psalms 75:8

Habakkuk 2:16

Isaiah 51:17

Revelation 14:10

Jeremiah 25:15–29

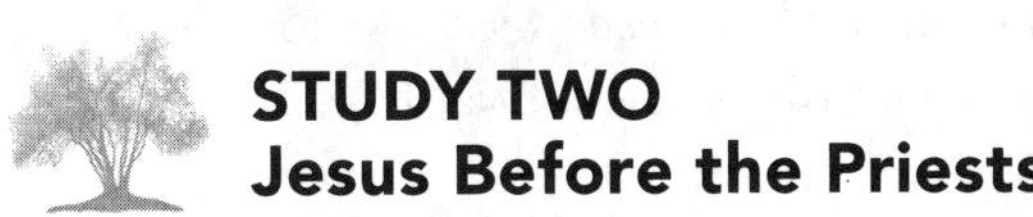

STUDY TWO
Jesus Before the Priests

As Jesus stood before the elder statesman of Israel, He was both directing and participating in the events as they unfolded. The Son of Man was also the Son of God, sovereign over every moment of the treacherous trial He had to bear. Outside, a charcoal fire served as the only light in the courtyard of the high priest, where Peter endured a trial of his own. A young slave girl questioned Peter's ties to Jesus, but Peter kept her in the dark. The high priest interrogated Jesus about His ministry, and Jesus pointed them to the light: His instruction that had been proclaimed in the open and the many witnesses to the truth. Jesus' transparency earned Him undeserved injury—the first of many blows. Then Annas sent Jesus on to Caiaphas and the Council, a brood of vipers waiting to strike His heel.

John 18:12–24

"**12** So the Roman cohort and the commander and the officers of the Jews, arrested
Jesus and bound Him, **13** and led Him to Annas first; for he was father-in-law of
Caiaphas, who was high priest that year. **14** Now Caiaphas was the one who had
advised the Jews that it was expedient for one man to die on behalf of the people.
15 Simon Peter was following Jesus, and so was another disciple. Now that

disciple was known to the high priest, and entered with Jesus into the court of the
high priest, **16** but Peter was standing at the door outside. So the other disciple,
who was known to the high priest, went out and spoke to the doorkeeper, and
brought Peter in. **17** Then the slave-girl who kept the door said to Peter, 'You are
not also one of this man's disciples, are you?' He said, 'I am not.' **18** Now the slaves
and the officers were standing there, having made a charcoal fire, for it was cold
and they were warming themselves; and Peter was also with them, standing and
warming himself.

19 The high priest then questioned Jesus about His disciples, and about His
teaching. **20** Jesus answered him, 'I have spoken openly to the world; I always
taught in synagogues and in the temple, where all the Jews come together; and
I spoke nothing in secret. **21** Why do you question Me? Question those who
have heard what I spoke to them; they know what I said.' **22** When He had said
this, one of the officers standing nearby struck Jesus, saying, 'Is that the way You
answer the high priest?' **23** Jesus answered him, 'If I have spoken wrongly, testify
of the wrong; but if rightly, why do you strike Me?' **24** So Annas sent Him bound
to Caiaphas the high priest."

1. Who arrested Jesus and where did they take Him? (vv. 12–13)

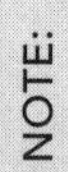

Annas was the former high priest and patriarch of this prominent Jewish family. Caiaphas was the high priest at this time (AD 33). Scholars believe it is highly likely that they lived in the same house.

2. Who was following Jesus and how did they get access to the court where Jesus was? (vv. 15–16) What happened when Peter was brought in? (v. 17) Describe the scene inside the courtyard. (v. 18)

3. What did Annas question Jesus about? (v. 19)

4. What did Jesus say about His teaching? (vv. 20–21) What Old Testament law was Jesus referring to in verse 21? (Deuteronomy 19:15)

5. What happened to Jesus in verse 22? How did He respond to that? (v. 23)

6. Where did Jesus go from here? (v. 24)

Application

What does it mean to be "in the world but not of the world?" How does Peter's example in verses 17–18 illustrate the influence the world can have on the strongest follower of Jesus? (Romans 12:2, Ephesians 4:22–24)

STUDY THREE
Jesus Before Caiaphas and Peter's Denial

The religious leaders wanted to deal in deception. Jesus was a problem that needed to go away, and they knew witnesses with shady stories would be the only way to permanently remove Him. At last, a twisted truth emerged and blasphemy was pronounced. With the death of Jesus assured, the Son of Man absorbed merciless beatings by the hand of those He had come to save. At the same time, Peter was facing his own demons. Laid low by the accusation of another servant girl, Peter swore the Nazarene was a stranger to him. Then the whole crowd challenged Peter, saying his own words gave him away. Self-preservation and pride wrestled with the truth in his heart, and Peter was overcome by the darkness. With curses, Peter denied His Lord one last time. And when the rooster crowed, Peter remembered and broke under the weight of Jesus' words. He had been sifted and shaken but, even in that moment, Jesus bore his grief.

Matthew 26:57–75
"57 Those who had seized Jesus led Him away to Caiaphas, the high priest, where
the scribes and the elders were gathered together.58 But Peter was following Him
at a distance as far as the courtyard of the high priest, and entered in, and sat
down with the officers to see the outcome. 59 Now the chief priests and the whole
Council kept trying to obtain false testimony against Jesus, so that they might
put Him to death. 60 They did not find any, even though many false witnesses
came forward. But later on two came forward, 61 and said, 'This man stated, 'I
am able to destroy the temple of God and to rebuild it in three days.' 62 The high
priest stood up and said to Him, 'Do You not answer? What is it that these men
are testifying against You?' 63 But Jesus kept silent. And the high priest said to
Him, 'I adjure You by the living God, that You tell us whether You are the Christ,
the Son of God.' 64 Jesus said to him, 'You have said it yourself; nevertheless I tell
you, hereafter you will see the Son of Man sitting at the right hand of Power, and
coming on the clouds of heaven.'

65 Then the high priest tore his robes and said, 'He has blasphemed! What
further need do we have of witnesses? Behold, you have now heard the blasphemy; **66** what do you think?' They answered, 'He deserves death!'
67 Then they spat in His face and beat Him with their fists; and others slapped
Him, **68** and said, 'Prophesy to us, You Christ; who is the one who hit You?'

69 Now Peter was sitting outside in the courtyard, and a servant-girl came to
him and said, 'You too were with Jesus the Galilean.' **70** But he denied it before
them all, saying, 'I do not know what you are talking about.' **71** When he [Peter]
had gone out to the gateway, another servant-girl saw him and said to those who
were there, 'This man was with Jesus of Nazareth.' **72** And again he denied it with
an oath, 'I do not know the man.' **73** A little later the bystanders came up and
said to Peter, 'Surely you too are one of them; for even the way you talk gives
you away.' **74** Then he began to curse and swear, 'I do not know the man!' And
immediately a rooster crowed. **75** And Peter remembered the word which Jesus
had said, 'Before a rooster crows, you will deny Me three times.' And he went out
and wept bitterly."

NOTE: The high priest presided over the Sanhedrin, the highest court in Israel at the time. Scribes were the teachers of the Law; elders represented the people. The groups, along with the chief priest, made up Israel's governing body.

1. Who was Caiaphas? (v. 57)

2. What had been going on behind the scenes in verses 59–60? What does the Old Testament law say about this kind of behavior? (Deuteronomy 19:16–21)

3. What was the "charge" brought against Jesus in verse 61? Was this a legitimate allegation? (see John 2:19–21)

4. Why did Caiaphas want to compel Jesus to answer His charge in verse 63? (see vv. 65–66)

5. How did Jesus respond in verse 64? How does this connect back to what is promised in Psalms 110:1–2 and Daniel 7:13–14?

6. What did the high priest call Jesus' words in verse 65? How did the Council respond to His proclamation?

7. Where in this scene do we see fulfillment of Isaiah 53:3–8?

8. Who challenges Peter in Matthew 26:71 and 73? What was the additional evidence mentioned in verse 73? What added detail do we get from John 18:26?

9. What did Peter say to his accusers in verses 72 and 74? What happened in verses 74–75?

Application

Even though Jesus knew Peter would deny Him (Matthew 26:31–35), this moment was still part of the suffering of our Servant. Meditate on the truth of Jesus' humanity at this hour. What might He have experienced as a Man abandoned by His friends during a time of great need?

STUDY FOUR
Jesus Before Pilate

Pontius Pilate made a name for himself in history not because of his wise judgments, strong leadership, or strategic use of force, but because he handed down the death sentence to the Messiah. Pilate is a tragic figure. He was granted the opportunity of a lifetime—a private audience with the Savior of the world, God incarnate, the Word made flesh. But his hard heart and unwavering pride prevented him from seeing the Truth. The Roman ruler was in the presence of the King of kings, but instead of bowing his knee, he turned a blind eye. As the keeper of law, Pilate's charge was to determine Jesus' innocence or guilt, and he struggled to stay on the side of right. Pressure from the Jews forced Pilate's unsteady hand. Nothing pointed to Jesus' guilt, but it was becoming impossible to set the Truth free.

Luke 22:66–71

"66 When it was day, the Council of elders of the people assembled, both chief
priests and scribes, and they led Him away to their council chamber, saying, 67 'If
You are the Christ, tell us.' But He said to them, 'If I tell you, you will not believe;
68 and if I ask a question, you will not answer. 69 But from now on the Son of
Man will be seated at the right hand of the power of God.' 70 And they all said,
'Are You the Son of God, then?' And He said to them, 'Yes, I am.' 71 Then they
said, 'What further need do we have of testimony? For we have heard it ourselves
from His own mouth.'"

John 18:28–38

"28 Then they led Jesus from Caiaphas into the Praetorium, and it was early; and
they themselves did not enter into the Praetorium so that they would not be
defiled, but might eat the Passover. 29 Therefore Pilate went out to them and said,
'What accusation do you bring against this Man?' 30 They answered and said to
him, 'If this Man were not an evildoer, we would not have delivered Him to you.'
31 So Pilate said to them, 'Take Him yourselves, and judge Him according to
your law.' The Jews said to him, 'We are not permitted to put anyone to death,'
32 to fulfill the word of Jesus which He spoke, signifying by what kind of death
He was about to die.

33 Therefore Pilate entered again into the Praetorium, and summoned Jesus
and said to Him, 'Are You the King of the Jews?' 34 Jesus answered, 'Are you
saying this on your own initiative, or did others tell you about Me?' 35 Pilate
answered, 'I am not a Jew, am I? Your own nation and the chief priests delivered
You to me; what have You done?' 36 Jesus answered, 'My kingdom is not of this
world. If My kingdom were of this world, then My servants would be fighting so
that I would not be handed over to the Jews; but as it is, My kingdom is not of
this realm.' 37 Therefore Pilate said to Him, 'So You are a king?' Jesus answered,
'You say correctly that I am a king. For this I have been born, and for this I have
come into the world, to testify to the truth. Everyone who is of the truth hears
My voice.' 38 Pilate said to Him, 'What is truth?'

And when he had said this, he went out again to the Jews and said to them,
'I find no guilt in Him.'"

"Day" refers to early Friday morning.

1. What predictions and proclamation did Jesus make in Luke 22: 67–70?

NOTE: *Praetorium* is a military word and was the official residence of the Roman governor. For more information, see the International Standard Bible Encyclopedia found at www.biblestudytools.com.

2. Why didn't the Jews want to enter the Praetorium? (John 18:28–29)

3. What can you discern, from tone and intent, about the conversation between Pilate and the Jewish leaders in verses 29–32? (see Luke 23:2–5 for more detail)

NOTE: If the Jewish Council would have carried out the death sentence against Jesus, it would have been by stoning (Leviticus 24:16, Galatians 3:13). Romans executed their criminals by crucifixion.

4. What questions did Pilate ask Jesus? (vv. 33, 35, 37–38)

5. Did Jesus provide a defense or an explanation in answer to Pilate's questions? Summarize His words.

6. What truth has Jesus revealed to Pilate in this brief exchange? (vv. 36–37)

7. How does God's Word define truth in Psalms 119:160, John 14:6, and John 17:17?

8. What was Pilate's conclusion after speaking with Jesus? (v. 38)

Application

What in the past has prevented you from recognizing truth? How do you decide what is truth?

A DEEPER LOOK

What does the Bible say about truth and its role in the life of a believer? Why is knowing "what is truth" important?

Psalms 15:1–2

Psalms 25:5

Psalms 43:3

Psalms 86:11

Proverbs 30:5

Zechariah 8:16

Ephesians 1:13–14

Ephesians 4:25

Philippians 4:8

1 Peter 1:22–23

1 John 3:18, 5:20

STUDY FIVE
Crucify Him!

In His sovereignty, God had been moving toward the sacrificial death of His Son Jesus since before time began. Yet it is still hard to imagine that anyone would so eagerly accept responsibility for the murder of the Messiah. But in this passion-infused scene, that is exactly what happened: HIS BLOOD SHALL BE ON

US AND ON OUR CHILDREN! *We accept the guilt for the execution of Jesus.* And so this demand was met. Indeed, it was their sin and ours and the sin of all who came before and after us that nailed Jesus to the cross. We spit in His face. We stripped and mocked Him. We held the whip that tore the flesh from His back. We pressed the crown of thorns into his head. Our hands drove the nails. And we abandoned Him in the darkness. It was not just "those people." It was us. He took on our sin and drank the cup of God's wrath, poured for us, until it was dry.

Luke 23:6–16

"**6** When Pilate heard it, he asked whether the man was a Galilean. **7** And when he learned that He belonged to Herod's jurisdiction, he sent Him to Herod, who himself also was in Jerusalem at that time.

8 Now Herod was very glad when he saw Jesus; for he had wanted to see Him for a long time, because he had been hearing about Him and was hoping to see some sign performed by Him. **9** And he questioned Him at some length; but He answered him nothing. **10** And the chief priests and the scribes were standing there, accusing Him vehemently. **11** And Herod with his soldiers, after treating Him with contempt and mocking Him, dressed Him in a gorgeous robe and sent Him back to Pilate. **12** Now Herod and Pilate became friends with one another that very day; for before they had been enemies with each other.

13 Pilate summoned the chief priests and the rulers and the people, **14** and said to them, 'You brought this man to me as one who incites the people to rebellion, and behold, having examined Him before you, I have found no guilt in this man regarding the charges which you make against Him. **15** No, nor has Herod, for he sent Him back to us; and behold, nothing deserving death has been done by Him. **16** Therefore I will punish Him and release Him.'"

Matthew 27:15–26

"**15** Now at the feast the governor was accustomed to release for the people any one prisoner whom they wanted. **16** At that time they were holding a notorious prisoner, called Barabbas. **17** So when the people gathered together, Pilate said to them, 'Whom do you want me to release for you? Barabbas, or Jesus who is called Christ?' **18** For he knew that because of envy they had handed Him over.

19 While he was sitting on the judgment seat, his wife sent him a message, saying, 'Have nothing to do with that righteous Man; for last night I suffered greatly in a dream because of Him.' **20** But the chief priests and the elders persuaded the crowds to ask for Barabbas and to put Jesus to death. **21** But the governor said to them, 'Which of the two do you want me to release for you?' And they said, 'Barabbas.' **22** Pilate said to them, 'Then what shall I do with Jesus who is called Christ?' They all said, 'Crucify Him!' **23** And he said, 'Why, what evil has He done?' But they kept shouting all the more, saying, 'Crucify Him!'

24 When Pilate saw that he was accomplishing nothing, but rather that a riot was starting, he took water and washed his hands in front of the crowd, saying, 'I am innocent of this Man's blood; see to that yourselves.' **25** And all the people said, 'His blood shall be on us and on our children!' **26** Then he released Barabbas for them; but after having Jesus scourged, he handed Him over to be crucified."

1. What do we already know about Herod from Scripture? (see Matthew 14:1–12, Luke 3:1–2)

NOTE: This was Herod Antipas who ruled from 4 BC–39 BC after his father, Herod the Great, died.

2. Why did Pilate send Jesus to Herod? (vv. 6–7) Why did Herod want to see Jesus? (v. 8)

3. Describe the scene in verses 9–11. Who is there? What are they doing?

4. What is the outcome for Herod and Pilate? (v. 12)

5. What conclusion did Herod and Pilate come to about Jesus? (vv. 13–16)

6. What tradition is introduced in Matthew 27:15?

7. Who enters this scene in verse 16 and what do we know about him? (see also Luke 23:19 and Mark 15:7)

NOTE: Barabbas means "son of the father."

8. We learn a few important but behind-the-scenes details in verses 18–20. What are they?

9. How is Pilate's question in verses 22–23 a fulfillment of prophecy? (see also Psalms 38:20–21 and Isaiah 53:9)

10. What did Pilate do in verse 24? As the ruler of this realm, what could he have done instead?

11. What does verse 25 indicate about the people? Why are their words significant?

12. What was the ultimate result for Jesus in verse 26?

NOTE: Scourging was often the first step in Roman punishment. The leather whip was composed of several strands with pieces of bone and metal attached to each end. The purpose was to remove the flesh from the bones of the victim, hastening blood loss and often leaving them near death. (Isaiah 50:6, 52:14)

Application

Imagine yourself in the scene in verses 21–23. Consider the various characters that were or could have been there: the religious leaders, the disciples, the common people or "good Jews" who had come to observe the Feast, those Jesus had healed and taught, His mother Mary. What might have been the emotional experience of those very real people in this almost surreal moment in history?

A DEEPER LOOK

What does Scripture say about the power of the blood of Jesus?

Romans 5:9

Hebrews 9:12

Ephesians 1:7

1 John 1:7

Ephesians 2:13

Revelation 5:9–10

Colossians 1:20

WRAPPING UP

We have just walked through one of the heaviest passages in all of the Bible with the Son of Man. Jesus ended His last meal with His disciples. He was betrayed and denied by His own, spat upon, beaten, and mocked through the night in an illegal trial hosted by the religious leaders of Israel. And He perplexed Pilate with His humility, gentleness, and startling truth. All this with His deity restrained and humanity resolved.

While undeserved, we knew it was coming. More than 700 years before it occurred, Isaiah wrote, "But the Lord was pleased To crush Him, putting Him to grief…." (Isaiah 53:10)

It was the inevitable and perfect plan of God, but only necessary because of the wickedness in our hearts. The 19th century British preacher Charles Spurgeon said it this way: *"I slew him—this right hand struck the dagger to his heart. My deeds slew Christ. Alas! I slew my best beloved; I killed him who loved me with an everlasting love. Oh eyes, why do you refuse to weep when you see Jesus' body mangled and torn? Give vent to your sorrow, Christians, for you have good reason to do so."*

While this vicious call indicts us—"His blood shall be on us and on our children!"—the words take a different tone on this side of the cross. The blood of Jesus is our redemption, justification, nearness to God, fellowship with Jesus, security and forgiveness, atonement and reconciliation, our present peace and future hope. This cry from the depths of hell has become the song of the redeemed. A once-fatal indictment has become a desperate yearning and a precious promise. All was satisfied by the death of Jesus, and so these words become a plea. A confession. The eternal desire of our hearts.

Oh Father, let the blood of Jesus be on us and on our children.

Notes

~ Map of Passion Week ~

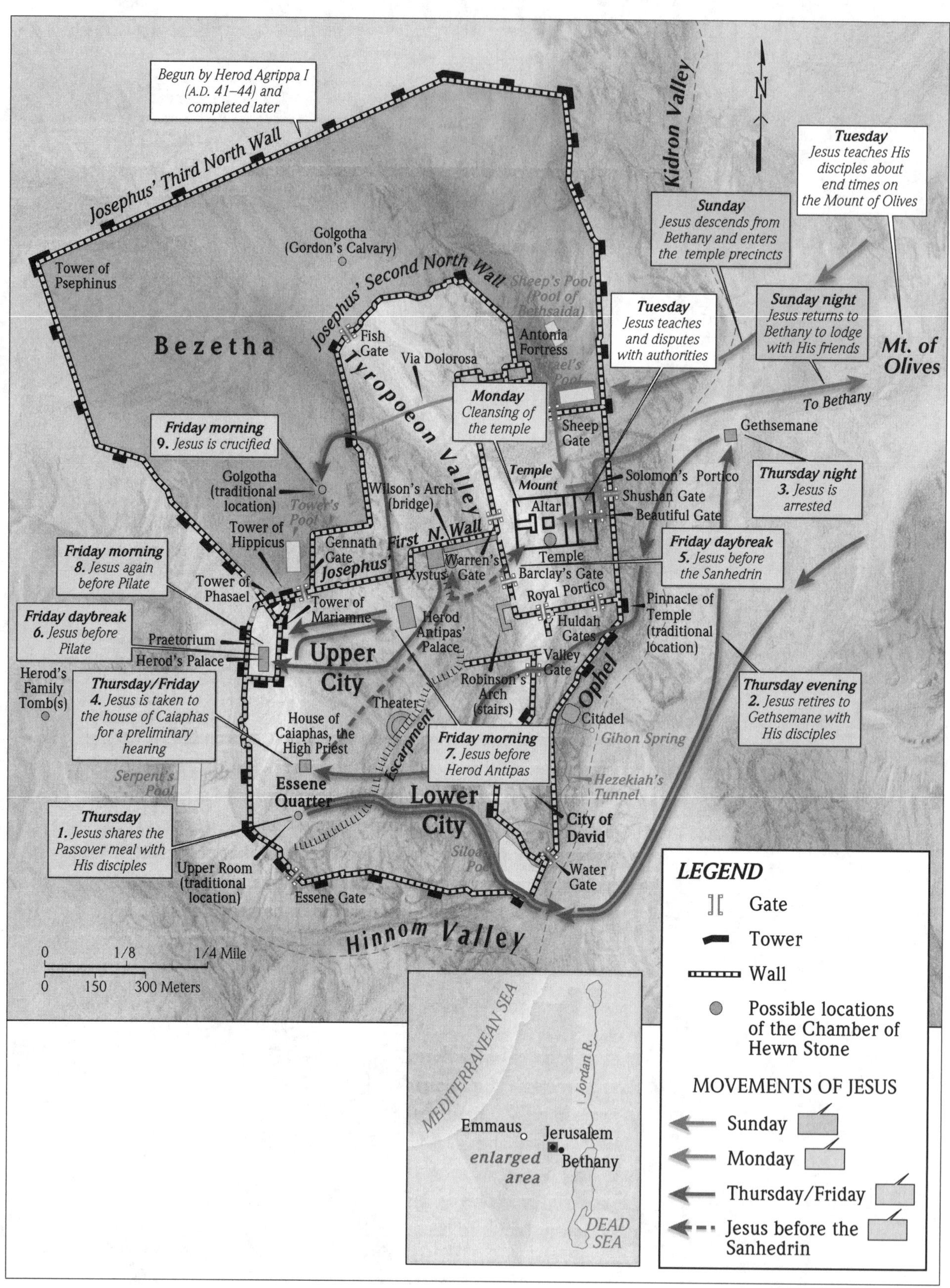

WEEK 22

JESUS, THE SUFFERING SERVANT

"When they came to the place called The Skull, there they crucified Him and the criminals, one on the right and the other on the left."
LUKE 23:33

We speak of suffering in hushed tones—whispered in hospital hallways, shared in confidence with mediators or counselors, talked through tears at the kitchen table. No one shouts about their suffering from the rooftops. At best, trials are something people tolerate or, if possible, diminish. And most, if they are honest, would choose to avoid them at all costs.

In contrast, the suffering of Jesus is on display for the all world to see. And Scripture says believers, instead of avoiding it, should rejoice to share in the suffering of Christ. (1 Peter 4:13) Isaiah 53 is about the Suffering Servant, written 700 years before Jesus was born. Jesus is not named in this passage, but no one else could or has fulfilled the prophet's predictions.

When we think of Jesus suffering, we remember the nails that pierced through the flesh of His hands and feet. But beyond physical torture, Jesus also suffered injustice. Completely innocent, Jesus did not fight the false accusations as He could have—with legions of angels or by unleashing His power over creation or ending life as we know it. Instead, *"Like a lamb that is led to slaughter...So He did not open His mouth."* (Isaiah 53:7)

But an even greater agony came spiritually. Not only was He *"despised and forsaken of men"* (v. 3)—including His closest friends—He experienced the most devastating divide of all: He was forsaken by His Father. Jesus was *"Smitten of God, and afflicted ... the LORD was pleased to crush Him ...* [and] *... caused the iniquity of us all to fall on Him."* (vv. 4–10)

Jesus was intimately acquainted with anguish, so He sympathizes with our desire to steer clear. But when we live looking for an escape route, we miss out on great blessing. Because what we call affliction Jesus calls fellowship. What we see as a burden Jesus says is a gift. It is through trials that we hold on to the hope of the unseen—identification with our Savior now and the weight of glory that awaits us in eternity.

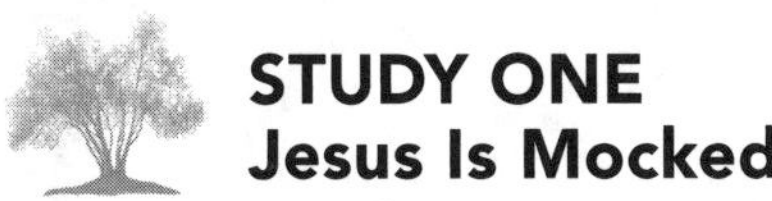

STUDY ONE
Jesus Is Mocked

What happens here takes our breath away. Even Hollywood at its best cannot capture the full extent of what took place on that day. The thorns the soldiers forced into Jesus' head stung and sliced like razors. The spit that ran down His face was as vile and obscene as the venom they spewed with their words. Jesus felt every slap, every blow from the rod that mocked His royalty. The robe that draped across the open wounds on His back hung heavy with contempt. His body was already so broken, a bystander named Simon had to carry His crossbeam up the hill where Jesus would die. The nails they drove through His hands and feet held firm only because Jesus willingly gave Himself as the atonement for the sins of the world. Luke notes the women in particular knew this was not a day for rejoicing. Their Friend and Savior would be dead in hours, and all they could do was weep.

Matthew 27:27–32

"27 Then the soldiers of the governor took Jesus into the Praetorium and gathered the whole Roman cohort around Him. 28 They stripped Him and put a scarlet robe on Him. 29 And after twisting together a crown of thorns, they put it on His head, and a reed in His right hand; and they knelt down before Him and mocked Him, saying, 'Hail, King of the Jews!' 30 They spat on Him, and took the reed and began to beat Him on the head. 31 After they had mocked Him, they took the scarlet robe off Him and put His own garments back on Him, and led Him away to crucify Him.

32 As they were coming out, they found a man of Cyrene named Simon, whom they pressed into service to bear His cross."

Luke 23:27–33

"27 And following Him was a large crowd of the people, and of women who were mourning and lamenting Him. 28 But Jesus turning to them said, 'Daughters of Jerusalem, stop weeping for Me, but weep for yourselves and for your children. 29 For behold, the days are coming when they will say, 'Blessed are the barren, and the wombs that never bore, and the breasts that never nursed.' 30 Then they will begin to say to the mountains, 'Fall on us,' and to the hills, 'Cover us.' 31 For if they do these things when the tree is green, what will happen when it is dry?'

32 Two others also, who were criminals, were being led away to be put to death with Him.

33 When they came to the place called The Skull, there they crucified Him and the criminals, one on the right and the other on the left."

1. What did Jesus say would happen to Him in Matthew 20:19? What is taking place in Matthew 27:27–30?

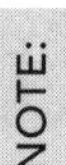

A cohort could be as many as 200–600 soldiers.

2. Consider: was Jesus a dangerous criminal? Was Jesus a "flight risk?" Recall Pilate's question in Matthew 27:23. With that in mind, what was the purpose of what the Roman soldiers did in verses 27–31?

3. What additional details do we learn about Simon from Mark 15:21 and Luke 23:26?

NOTE: Scholars estimate the weight of the whole cross to be around 300 pounds. Victims usually only carried the crossbeam, which weighed between 75–125 pounds.

4. Read Romans 16:13 and record the impact Simon's brief yet transforming encounter with Jesus seems to have had on his family.

5. Consider Jesus' physical, mental, and emotional state in this moment. What does He do and say in the midst of His suffering in Luke 23:28–31?

6. What was Jesus predicting in verses 29–30? (See also Matthew 24:1–8)

NOTE: The temple in Jerusalem was destroyed by Titus, son of the Roman Emperor Vespasian, in AD 70.

7. Who is Jesus associated with in verses 32–33? (See also Isaiah 53:12)

Application

What unexpected or unplanned events in your life have had the most significance? Has anything ever happened to you "by chance" that turned out to be life-changing? Share that testimony.

STUDY TWO
The Crucifixion

Words are inadequate to depict this horrific scene, which might be why it was written so simply. A Man was put to death on a Friday afternoon, which was nothing extraordinary considering the brutality of the Romans at the time. Except that this Man was perfectly innocent. His trial was unjust, the accusations were false, the abuse unnecessary. Rather than simply being imprisoned or exiled, He was nailed to a cross, an execution contrived to prolong pain and humiliation. Jesus hung between two criminals, when His true position was a seat at the right hand of the Father. He was subjected to a barrage of insults and disgrace, when what He deserved was all blessing and honor and glory and power. The soldiers plundered and placed bets for His possessions, when He was willing to graciously give them all things. (Romans 8:32) For one unbearable stretch of time, Jesus faced every hideous impulse of humanity, as all hell broke loose on earth.

Matthew 27:33–37

"33 And when they came to a place called Golgotha, which means Place of a
Skull, 34 they gave Him wine to drink mixed with gall; and after tasting it, He
was unwilling to drink.
35 And when they had crucified Him, they divided up His garments among
themselves by casting lots. 36 And sitting down, they began to keep watch over
Him there. 37 And above His head they put up the charge against Him which
read, 'THIS IS JESUS THE KING OF THE JEWS.'"

Luke 23:34a

"But Jesus was saying, 'Father forgive them; for they do not know what they are doing.' And they cast lots, dividing up His garments among themselves."

Matthew 27:38–44

"38 At that time two robbers were crucified with Him, one on the right and one
on the left. 39 And those passing by were hurling abuse at Him, wagging their
heads 40 and saying, 'You who are going to destroy the temple and rebuild it in
three days, save Yourself! If You are the Son of God, come down from the cross.'
41 In the same way the chief priests also, along with the scribes and elders, were
mocking Him and saying, 42 'He saved others; He cannot save Himself. He is the
King of Israel; let Him now come down from the cross, and we will believe in
Him. 43 He trusts in God; let God rescue Him now, if He delights in Him; for
He said, 'I am the Son of God.' 44 The robbers who had been crucified with Him
were also insulting Him with the same words."

1. What does this tell us about Jesus and His attitude toward sinners? How is this a picture of the hope, grace, and love we have in Christ?

2. What was written about Jesus and affixed to the cross? (Mark 15:26, Luke 23:38, John 19:19)

3. What does Colossians 2:13–14 say was also nailed to the cross? In what ways does that encourage you today?

4. What was given to Jesus in verse 34? Why do you think He did not drink it?

NOTE: Gall referred to a bitter poison that was often mixed into a drink for those suffering crucifixion, serving to numb the senses and, sometimes, hasten death.

5. What prophecy was fulfilled in verses 38–44? (See Psalms 22:7–8, Psalms 109:25)

6. What proof were the people and their leaders still looking for from Jesus? What is the irony in their words? (vv. 39–43)

Application

What does Luke 23:34 mean for believers today in terms of how mindful we are of our sin? How might being more mindful of sin affect how we live? (Psalms 19:12–14, Romans 7:22–23) How does Jesus' response in Luke 23:34 serve as an example to us as we seek to forgive those who have sinned against us?

A DEEPER LOOK

Read and meditate on Psalms 22. Write down your observations from this psalm that correlate to Jesus' crucifixion.

STUDY THREE
Remember Me

Wherever we find Christ, we find hope. The exchange between the Son of Man and a son of man reminds us of this truth. While there seems to be no end to our capacity to sin, we are never beyond the bounds of His grace. By the mercy of God, one thief was given eyes to see during the darkest day of his life. He knew his punishment was deserved; he also knew he was dying beside the One whose rightful place was on the throne. With the little breath he had left, this thief boldly and humbly drew near to Grace, begging only to be remembered in eternity. And, as grace would have it, Jesus promised so much more. You won't just be a memory, He told him—you will be *with Me*. Jesus also secured an earthly home for His mother with His beloved friend, John. Over and over, in the midst of great sacrifice, Jesus displayed His perfect love.

Luke 23:39–43
"[39] One of the criminals who were hanged there was hurling abuse at Him, saying,
'Are You not the Christ? Save Yourself and us!' [40] But the other answered, and
rebuking him said, 'Do you not even fear God, since you are under the same sentence of condemnation? [41] And we indeed are suffering justly, for we are receiving
what we deserve for our deeds; but this man has done nothing wrong.' [42] And he
was saying, 'Jesus, remember me when You come in Your kingdom!' [43] And He
said to him, 'Truly I say to you, today you shall be with Me in Paradise.'"

John 19:25–27
"[25] Therefore the soldiers did these things.
But standing by the cross of Jesus were His mother, and His mother's sister,
Mary the wife of Clopas, and Mary Magdalene. [26] When Jesus then saw His
mother, and the disciple whom He loved standing nearby, He said to His mother,
'Woman, behold, your son!' [27] Then He said to the disciple, 'Behold, your
mother!' From that hour the disciple took her into his own household."

1. How does the thief on the cross demonstrate his rejection of Jesus in verse 39?

2. What did the second thief ask for in verses 40–42? What did Jesus promise in verse 43?

3. Isaiah 51:3 and Revelation 2:7 contain references to paradise, Eden, or heaven. What does Scripture tell us is found there?
For in-depth study, look up "paradise" in the Quick Reference Dictionary at biblestudytools.com

4. Who else does John tell us was at the cross with Jesus in verse 25? What "transaction" was taking place in verses 26–27? Read Mark 6:3–4. What might be another reason Jesus did this for His mother?

5. What do we see about Jesus and His relationships in John 19:26–27, even in His darkest hour on earth?

6. Below, reflect on Jesus' words on the cross. How do they demonstrate His humanity? How do they demonstrate His deity?

   Matthew 27:46

   Luke 23:34

   Luke 23:43

   Luke 23:46

   John 19:26–27

   John 19:30

   John 19:28

Application

How does the salvation of the thief encourage and/or instruct you?

STUDY FOUR
It Is Finished

God-forsaken. A term used to describe a desolate place where nothing can survive. A place full of neglect and misery, a place with no evidence of hope. On this day of shadows, as heaven turned its back on the only begotten Son, these words described Jesus. And this caused Him the deepest pain of all. Here, on history's darkest day, Jesus became sin (2 Corinthians 5:21). It is important to understand that this goes beyond the idea of "bearing" or "representing" our sin. Jesus *became* sin. Every murder, lie, rape, robbery, war, abuse, idolatry, racial slur, prideful attitude, lustful thought, careless word—everything you can think of and everything unthinkable. That was Jesus on the cross, cursed and cast off. Why? Because we were cursed. Flawlessly keeping the law was an impossible burden for our hearts of stone, forever separating us from God. And He didn't want it to stay that way. So Jesus became the perfect sacrifice, drinking to the dregs the cup of God's wrath, substituting Himself for our every past, present, and future sin, and bringing us peace.

Matthew 27:45–49

"**45** Now from the sixth hour darkness fell upon all the land until the ninth hour.
46 About the ninth hour Jesus cried out with a loud voice, saying, 'Eli, Eli, lama
sabachthani?' that is, 'My God, My God, why have You forsaken Me?' **47** And
some of those who were standing there, when they heard it, began saying, 'This
man is calling for Elijah.' **48** Immediately one of them ran, and taking a sponge,
he filled it with sour wine and put it on a reed, and gave Him a drink. **49** But the
rest of them said, 'Let us see whether Elijah will come to save Him.'"

John 19:28–30

"**28** After this, Jesus, knowing that all things had already been accomplished, to
fulfill the Scripture, said, 'I am thirsty.' **29** A jar full of sour wine was standing
there; so they put a sponge full of the sour wine upon a branch of hyssop and
brought it up to His mouth. **30** Therefore when Jesus had received the sour wine,
He said, 'It is finished!' And He bowed His head and gave up His spirit."

Matthew 27:51–56

"**51** And behold, the veil of the temple was torn in two from top to bottom; and
the earth shook and the rocks were split. **52** The tombs were opened, and many
bodies of the saints who had fallen asleep were raised; **53** and coming out of the
tombs after His resurrection they entered the holy city and appeared to many.
54 Now the centurion, and those who were with him keeping guard over Jesus,
when they saw the earthquake and the things that were happening, became very
frightened and said, 'Truly this was the Son of God!'

55 Many women were there looking on from a distance, who had followed Jesus
from Galilee while ministering to Him. **56** Among them was Mary Magdalene, and
Mary the mother of James and Joseph, and the mother of the sons of Zebedee."

1. How does creation respond to Jesus' death? (Matthew 27:45) See also Luke 23:44–45.

2. What did Jesus say in Matthew 27:46? What did He mean? (Isaiah 53: 3–6, 10–12, 2 Corinthians 5:21, Galatians 3:13)

3. Jesus speaks again from the cross in John 19:28. What was the purpose of this? (see Psalms 69:21)

4. What else might Jesus have been thirsty for in John 19:28, according to Psalms 42:1–2?

5. Jesus speaks for the last time in John 19:30 and Luke 23:46. What does He say? How do those statements demonstrate the sovereignty and authority of the Son of God?

6. Matthew 27:51–53 describes the miraculous events surrounding Jesus' death. What were they?

7. What was the purpose of the veil or curtain in the temple? (Exodus 26:31–33) What did the tearing symbolize (notice the direction of the tear)? (Hebrews 6:19–20)

8. What is the response of the people in Matthew 27:54 and Luke 23:48? How is this a fitting resolve?

NOTE: "It is finished" is one word in Greek: *tetelestai.* The phrase was often written on business documents after financial transactions to confirm the debt on the account was paid in full.

9. In Matthew 27:55–56, who remained with Jesus to the end?

Application

Using the past four studies and putting yourself in each scene, what evidence or signs recorded in Scripture would have proven to you the deity of Christ?

A DEEPER LOOK

Meditate on these verses in the context of this scene:

Romans 5:8

Hebrews 9:14, 22

Romans 8:32

Hebrews 10:10–13

2 Corinthians 5:18–19

1 Peter 2:24

Ephesians 5:2

1 John 4:9–10

STUDY FIVE
Jesus Is Buried

In some ways, this scene is a relief. The suffering of Jesus is over. His broken body can rest now, in a newly cut tomb given by a friend. At the same time, for some, suffering begins. His disciples and friends still have not put all the pieces together. All they know is their Teacher is gone. They thought He had come to save them—they did not expect Him to die. They thought He would be a ruler, not a martyr. Now they were alone and afraid, and only the women bravely mourned at His grave. John tells us two wealthy men—Joseph of Arimathea and Nicodemus—claimed and buried Jesus. Scripture calls them "secret disciples," too fearful in life to follow Him publicly, only revealing their true hearts in His death. Still scheming, the Pharisees and priests worried the disciples would try to stage a resurrection and incite the people once more. So Pilate sent off the Pharisees and priests with a guard and his seal, hoping for an uneventful third day.

John 19:31–39

"**31** Then the Jews, because it was the day of preparation, so that the bodies would not remain on the cross on the Sabbath (for that Sabbath was a high day), asked Pilate that their legs might be broken, and that they might be taken away. **32** So the soldiers came, and broke the legs of the first man and of the other who was crucified with Him; **33** but coming to Jesus, when they saw that He was already dead, they did not break His legs. **34** But one of the soldiers pierced His side with a spear, and immediately blood and water came out. **35** And he who has seen has testified, and his testimony is true; and he knows that he is telling the truth, so that you also may believe. **36** For these things came to pass to fulfill the Scripture, 'Not a bone of Him shall be broken.' **37** And again another Scripture says, 'They shall look on Him whom they pierced.'

38 After these things Joseph of Arimethea, being a disciple of Jesus, but a secret one for fear of the Jews, asked Pilate that he might take away the body of Jesus; and Pilate granted permission. So he came and took away His body. **39** Nicodemus, who had first come to Him by night, also came, bringing a mixture of myrrh and aloes, about a hundred pounds weight."

Matthew 27:57–66

"**57** When it was evening, there came a rich man from Arimathea, named Joseph, who himself had also become a disciple of Jesus. **58** This man went to Pilate and asked for the body of Jesus. Then Pilate ordered it to be given to him. **59** And Joseph took the body and wrapped it in a clean linen cloth, **60** and laid it in his own new tomb, which he had hewn out in the rock; and he rolled a large stone against the entrance of the tomb and went away. **61** And Mary Magdalene was there, and the other Mary, sitting opposite the grave.

62 Now on the next day, the day after the preparation, the chief priests and the Pharisees gathered together with Pilate, **63** and said, 'Sir, we remember that when He was still alive that deceiver said, 'After three days I am to rise again.' **64** Therefore, give orders for the grave to be made secure until the third day, otherwise His disciples may come and steal Him away and say to the people, 'He has risen from the dead,' and the last deception will be worse than the first.' **65** Pilate said to them, 'You have a guard; go, make it as secure as you know how.' **66** And they went and made the grave secure, and along with the guard they set a seal on the stone."

1. John 19:31–37 is the only record of this event and the fulfilled prophecy. What does this scene confirm and why is it important? (Exodus 12:46)

2. What does Scripture tell us about the men who buried Jesus? (Matthew 27:57–59 and John 19:38–39)

3. What prophecy is fulfilled in these passages? See Isaiah 53:9.

NOTE: Jesus' death and burial take place Friday before the Sabbath. For more details about the importance of burial to the Jews, visit Baker's Evangelical Dictionary of Biblical Theology at biblestudytools.com.

4. Who else attended the burial of Jesus? (v. 61) What details are notable about His burial?

5. Who came together in verse 62? What day was it? What is significant (and hypocritical) about this scene? (Matthew 12:10, Mark 3:2, John 9:14–16)

6. What was their complaint? What was their solution? (vv. 63–64)

7. How did Pilate respond? (v. 65)

Application

Has your heart ever been hard toward Jesus, as the Pharisees' hearts were in this passage? What did He do to soften it?

WRAPPING UP

Suffering is the gift no one wants. But, for believers, what makes suffering a form of grace is that, while we look like Jesus when we love and forgive, we can also reflect Him when we are called to walk through affliction. But this isn't suffering for the sake of suffering. He promises us that, one day, every temptation, every trial, and every tear will somehow be worth it: *"For momentary, light affliction is producing for us an eternal weight of glory far beyond all comparison. . . ."* (2 Corinthians 4:17)

The suffering of Jesus displayed the depths of man's wickedness and was the penalty we all should have paid for offending a Holy God, who hates our sin because He loves us so much. The Lord laid the weight of His wrath and our transgressions on His Son so that we could live, forgiven and free, as children of God.

Jesus wasn't forced to die—He freely gave His life for us (John 10:17–18, 1 John 3:16). Saint Augustine of Hippo frames it this way: "He gave up His life because He willed it, when He willed it, and as He willed it." And that truth should give us great joy!

Suffering and joy are unlikely companions, and only add up in the economy of God. What a blessing that, in times of trial, we have a place to fix our eyes and find our hope—*"on Jesus, the author and perfecter of faith, who for the joy set before Him endured the cross, despising the shame, and has sat down at the right hand of the throne of God."* (Hebrews 12:2)

Notes

JESUS, REDEEMER AND SAVIOR

"...knowing that you were not redeemed with perishable things like silver or gold from your futile way of life inherited from your forefathers, but with precious blood, as of a lamb unblemished and spotless, the blood of Christ."
1 PETER 1:18–19

Dawn crept slowly over the Judean hills, the air still heavy with grief. No doubt the followers of Jesus were hoping the previous forty-eight hours were all just a horrible dream. The words of the ancients came to pass on this somber morning: "*...and they will mourn for Him, as one mourns for an only son, and they will weep bitterly over Him like the bitter weeping over a firstborn.*" (Zechariah 12:10)

Still in the throes of deep sorrow, women once again came to tend their Teacher. Like so many, when sleep won't come and there are no tears left to cry, they needed to work out their grief. But this time, there was nothing left to do. Everything had been accomplished.

Confusion and fear came first. Why was the stone moved? And how? *And where was Jesus?* Mary rushed to tell Peter and John, who ran to also find nothing where His body should have been. Faith and understanding began to stir.

But Mary Magdalene was overcome. It's likely her broken heart could hardly take in the angels sitting inside His tomb, speaking words of hope. Then, He said her name. The same tone, same inflection He used the day He freed her from slavery and suffering, when He called her His child for the first time. On this beautiful day, Jesus again expressed His love for Mary—a woman once possessed by legions of demons was the first to see the risen Savior face-to-face.

From the Emmaus road to the upper room to breakfast by the sea, Jesus continued to reveal Himself to His redeemed—gracious with the grieving, patient with the doubting, faithful to the faithless. Like the slow rise of the sun, Jesus turned mourning to joy everywhere He went. And so often to so many, it was impossible to record it all. But the reason was the same: that we may know our Redeemer lives! May that truth thrill our hearts each day, just as it did that glorious day in the Garden, when Jesus spoke all of our names to life.

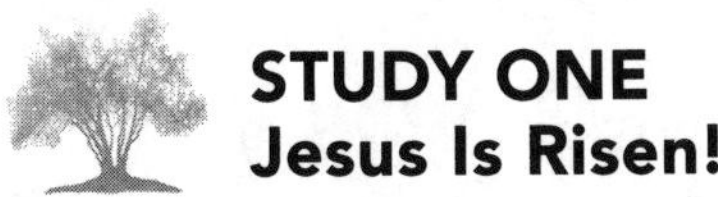

STUDY ONE
Jesus Is Risen!

The earth shook in response to the presence of the angel of the Lord, and the stone rolled away. The armed guards fell over like feathers, while the women stood in awed silence, waiting for what was next. Their hearts finally filled with hope as the angel spoke words of life: *He has risen from the dead.* Fear and joy pulsed like lightning in their veins as they ran to share the good news with the disciples. And on the way, they received a great gift—Jesus in all His glory appeared, so that they might know the message was true. At the same time, the event aroused another kind of fear in Israel. Hearing the news was an offer of grace; the religious leaders could have repented even then and acknowledged their Messiah. Instead, they reached into their pockets and tried to pay for their own salvation. Redemption was the offer, and they chose rejection once and for all.

Matthew 28:1–15

"Now after the Sabbath, as it began to dawn toward the first day of the week,
Mary Magdalene and the other Mary came to look at the grave. 2 And behold, a
severe earthquake had occurred, for an angel of the Lord descended from heaven
and came and rolled away the stone and sat upon it. 3 And his appearance was like
lightning, and his clothing as white as snow. 4 The guards shook for fear of him
and became like dead men. 5 The angel said to the women, 'Do not be afraid; for
I know that you are looking for Jesus who has been crucified. 6 He is not here,
for He has risen, just as He said. Come, see the place where He was lying. 7 Go
quickly and tell His disciples that He has risen from the dead; and behold, He is
going ahead of you into Galilee, there you will see Him; behold, I have told you.'
8 And they left the tomb quickly with fear and great joy and ran to report it
to His disciples. 9 And behold, Jesus met them and greeted them. And they came
up and took hold of His feet and worshiped Him. 10 Then Jesus said to them,
'Do not be afraid; go and take word to My brethren to leave for Galilee, and there
they will see Me.'
11 Now while they were on their way, some of the guard came into the city
and reported to the chief priests all that had happened. 12 And when they had
assembled with the elders and consulted together, they gave a large sum of money
to the soldiers, 13 and said, 'You are to say, 'His disciples came by night and stole
Him away while we were asleep.' 14 And if this should come to the governor's
ears, we will win him over and keep you out of trouble.' 15 And they took the
money and did as they had been instructed; and this story was widely spread
among the Jews, and is to this day."

1. When and where does this scene take place? Who was there? (v. 1) See Mark 16:1 and Luke 24:10 for more details.

2. Read Mark 16:3. What might have been your questions, concerns, or emotions as a follower of Jesus on this day?

3. How does Scripture tell us the stone was removed from the tomb? (v. 2)

4. Describe who was waiting at the tomb. (vv. 2–3) How did the guards respond? (v. 4) How did the women respond? (see also Mark 16:5, Luke 24:4–6)

5. Angels have been delivering messages about Jesus since before He was born. What was the angel's message this time? (vv. 5–7) What promises, commands, or instruction were given?

6. Note in verse 5 who the message was given to first—an historical detail recorded without exception by all four gospel writers. What was their response to the message? (v. 8)

7. What extra measure of grace do we see these women receive in verses 9–10? What was His message? How did they respond?

8. What takes place in verses 11–15?

9. Where do you see the power of God displayed in this passage? Where do you see the weakness of man revealed in this passage?

Application

In what ways has the Lord strengthened your faith, particularly in the face of a trial or difficult time? How did this contribute to your spiritual growth?

A DEEPER LOOK

What does Scripture say Christ's death and resurrection accomplished?

Romans 1:4

Romans 3:25–26

Romans 4:25

Romans 5:10–11

Romans 6:9–11

1 Peter 1:3–4

STUDY TWO
At the Tomb

John records that it was still very dark when an emotionally spent Mary arrived at Jesus' grave, probably because sleep had evaded her all night. But what she saw in the darkness got her adrenaline flowing, and she ran to the disciples for help. Peter and John encountered the same mystery as Mary: neatly folded linen cloths as the only earthly witnesses to what transpired in the tomb. The scene awakened belief in some, but Mary was still overwhelmed by despair, not yet aware of the high calling she would receive. First, angels appeared as a picture of hope, then Jesus Himself commissioned her to carry a message of joy: *I'm here, but not for long. I will soon be seated again with My Father and yours, accomplishing more on your behalf than you can ask or imagine.* This was Good News indeed!

John 20:1–18

"Now on the first day of the week Mary Magdalene came early to the tomb, while
it was still dark, and saw the stone already taken away from the tomb. 2 So she
ran and came to Simon Peter and to the other disciple whom Jesus loved, and
said to them, 'They have taken away the Lord out of the tomb, and we do not
know where they have laid Him.' 3 So Peter and the other disciple went forth,
and they were going to the tomb. 4 The two were running together; and the other
disciple ran ahead faster than Peter and came to the tomb first; 5 and stooping
and looking in, he saw the linen wrappings lying there; but he did not go in.
6 And so Simon Peter also came, following him, and entered the tomb; and he
saw the linen wrappings lying there, 7 and the face-cloth which had been on His
head, not lying with the linen wrappings, but rolled up in a place by itself. 8 So
the other disciple who had first come to the tomb then also entered, and he saw
and believed. 9 For as yet they did not understand the Scripture, that He must
rise again from the dead. 10 So the disciples went away again to their own homes.

11 But Mary was standing outside the tomb weeping; and so, as she wept, she
stooped and looked into the tomb; 12 and she saw two angels in white sitting, one
at the head and one at the feet, where the body of Jesus had been lying. 13 And
they said to her, 'Woman, why are you weeping?' She said to them, 'Because
they have taken away my Lord, and I do not know where they have laid Him.'
14 When she had said this, she turned around and saw Jesus standing there, and
did not know that it was Jesus. 15 Jesus said to her, 'Woman, why are you weeping? Whom are you seeking?' Supposing Him to be the gardener, she said to
Him, 'Sir, if you have carried Him away, tell me where you have laid Him, and I
will take Him away.' 16 Jesus said to her, 'Mary!' She turned and said to Him in
Hebrew, 'Rabboni!' (which means, Teacher). 17 Jesus said to her, 'Stop clinging
to Me, for I have not yet ascended to the Father; but go to My brethren and say
to them, 'I ascend to My Father and your Father, and My God and your God.'
18 Mary Magdalene came, announcing to the disciples, 'I have seen the Lord,' and
that He had said these things to her."

1. In verse 1, note who "she" was and what she saw in the rest of this passage.

2. John provides a different yet still accurate account of the scene at the tomb. Verses 2–10 may leave us with more questions than answers but, from the details provided, what do we know about:

   Mary Magdalene:

   Peter:

   Disciple Jesus loved (John):

   The tomb:

   What could have been going through the minds of Mary, Peter, and John in this scene? What questions would you have had?

3. What was Mary's emotional state in verse 11? What was different about the tomb when she looked inside? (v. 12)

4. How does Mary's witness to the resurrection of Jesus testify to the grace of God? (Luke 8:2)

5. What question did the angels and Jesus ask Mary? (vv. 13, 15) Why do you think they asked questions rather than immediately announce the good news of Jesus' resurrection? How do Proverbs 8:17 and Psalms 30:5b speak into this scene?

6. Who does Mary think Jesus is? (vv. 14–15) How does she recognize Him? (v. 16) (John 10:4, 27)

7. What command did Jesus give Mary in verse 17? Why? (Matthew 28:9) What commission did Jesus give Mary? What is the focus of the messages she is to relay?

8. How does this mark a change in His ministry and relationship with the disciples?

9. Think of all the people Jesus could have appeared to: the Pharisees, Sadducees and scribes, Caiaphas, Herod and Pilate, even His disciples in the Upper Room or to the crowd in the middle of Jerusalem. What might be significant about His appearance to Mary?

10. What is Jesus communicating to His disciples about their relationship with the Lord? (v. 17) Read John 15:14–16. How has their relationship progressed? In verse 17, what is Jesus saying His death and resurrection accomplished for His disciples? (Romans 8:15–16)

11. What does Scripture record was the disciples' response to Mary's message about Jesus? (Mark 16:10–11, Luke 24:11)

Application

Are you holding on to something from your past—a sin, dream, regret, or goal—that your Father wants you to let go of? How can holding on to the past prevent God from working in our present and moving us into the future? (Isaiah 43:18–19)

STUDY THREE
The Road to Emmaus

It was a peculiar experience. This Man, a Perfect Stranger who claimed to know nothing about recent events, was unfolding Truths from the Law and the Prophets about the coming of the Messiah. And they were spellbound. How did He seem to know so little and yet, know so much? Their sadness was deep, but His words kindled something inside that reminded them of joy. When it came time to part, the travelers begged their Teacher not to go. What else might He say that could bring light into their darkest day? So He stayed and shared a meal. Acting as Host, Jesus prayed and broke the bread, and at last, Cleopas and his companion recognized Jesus as the spiritual and physical Provider they had been longing for. With their hearts and eyes opened, Jesus disappeared. But He left behind two believers, eager to proclaim the message that burned inside them.

Luke 24:13–35

"**13** And behold, two of them were going that very day to a village named Emmaus,
which was about seven miles from Jerusalem. **14** And they were talking with each
other about all these things which had taken place. **15** While they were talking
and discussing, Jesus Himself approached and began traveling with them. **16** But
their eyes were prevented from recognizing Him. **17** And He said to them, 'What
are these words that you are exchanging with one another as you are walking?'
And they stood still, looking sad. **18** One of them, named Cleopas, answered and
said to Him, 'Are You the only one visiting Jerusalem and unaware of the things
which have happened here in these days?' **19** And He said to them, 'What things?'
And they said to Him, 'The things about Jesus the Nazarene, who was a prophet
mighty in deed and word in the sight of God and all the people, **20** and how the
chief priests and our rulers delivered Him to the sentence of death, and crucified
Him. **21** But we were hoping that it was He who was going to redeem Israel.
Indeed, besides all this, it is the third day since these things happened. **22** But
also some women among us amazed us. When they were at the tomb early in the
morning, **23** and did not find His body, they came, saying that they had also seen
a vision of angels who said that He was alive. **24** Some of those who were with us
went to the tomb and found it just exactly as the women also had said; but Him
they did not see.' **25** And He said to them, 'O foolish men and slow of heart to
believe in all that the prophets have spoken! **26** Was it not necessary for the Christ
to suffer these things and to enter into His glory?' **27** Then beginning with Moses
and with all the prophets, He explained to them the things concerning Himself
in all the Scriptures.

28 And they approached the village where they were going, and He acted as
though He were going farther. 29 But they urged Him, saying, 'Stay with us, for it
is getting toward evening, and the day is now nearly over.' So He went in to stay
with them. 30 When He had reclined at the table with them, He took the bread
and blessed it, and breaking it, He began giving it to them. 31 Then their eyes
were opened and they recognized Him; and He vanished from their sight. 32 They
said to one another, 'Were not our hearts burning within us while He was speaking to us on the road, while He was explaining the Scriptures to us?' 33 And they
got up that very hour and returned to Jerusalem, and found gathered together the
eleven and those who were with them, 34 saying, 'The Lord has really risen and
has appeared to Simon.' 35 They began to relate their experiences on the road and
how He was recognized by them in the breaking of the bread."

1. Based on what we know in Scripture and from the context, who is "them" in verse 13? What were they doing and saying? (vv. 14–15) Looking ahead to verse 17b, what was the mood in this scene?

NOTE: The exact location of Emmaus is unknown.

2. Who joined them? What is important to note from verse 16?

3. Jesus asked a question in verse 17. Who and how was it answered in verses 18–24? What does this tell us about how the disciples still viewed Jesus?

4. What is ironic about the hope these two disciples expressed in verse 21?

5. How did Jesus respond to the men and their report? (vv. 25–26)

6. What does Jesus' rebuke in verse 25 say to us today about knowing, understanding, and trusting in Scripture?

7. What does verse 27 say Jesus did? What does that tell us about seeing Jesus in the Old Testament? What are the implications of that regarding Jesus and the OT?

8. What did Jesus say was necessary in verse 26?

9. Circle the word "all" in verse 27. What does that tell us about the focus and purpose of God's Word? How does this clarify God's eternal plan for redemption?

10. What is the setting in verses 28–30? Why do you think the disciples urged Jesus to stay with them? (v. 29)

11. The disciples' eyes were opened in an instant but their understanding was progressive. What about their encounter with Jesus led to their realization of who He was? (vv. 25–30)

12. How did the disciples reflect on their time with Jesus in verse 32?

13. How did the disciples respond to the good news about Jesus? (vv. 33–35)

Application

Jesus wasn't being cruel to the men on the road by not revealing Himself; He was building their faith. In what ways does Jesus' gradual revelation of Himself help grow your faith and trust in Him?

A DEEPER LOOK

The following are Old Testament passages Jesus might have referred to on the Emmaus road. Read them and note how they reveal Christ.

Deuteronomy 18:15

Psalms 110:1

Psalms 2:7

Daniel 7:13–14

STUDY FOUR
Why This Gospel Was Written

News of Jesus traveled as fast as the feet of the men from Emmaus could carry them. As they relayed their story to His followers, in mid-sentence, Jesus appeared, bringing grace and peace with His presence. Jesus offered His hands and feet as evidence of His love and sacrifice, but the disciples could not take it all in. Fear and doubt held fast to the joy and wonder quickening in their spirits. Jesus ate a piece of fish to prove He was flesh and bone, then He taught them as if for the first time, opening their minds to all the prophesies and promises of Scripture. Thomas was missing from this gathering and unimpressed with their testimonies but, in His grace, Jesus later appeared to help his unbelief. And what a kindness that we are also in this scene—the blessed unseeing, believing by faith in our resurrected King.

Luke 24:36–49
"36 While they were telling these things, He Himself stood in their midst and said
to them, 'Peace be to you.' 37 But they were startled and frightened and thought
that they were seeing a spirit. 38 And He said to them, 'Why are you troubled,
and why do doubts arise in your hearts? 39 See My hands and My feet, that it is
I Myself; touch Me and see, for a spirit does not have flesh and bones as you see
that I have.' 40 And when He had said this, He showed them His hands and His
feet. 41 While they still could not believe it because of their joy and amazement,
He said to them, 'Have you anything here to eat?' 42 They gave Him a piece of a
broiled fish; 43 and He took it and ate it before them.

44 Now He said to them, 'These are My words which I spoke to you while I
was still with you, that all things which are written about Me in the Law of Moses
and the Prophets and the Psalms must be fulfilled.' 45 Then He opened their
minds to understand the Scriptures, 46 and He said to them, 'Thus it is written,
that the Christ would suffer and rise again from the dead the third day, 47 and
that repentance for forgiveness of sins would be proclaimed in His name to all the
nations, beginning from Jerusalem. 48 You are witnesses of these things. 49 And
behold, I am sending forth the promise of My Father upon you; but you are to
stay in the city until you are clothed with power from on high.'"

John 20:24–31

"24 But Thomas, one of the twelve, called Didymus, was not with them when
Jesus came. 25 So the other disciples were saying to him, 'We have seen the Lord!'
But he said to them, 'Unless I see in His hands the imprint of the nails, and put
my finger into the place of the nails, and put my hand into His side, I will not
believe.'

26 After eight days His disciples were again inside, and Thomas with them.
Jesus came, the doors having been shut, and stood in their midst and said, 'Peace
be with you.' 27 Then He said to Thomas, 'Reach here with your finger, and see
My hands; and reach here your hand and put it into My side; and do not be unbelieving, but believing.' 28 Thomas answered and said to Him, 'My Lord and my
God!' 29 Jesus said to him, 'Because you have seen Me, have you believed? Blessed
are they who did not see, and yet believed.'

30 Therefore many other signs Jesus also performed in the presence of the disciples, which are not written in this book; 31 but these have been written so that
you may believe that Jesus is the Christ, the Son of God; and that believing you
may have life in His name."

1. There would have been dramatic shifts in the mood among the disciples in Jerusalem in Luke 24. Describe what you think the emotion and atmosphere would have been like:

    - Before the men from the Emmaus arrived (Luke 24:33)

    - While they were sharing stories (v. 36)

    - When Jesus appeared in their midst (vv. 36–37)

2. Based on all the accounts so far in the resurrection story, was Thomas the only one who doubted?

3. What did Jesus invite the disciples to do? (vv. 38–40) Why do you think He did that?

4. Write down the words indicating the disciples' emotion in this passage. (vv. 37, 41) What is one more practical thing Jesus did to build their faith in the midst of swirling feelings? (vv. 42–43)

5. What does Jesus tell His disciples He fulfills in verse 44? What does he do for His disciples in verse 45?

6. What is the order of events as proclaimed by Jesus from Scripture in verses 46–47? What is left to be accomplished at that moment in history?

7. What does He call His disciples in verse 48? After explaining their responsibility, what promise does Jesus give in verse 49? (see John 14:16–17) What command does He give them?

8. What do we learn about Thomas in John 20:24?

9. What did Thomas say was required for him to believe? (v. 25)

10. What is the scene of verse 26 and when does it take place?

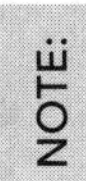

The day of the week both appearances of Jesus were recorded took place on a Sunday.

11. What is the invitation and command in verse 27? How does Thomas respond? (v. 28) What is significant about Thomas' confession?

This marks the first time one of Jesus' disciples addressed Him as "God."

12. Jesus had already appeared to all His disciples except Thomas. What does this account tell us about the grace and love of Jesus for all of His children?

13. What do we learn in verse 30? What does John tell us the purpose of his book is? (v. 31)

14. Let's reframe Thomas in our minds for a moment. How might his "doubt" be considered a kind of "discernment" instead? And why would discernment be important in this situation?

Application

In what ways have you been asked to "walk by faith and not by sight" in your life? How does the disciples' progression from despair to disbelief to faith encourage you in your walk with Jesus?

A DEEPER LOOK

Just like Thomas missed the first appearance of Jesus, what do we miss out on when we neglect to meet with other believers?

Acts 2:42

Romans 12:6–8, 10

1 Corinthians 12:25–26

Galatians 6:2

Colossians 3:13–16

1 Thessalonians 5:11

Hebrews 10:25

1 Peter 5:1–3

STUDY FIVE
Jesus and the Disciples at the Sea of Galilee

The fish just weren't biting. The disciples had been out on the water all night and were coming in empty-handed. As the sun rose over the hillside, a voice called out a strange instruction: *Try again on the other side.* They followed the order and at once their net filled with fish, a miraculous catch orchestrated by the hand of the Lord. When John realized it was Jesus on the shore, Peter dove into the sea, eager to be with his Savior. Breakfast over an open fire waited for them, but Jesus had an even greater purpose for this morning meal together. Jesus' call on Peter's life was irrevocable, but it required restoration. After three denials by a charcoal fire in the accusers' courtyard, Peter gets three chances to proclaim his love for His Savior by another fire near the sea. Peter's relationship with his Redeemer is renewed, and his course is sure. This disciple will tend the Good Shepherd's sheep, proclaiming the same message he received by grace that day: *you are loved, you are forgiven, and you are Mine.*

John 21:1–25

"After these things Jesus manifested Himself again to the disciples at the Sea of
Tiberias, and He manifested Himself in this way. 2 Simon Peter, and Thomas
called Didymus, and Nathanael of Cana in Galilee, and the sons of Zebedee, and
two others of His disciples were together. 3 Simon Peter said to them, 'I am going
fishing.' They said to him, 'We will also come with you.' They went out and got
into the boat; and that night they caught nothing.

4 But when the day was now breaking, Jesus stood on the beach; yet the disciples did not know that it was Jesus. 5 So Jesus said to them, 'Children, you do
not have any fish, do you?' They answered Him, 'No.' 6 And He said to them,
'Cast the net on the right-hand side of the boat and you will find a catch.' So they
cast, and then they were not able to haul it in because of the great number of fish.
7 Therefore that disciple whom Jesus loved said to Peter, 'It is the Lord.' So when
Simon Peter heard that it was the Lord, he put his outer garment on (for he was
stripped for work), and threw himself into the sea. 8 But the other disciples came
in the little boat, for they were not far from the land, but about one hundred
yards away, dragging the net full of fish.

9 So when they got out on the land, they saw a charcoal fire already laid and
fish placed on it, and bread. 10 Jesus said to them, 'Bring some of the fish which
you have now caught.' 11 Simon Peter went up and drew the net to land, full of
large fish, a hundred and fifty-three; and although there were so many, the net
was not torn.

12 Jesus said to them, 'Come and have breakfast.' None of the disciples ventured
to question Him, 'Who are You?' knowing that it was the Lord. 13 Jesus came and
took the bread and gave it to them, and the fish likewise. 14 This is now the third
time that Jesus was manifested to the disciples, after He was raised from the dead.

15 So when they had finished breakfast, Jesus said to Simon Peter, 'Simon, son of
John, do you love Me more than these?' He said to Him, 'Yes, Lord; You know
that I love You.' He said to him, 'Tend My lambs.' 16 He said to him again a
second time, 'Simon, son of John, do you love Me?' He said to Him, 'Yes, Lord;
You know that I love You.' He said to him, 'Shepherd My sheep.' 17 He said to
him the third time, 'Simon, son of John, do you love Me?' Peter was grieved
because He said to him the third time, 'Do you love Me?' And he said to Him,
'Lord, You know all things; You know that I love You.' Jesus said to him, 'Tend
My sheep.

18 Truly, truly, I say to you, when you were younger, you used to gird yourself
and walk wherever you wished; but when you grow old, you will stretch out your
hands and someone else will gird you, and bring you where you do not wish to
go.' 19 Now this He said, signifying by what kind of death he would glorify God.
And when He had spoken this, He said to him, 'Follow Me!'

20 Peter, turning around, saw the disciple whom Jesus loved following them;
the one who also had leaned back on His bosom at the supper and said, 'Lord,
who is the one who betrays You?' 21 So Peter seeing him said to Jesus, 'Lord, and
what about this man?' 22 Jesus said to him, 'If I want him to remain until I come,
what is that to you? You follow Me!' 23 Therefore this saying went out among the
brethren that that disciple would not die; yet Jesus did not say to him that he
would not die, but only, 'If I want him to remain until I come, what is that to
you?'

24 This is the disciple who is testifying to these things and wrote these things,
and we know that his testimony is true.

25 And there are also many other things which Jesus did, which if they were
written in detail, I suppose that even the world itself would not contain the books
that would be written."

1. Note and record the people, time, location and events described in verses 1–2. What are the disciples doing in verse 3?

NOTE: The Sea of Tiberias was also known as the Sea of Galilee. (See John 6:1)

2. What pattern between the resurrected Jesus and His disciples do we see repeated in verse 4?

3. How were their eyes opened to the presence of Jesus and who was (again) the first to see Him? (vv. 5–7)

4. What attributes of God do we see in this small scene that could have led to their recognition of their Savior?

5. How did Peter respond once he recognized Jesus? (v. 7)

6. How is Jesus practically showing His love for His friends in this scene? (vv. 9–14)

7. John 18:18–27 is the scene of another charcoal fire for Peter. When was the last time Scripture records Peter being near a fire? What emotions might he have been experiencing in the presence of Jesus?

8. What question does Jesus ask Peter in verses 15–17? How many times does He ask that? What might be significant about that? (Matthew 26:34)

9. How did Peter respond? How does Scripture tell us Peter felt? (v. 17)

10. What is notable about verses 18–19?

NOTE: Church tradition holds that Peter was crucified, as Jesus was. One ancient scholar records that Peter was crucified upside down, at his own request.

11. As we have progressed in our study of the life of Jesus, we have gotten to know Peter as well. Read 1 Peter 5:1–11 with the backstory of this man in mind. How does a deeper understanding of Peter's relationship with Jesus enrich the reading of this passage?

12. What distracted Peter in verses 20–21? How does Jesus correct his focus? (v. 22)

13. How do verses 24–25 speak to us about the truth and integrity of Scripture and the magnitude and magnificence of Jesus?

Application

How are obedience and blessing connected in Scripture? (See Joshua 1:8, 1 Kings 2:3, Psalms 128:1)

A DEEPER LOOK

Read 1 Corinthians 13. How is love a distinguishing feature of the work and ministry Jesus calls us to do?

How did Jesus demonstrate this for us during His time of ministry on earth?

WRAPPING UP

What a strange jumble of emotions for the followers of Jesus: fear in the presence of joy, doubt in the midst of worship. But who could blame them? They saw Jesus beaten within an inch of His life and hung on a Roman cross until He died. They knew His body was taken down by trustworthy, God-fearing men and placed securely in a guarded tomb. And yet, there He was. Flesh and blood and bone. Speaking and eating and breathing. More alive than anyone they had ever seen.

But why does this even matter? The resurrection is an incredible miracle, but what difference does it make in our lives?

Paul, in his letter to the Romans, explains the reason for Christ's resurrection. It is a picture not only of our impossible, sinful condition, but the beautiful redemption our Savior has provided—by His grace and for His glory, to bring us peace:

"For while we were still helpless, at the right time Christ died for the ungodly. For one will hardly die for a righteous man; though perhaps for the good man someone would dare even to die. But God demonstrates His own love toward us, in that while we were yet sinners, Christ died for us. Much more then, having now been justified by His blood, we shall be saved from the wrath of God through Him. For if while we were enemies we were reconciled to God through the death of His Son, much more, having been reconciled, we shall be saved by His life. And not only this, but we also exult in God through our Lord Jesus Christ, through whom we have now received the reconciliation."
(Romans 5:6–11)

These words of truth should erase all fear and doubt, move us to worship, and fill us with joy!

JESUS, KING OF KINGS

"These will wage war against the Lamb, and the Lamb will overcome them, because He is Lord of lords and King of kings, and those who are with Him are the called and chosen and faithful."
REVELATION 17:14

It is fitting we end our time studying *The Amazing Life of Jesus Christ* with a view to "*The* End," the point in history when the preexistent Son of God—who took His first human breath in an animal stall and breathed His last while nailed to a cross—returns to rule and reign and claim His own.

The book of Revelation is an account, as best human words can express, of this future time, and begins by distinguishing Jesus as "the ruler of the kings of the earth." (Revelation 1:5)

In other words, the King of kings. The One who leads leaders and conquers conquerors, who is Master of every other master and possesses authority over all authority.

This coming King will be unlike the kings of old, who burdened their subjects with wicked governance and demanded sacrificial adoration without reciprocity. King Jesus *"loves us and released us from our sins by His blood—and He has made us to be a kingdom, priests to His God and Father—to Him be the glory and the dominion forever and ever. Amen."* (Revelation 1:5–6)

Scripture says, as citizens of this Kingdom, we "share in the inheritance of the saints in light." Which means, because of Jesus, some day all that belongs to God will also belong to us. While unbelievable, these words aren't myth or fairy tale; it is a true and everlasting story of an infinitely loving King who blesses His people with a beautiful gift: the power and privilege to expand His Kingdom. (Colossians 1:12–13)

Through Jesus, the unworthy have been made worthy. Outcasts have been brought near. Enemies have become heirs. And we have a message of grace to proclaim: *Come know and enjoy this glorious King—the only King who invites us to share His crown!*

STUDY ONE
The Great Commission

They must have held some amount of faith just to show up at the mountain. But ironically, when Jesus appeared, so did their doubt. It is hard to believe that these men who had seen so much—the blind and broken, the demon-possessed and dead, restored before their eyes—would still have questions in their heart. While unsettling at the time, this scene brings us comfort because that mingling of fear and faith are familiar to us as well. Their feelings did not change Jesus' message. He was there to commission them to carry on, but this was more than a pep talk. There was work to do, centuries of souls to save. And Jesus gives us the same charge He left His disciples: *Go and grow My Kingdom. Teach the world about Me and trust the Spirit to show you how.*

Matthew 28:16–20
"**16** But the eleven disciples proceeded to Galilee, to the mountain which Jesus
had designated. **17** When they saw Him, they worshiped Him; but some were
doubtful. **18** And Jesus came up and spoke to them, saying, 'All authority has been
given to Me in heaven and on earth. **19** Go therefore and make disciples of all
the nations, baptizing them in the name of the Father and the Son and the Holy
Spirit, **20** teaching them to observe all that I commanded you; and lo, I am with
you always, even to the end of the age.'"

1. Who is in the scene in verse 16 and where are they?

2. What is their response to Jesus in verse 17?

3. What was the first thing Jesus proclaimed about Himself to His disciples in verse 18?

4. What was the commission Jesus gave His followers? What are the steps required in making disciples of Jesus? (vv. 19–20) What are the elements of the Great Commission that are imperative for Christians to carry out still today?

5. What assurance do we—along with the disciples—have from Jesus in verse 20?

6. You are where you are right now because the disciples obeyed Jesus' command in verses 19–20. Stop and express your gratitude for the impact their faithfulness has had on your life and on those you know and love. In what ways are you fulfilling this command in the world right now?

Application

Have you ever experienced doubt and worship at the same time? (v.17) What does this scene tell us about God's grace in those times?

STUDY TWO
Forty Days

Scripture refrains from sharing many details, choosing instead to give the 10,000-foot view of the forty days Jesus spent on earth in His resurrected body. We are left for the most part to imagine what it was like for those followers who were grieving and confused to see their Savior once again, their hope restored, and mission seemingly back on track. Surely the disciples would have been emboldened in their faith and understanding of His life and death. But this scene in Acts seems to indicate they were still hoping for an earthly and immediate reign of their resurrected King. Jesus did not discount their future hope, but He did delay it. These men were thinking politically, but Jesus wanted to grant them power and influence beyond anything the world had ever seen.

1 Corinthians 15:6–7

"6 After that He appeared to more than five hundred brethren at one time, most
of whom remain until now, but some have fallen asleep; 7 then He appeared to
James, then to all the apostles;"

Acts 1:3–8

"3 To these He also presented Himself alive after His suffering, by many con-
vincing proofs, appearing to them over a period of forty days and speaking of
the things concerning the kingdom of God. 4 Gathering them together, He commanded them not to leave Jerusalem, but to wait for what the Father had promised, 'Which,' He said, 'you heard of from Me; 5 for John baptized with water, but
you will be baptized with the Holy Spirit not many days from now.'

6 So when they had come together, they were asking Him, saying, 'Lord, is it
at this time You are restoring the kingdom to Israel?' 7 He said to them, 'It is not
for you to know times or epochs which the Father has fixed by His own authority;
8 but you will receive power when the Holy Spirit has come upon you; and you
shall be My witnesses both in Jerusalem, and in all Judea and Samaria, and even
to the remotest part of the earth.'"

1. What additional details do we learn from Paul in 1 Corinthians 15: 6–7 about the resurrection of Jesus?

2. How does Luke describe Jesus' life on earth after His resurrection from the dead? (Acts 1:3)

NOTE: Luke, a Gentile physician, missionary, and friend of Paul, is the author of Acts.

3. What did Jesus command His disciples to do in verse 4? For what purpose? (v. 5)

4. How did the disciples get off track in verse 6?

5. How does Jesus reset their thinking in verse 7?

6. What is the order of events in verse 8? Why is the order important?

7. What was the Holy Spirit specifically empowering the disciples to do in verse 8?

Application

The same power that enabled the disciples to "be My witnesses" all over the earth is alive and working in you today. If sharing the Gospel is intimidating for you, how does this truth about the Holy Spirit empower you? Have you ever had an experience of the Holy Spirit empowering you as you shared the gospel with an unbeliever?

A DEEPER LOOK

In addition to eternal life with Him in heaven, what does Scripture tell us Christ secured for us through His death and resurrection?

Romans 5:9

Colossians 3:15

Romans 8:15–17

Titus 3:4–6

2 Corinthians 5:15, 21

1 Peter 2:24

Ephesians 2:6, 13

STUDY THREE
The Ascension

The followers of Jesus were wrestling with a mix of emotions and expectations—"We believe, but... We trust You, but..."—and their agenda had been rearranged in a way they had not foreseen. What a blessing that Jesus, who had just called them to be "My witnesses," allowed them to look on as He returned in a cloud of glory to His Father. The sight was so spectacular, only the exhortation of angels brought them back to reality. They returned to Jerusalem, gathered with believers in the upper room, and did the only thing they could do—something they saw their Savior do time and again: they devoted themselves to prayer to the One who gave them the power to serve.

Acts 1:9–14

"9 And after He had said these things, He was lifted up while they were looking on, and a cloud received Him out of their sight. 10 And as they were gazing
intently into the sky while He was going, behold, two men in white clothing
stood beside them. 11 They also said, 'Men of Galilee, why do you stand looking
into the sky? This Jesus, who has been taken up from you into heaven, will come
in just the same way as you have watched Him go into heaven.'

12 Then they returned to Jerusalem from the mount called Olivet, which is near
Jerusalem, a Sabbath day's journey away. 13 When they had entered the city, they

went up to the upper room where they were staying; that is, Peter and John and James and Andrew, Philip and Thomas, Bartholomew and Matthew, James the son of Alphaeus, and Simon the Zealot, and Judas the son of James. [14] These all with one mind were continually devoting themselves to prayer, along with the women, and Mary the mother of Jesus, and with His brothers."

Acts 2:1–4

"When the day of Pentecost had come, they we all together in one place. [2] And suddenly there came from heaven a noise like a violent rushing wind, and it filled the whole house where they were sitting. [3] And there appeared to them tongues as of fire distributing themselves, and they rested on each one of them. [4] And they were all filled with the Holy Spirit and began to speak with other tongues, as the Spirit was giving them utterance."

1. What happened in verse 9? How does Luke 24:50–53 expand this scene?

2. Who appeared in verse 10? What assurance did they give the disciples (and us) in verse 11?

3. How is the promise of John 16:7 fulfilled in this scene?

4. What did the disciples do next? (vv. 12–13) Note their obedience in verse 14.

5. Who is part of the group in the upper room in verses 13–14? According to Acts 1:15, how many people are there?

6. How does verse 14 give you a picture of the effect of their devotion, trust, and obedience to Christ?

Application

Jesus' disciples and those who had denied Him (John 7:5) came together after His ascension. Are you willing to rise above differences within the body of Christ and pursue unity for the sake of the Gospel? Do you believe the Holy Spirit can enable you to do that?

STUDY FOUR
All Things Under His Feet

This short passage presents a big picture of the past, present, and future along with a significant order of events. Sin and the curse that came with it entered the world and our souls long ago through Adam, bringing death to all mankind. At just the right time, Christ appeared and, through His death, provided our redemption, restoration to God, and the only way we can be made alive, right now and forever. Our resurrection to life after death reveals that the death and resurrection of Christ accomplished its purpose. However, the battle between our old flesh and our new heart remains until we enter heaven. But at the return of Jesus, that long war will finally be over. Scripture promises that some future day, death itself will be no more. Jesus the Son will present His Bride, the Church, to God the Father, subjecting all things to Him. And on that day, as the poet John Donne proclaimed, "Death, thou shalt die."

1 Corinthians 15:20–28

"**20** But now Christ has been raised from the dead, the first fruits of those who are
asleep. **21** For since by a man came death, by a man also came the resurrection of
the dead. **22** For as in Adam all die, so also in Christ all will be made alive. **23** But
each in his own order: Christ the first fruits, after that those who are Christ's at
His coming, **24** then comes the end, when He hands over the kingdom to the God
and Father, when He has abolished all rule and all authority and power. **25** For
He must reign until He has put all His enemies under His feet. **26** The last enemy
that will be abolished is death. **27** For He has put all things in subjection under
His feet. But when He says, 'All things are put in subjection,' it is evident that
He is excepted who put all things in subjection to Him. **28** When all things are
subjected to Him, then the Son Himself also will be subjected to the One who
subjected all things to Him, so that God may be all in all."

1. What fact does Paul present to us in verse 20?

2. In Scripture, "first fruits" were given to God as an offering and a promise of the harvest to come. How, then, is Jesus the "first fruit" of the eventual harvest of God's people? (Look up "first fruits" in the dictionary on biblestudytools.com)

3. Circle the words "in Christ" in verse 22. What does that phrase mean? How does it affect how we interpret the rest of the verse? (for help, see Romans 6:11 and 8:1, Galatians 3:26, and Ephesians 3:6)

4. Paul predicts the culmination of history in verses 23–26. What does he say happens, in their order, when the King returns?

5. What does Paul remind us is the great enemy? (v. 26) Who is Death subjected to? (v. 27)

6. Who does Jesus subject Himself to? (v. 28) Why does He do this?

Application

In subjecting Himself to the Father, what does the humility of Christ the King teach us about having a submissive spirit?

A DEEPER LOOK

Jesus defeated death through His resurrection but we still live in mortal, sinful bodies. Read Revelation 20:7–15 for a preview of death's final destruction along with the defeat of enemies by the hand of Christ. Record your observations.

STUDY FIVE
The Future Return of Christ

What else can possibly be added to the picture of Jesus painted in these passages? Awe-inspiring and almighty. Formidable and fearsome. Dazzling and dreadful. Marvelous and moving. This is the best man's prose can do when describing the most compelling vision human eyes have been allowed to behold. One glance at His glory would kill you. And yet, some day, we will see Him face-to-face. What a horror to be on the end of His sword and fierce wrath. What a grace to live forever with the One who will wipe away even the memory of our tears, who will replace sorrow with so much joy that even the language for pain will pass away. Even now, in every ray of sunlight and drop of falling rain, He proclaims His everlasting, coming-soon promise: *Look and see, I am making all things new!*

Revelation 19:11–16

"**11** And I saw heaven opened, and behold, a white horse, and He who sat on it is called Faithful and True, and in righteousness He judges and wages war. **12** His eyes are a flame of fire, and on His head are many diadems; and He has a name written on Him which no one knows except Himself. **13** He is clothed with a robe dipped in blood, and His name is called The Word of God. **14** And the armies which are in heaven, clothed in fine linen, white and clean, were following Him on white horses. **15** From His mouth comes a sharp sword, so that with it He may strike down the nations, and He will rule them with a rod of iron; and He treads the wine press of the fierce wrath of God, the Almighty. **16** And on His robe and on His thigh He has a name written, 'KING OF KINGS, AND LORD OF LORDS.'"

Revelation 21:2–27

"**2** And I saw the holy city, new Jerusalem, coming down out of heaven from God, made ready as a bride adorned for her husband. **3** And I heard a loud voice from the throne, saying, 'Behold, the tabernacle of God is among men, and He will dwell among them, and they shall be His people, and God Himself will be among them, **4** and He will wipe away every tear from their eyes; and there will no longer be any death; there will no longer be any mourning, or crying, or pain; the first things have passed away.'

5 And He who sits on the throne said, 'Behold, I am making all things new.' And He said, 'Write, for these words are faithful and true.' **6** Then He said to me, 'It is done. I am the Alpha and the Omega, the beginning and the end. I will give to the one who thirsts from the spring of the water of life without cost. **7** He who overcomes will inherit these things, and I will be his God and he will be My son. **8** But for the cowardly and unbelieving and abominable and murderers and immoral persons and sorcerers and idolaters and all liars, their part will be in the lake that burns with fire and brimstone, which is the second death.'

9 Then one of the seven angels who had the seven bowls full of the seven last plagues came and spoke with me, saying, 'Come here, I will show you the bride, the wife of the Lamb.'"

10 And he carried me away in the Spirit to a great and high mountain, and showed
me the holy city, Jerusalem, coming down out of heaven from God, 11 having the
glory of God. Her brilliance was like a very costly stone, as a stone of crystal-clear
jasper. 12 It had a great and high wall, with twelve gates, and at the gates twelve
angels; and names were written on them, which are the names of the twelve tribes
of the sons of Israel. 13 There were three gates on the east and three gates on the
north and three gates on the south and three gates on the west. 14 And the wall
of the city had twelve foundation stones, and on them were the twelve names of
the twelve apostles of the Lamb.

15 The one who spoke with me had a gold measuring rod to measure the city,
and its gates and its wall. 16 The city is laid out as a square, and its length is as
great as the width; and he measured the city with the rod, fifteen hundred miles;
its length and width and height are equal. 17 And he measured its wall, seven-
ty-two yards, according to human measurements, which are also angelic measurements. 18 The material of the wall was jasper; and the city was pure gold, like clear
glass. 19 The foundation stones of the city wall were adorned with every kind of
precious stone. The first foundation stone was jasper; the second, sapphire; the
third, chalcedony; the fourth, emerald; 20 the fifth, sardonyx; the sixth, sardius;
the seventh, chrysolite; the eighth, beryl; the ninth, topaz; the tenth, chrysoprase;
the eleventh, jacinth; the twelfth, amethyst. 21 And the twelve gates were twelve
pearls; each one of the gates was a single pearl. And the street of the city was pure
gold, like transparent glass.

22 I saw no temple in it, for the Lord God the Almighty and the Lamb are its
temple. 23 And the city has no need of the sun or of the moon to shine on it, for
the glory of God has illumined it, and its lamp is the Lamb. 24 The nations will
walk by its light, and the kings of the earth will bring their glory into it. 25 In the
daytime (for there will be no night there) its gates will never be closed; 26 and they
will bring the glory and the honor of the nations into it; 27 and nothing unclean,
and no one who practices abomination and lying, shall ever come into it, but
only those whose names are written in the Lamb's book of life."

Revelation 22:1–6a

"Then he showed me a river of the water of life, clear as crystal, coming from the
throne of God and of the Lamb, 2 in the middle of its street. On either side of
the river was the tree of life, bearing twelve kinds of fruit, yielding its fruit every
month; and the leaves of the tree were for the healing of the nations. 3 There will
no longer be any curse; and the throne of God and of the Lamb will be in it, and
His bond-servants will serve Him; 4 they will see His face, and His name will be
on their foreheads. 5 And there will no longer be any night; and they will not have
need of the light of a lamp nor the light of the sun, because the Lord God will
illumine them; and they will reign forever and ever.

6 And he said to me, 'These words are faithful and true'; and the Lord, the
God of the spirits of the prophets, sent His angel to show to His bond-servants
the things which must soon take place."

John, the disciple that Jesus loved, is the author of Revelation.

1. Where is this scene unfolding? (v. 11) Who does John see in verse 11?

2. How does John describe Jesus in verses 11–13? (see John 1:1, 14)

3. What does Isaiah 63:1–6 tell us about why His robe is dipped in blood? Did anyone else participate in the battle? Note the words "my" and "I."

4. How does verse 15 describe Jesus as a conquering warrior? Look back at Revelation 17:14 and Revelation 19:7–8. What do we learn about "the armies" in Revelation 19:14?

5. What is different about this second coming of Jesus compared to His first coming to earth? (Luke 2, Luke 23)

6. What does John see in Revelation 21:2?

7. What is the supreme eternal blessing in verse 3?

8. What does verse 4 tell us will be drastically different about our life in heaven compared with our life on earth?

9. Who speaks in verse 5? What does He have the ability and authority to do?

10. What contrast is drawn in verses 6–8?

11. Record your observations from the description of the Holy City—your future home—in Revelation 21:9–22:6a. How does this picture of eternity encourage you in your faith for today?

Application

As you complete this study, how has your view of Jesus changed or been enhanced? Is your response to Jesus today different than it was before you began your study of Him? If so, in what way?

A DEEPER LOOK

What does Scripture tell us God's desire has always been? How do you respond to this precious truth?

Genesis 3:8

Ezekiel 37:27

Exodus 6:7

Zechariah 2:10

Jeremiah 30:22

2 Corinthians 6:16

WRAPPING UP

In Philippians 2:10–11, Paul writes that the very *name* of Jesus has unparalleled power over every sphere of existence and that, one day, the universal response to our supreme Sovereign will be immediate awe and allegiance:

"...so that at the name of Jesus EVERY KNEE WILL BOW, of those who are in heaven and on earth and under the earth, and that every tongue will confess that Jesus Christ is Lord, to the glory of God the Father."

This is the only right response to the King of all kings. And there is no reason to wait!

Scripture tells us that right now, Jesus is seated at the right hand of God. (Hebrews 1:3, 8:1, 10:12) But He is not unapproachable. He desires that we come to Him to know His love and receive His free gift of eternal life. (Ephesians 3:17–19, 1 John 2:24–25)

Together, we have seen that Jesus is our Teacher and Healer, sent by God to carry our burdens and take away our sin. He is Truth and Light, providing all we need including the Way to eternal Life.

He is our Good Shepherd, Judge, Narrow Gate, and promised Messiah. He is the Son of David, Son of Man, and Son of God. He suffered and died in our place and redeemed us through His resurrection. He existed before creation and time began, and is our glorious King, who will for all eternity be worthy of our worship and praise.

What more do we need? And how could we ever seek anything less?

Praise God, from Whom all blessings flow;
Praise Him all creatures, here below;
Praise Him above, ye heavenly host;
Praise Father, Son, and Holy Ghost. Amen!

Notes

ENDNOTES

Week 24:

Donne, John. "Death, Be Not Proud" (Holy Sonnet 10), Public domain. 1633.

Ken, Thomas. *The Doxology,* Public domain. 1674.

TIMELINE FOR THE LIFE OF JESUS

Included in Part One:

1. Pre-ministry years

The Angel Gabriel appears to Zacharias and foretells the birth of John the Baptist
The Angel Gabriel appears to Mary and foretells Jesus' birth
Mary visits Elizabeth
John the Baptist is born
Jesus is born in Bethlehem
Shepherds visit the manger
Jesus is presented in the temple in Jerusalem
The Wisemen visit Jesus
Jesus' family escapes to Egypt
Jesus' family returns to Nazareth
Jesus astounds priests in the temple at age twelve
John the Baptist begins his ministry
Jesus is baptized
Jesus is tempted by Satan in the wilderness
Jesus returns to the Jordan; John proclaims "Behold the Lamb of God"
Andrew, Peter, Philip, Nathaniel, and perhaps John begin to follow Jesus
Jesus and disciples go to wedding in Cana; Jesus turns water into wine

2. First Year of Ministry (about 29–30 AD)

Passover: Jesus cleanses the temple in Jerusalem (first time)
Jesus meets with Nicodemus
Jesus ministers in Judea
John the Baptist probably arrested at this time
Jesus meets the woman at the well
The royal official's son is healed
Jesus is rejected at Nazareth, His hometown
He calls Andrew and Peter, James and John to be His disciples
He casts out an unclean demon
Jesus heals Peter's mother-in-law
Disciples experience a miraculous catch
He heals a leper
The paralytic is let down through the roof, forgiven, and healed
Matthew is called to be a disciple

3. Second Year of Ministry (about 30–31 AD)

Man healed at the pool of Bethesda in Jerusalem
Jesus proclaims He is equal with the Father
Controversy over the Sabbath with religious leaders
Man with crippled hand healed
The twelve appointed to follow Jesus
Sermon on the Mount given
The centurion's slave is healed
The widow of Nain's son is raised from the dead
Jesus answers John the Baptist's disciples' questions
Jesus curses Chorazin, Bethsaida, and Capernaum
Jesus is anointed by a disreputable woman
The blind-mute demonic spirit is cast out
Kingdom Parables
Calmed the stormy sea
Casts demons out into swine
Healed a woman who was hemorrhaging
Raised Jairus' daughter
Healed two blind men
Cast out demon from a mute and blind man
Taught and rejected again in Nazareth
The twelve disciples sent out
John the Baptist is beheaded
Jesus feeds the five thousand
Jesus appears as a ghost walking on water

4. Third Year of Ministry (about 31–32 AD)

Bread of Life discourse
Jesus withdrew to Tyre and Sidon
The Gentile woman's daughter delivered from demons
Jesus feeds the four thousand
Healed a blind man at Bethsaida
Peter proclaims Jesus is the Christ at Caesarea Philippi
The transfiguration
Demon cast out of boy
Temple tax paid
Teaches on forgiveness

INCLUDED IN PART TWO:

Jesus is ridiculed by His brothers
Journey to Jerusalem
Chief priests and Pharisees try to arrest Jesus
Jesus forgives an adulterous woman
The seventy are commissioned
Parable of Good Samaritan
Jesus visits Mary and Martha
Jesus teaches on prayer, hypocrisy, and wealth
Jesus heals a woman on the Sabbath
Jesus heals a blind man

Blind man excommunicated
Jesus teaches on the good shepherd
Jews tried to stone Jesus
Jesus heals a man with dropsy on the Sabbath
Parables of the lost sheep, lost coin, and lost son
Lazarus dies
Jesus raises Lazarus from the dead
Jesus teaches on the second coming
Jesus heals blind man
Zacchaeus meets Jesus
Jesus arrives in Bethany
(The Passion Week begins)
The Triumphant Entry
Jesus cleanses the temple the second time
Jesus teaches in Jerusalem
Jesus speaks "woes" to the Pharisees
The Olivet Discourse
Judas agrees to betray Christ
(The night before His death)
Washes disciples feet
Institutes the Lord's Supper
The Upper Room Discourse
The Garden of Gethsemane
Jesus is arrested
Tried before Annas
Peter denies Jesus
Tried before Caiaphas
Peter denies Jesus two more times
Judas regrets his betrayal
Jesus tried before Pilate
Jesus tried before Herod
Jesus sentenced by Pilate
Jesus' journey to Golgatha
He is crucified
Joseph of Arimathea takes Jesus' body
The body is placed in a tomb
Angel appears to Mary and Mary at the empty tomb
Peter and John arrive at the empty tomb
Jesus appears to Mary Magdalene
Soldiers report empty tomb
Disciples meet Jesus on road to Emmaus
Jesus appears in the upper room
Jesus appears again in the upper room with Thomas present
Jesus appears in Galilee to the disciples and prepares breakfast
Peter restored to ministry
Jesus appears to many
Jesus ascends into heaven

Memory Verses for *The Amazing Life of Jesus Christ*, Part Two

WEEK 13

JESUS, LIGHT OF THE WORLD

Then Jesus again spoke to them, saying, "I am the Light of the world; he who follows Me will not walk in the darkness, but will have the Light of life."

John 8:12

WEEK 14

JESUS, THE PROVIDER

And do not seek what you will eat and what you will drink, and do not keep worrying. For all these things the nations of the world eagerly seek; but your Father knows that you need these things. But seek His kingdom, and these things will be added to you.

Luke 12:29–31

WEEK 15

JESUS, THE GOOD SHEPHERD

I am the good shepherd, and I know My own and My own know Me, even as the Father knows Me and I know the Father; and I lay down My life for the sheep.

John 10:14–15

WEEK 16

JESUS, THE NARROW DOOR

Enter through the narrow gate; for the gate is wide and the way is broad that leads to destruction, and there are many who enter through it. For the gate is small and the way is narrow that leads to life, and there are few who find it.

Matthew 7:13–14

WEEK 17

JESUS, THE RESURRECTION AND THE LIFE

Jesus said to her, "I am the resurrection and the life; he who believes in Me will live even if he dies, and everyone who lives and believes in Me will never die. Do you believe this?"

John 11:25–26

WEEK 18

JESUS, SON OF DAVID

"The crowds going ahead of Him, and those who followed, were shouting, "Hosanna to the Son of David: BLESSED IS HE WHO COMES IN THE NAME OF THE LORD; Hosanna in the highest!"

Matthew 21:9

WEEK 19

JESUS, THE JUDGE

"But when the Son of Man comes in His glory, and all the angels with Him, then He will sit on His glorious throne. All the nations will be gathered before Him; and He will separate them from one another, as the shepherd separates the sheep from the goats."

Matthew 25:31–32

WEEK 20

JESUS, THE WAY, THE TRUTH, AND THE LIFE

"Jesus said to him, 'I am the way, and the truth, and the life; no one comes to the Father but through Me.'"

John 14:6

WEEK 21

JESUS, SON OF MAN

"Then He came to the disciples and said to them, 'Are you still sleeping and resting? Behold, the hour is at hand and the Son of Man is being betrayed into the hands of sinners.'"

Matthew 26:45

WEEK 22

JESUS, THE SUFFERING SERVANT

"When they came to the place called The Skull, there they crucified Him and the criminals, one on the right and the other on the left."

Luke 23:33

WEEK 23

JESUS, REDEEMER AND SAVIOR

"...knowing that you were not redeemed with perishable things like silver or gold from your futile way of life inherited from your forefathers, but with precious blood, as of a lamb unblemished and spotless, the blood of Christ."

1 Peter 1:18–19

WEEK 24

JESUS, KING OF KINGS

"These will wage war against the Lamb, and the Lamb will overcome them, because He is Lord of lords and King of kings, and those who are with Him are the called and chosen and faithful."

Revelation 17:14